Winifred Gérin
Biographer of the Brontës

"In an original and revealing biography . . . Helen MacEwan presents not just a fascinating study of Gérin's long and at times very personal preoccupation with the Brontës, but the story of a highly individual character . . . Using much previously unknown and unpublished material, MacEwan has painstakingly put together a portrait of one woman and her times that adds significantly to Brontë studies and literary biography, while her deftly-told narrative brings Gérin's private, feeling, thoughtful character to life with unerring sympathy."

CLAIRE HARMAN, biographer and critic, author of the major new biography, *Charlotte Brontë: A Life*, and of *Jane's Fame*.

"In this beautifully written and carefully researched biography of a biographer, Helen MacEwan shows us something of the European dimension of Gérin's experience and understanding, as well as revealing the deeply emotional character of her subject, in her joys, passions and losses . . . Helen MacEwan shines a fascinating light, not only on a remarkable woman of letters, but on a reader and writer of exceptional integrity."

STEVIE DAVIES, critic and novelist, author of *Emily Brontë: Heretic* and *Four Dreamers and Emily*

"For anyone, like me, who knows Winifred Gérin only as the biographer of the Brontës, this book will come as a revelation. Not only did Gérin have an astonishingly adventurous life, but Helen MacEwan has brought it before us in vivid and enthralling detail . . . MacEwan's book draws on extensive original research into unpublished papers and records, but she wears her erudition lightly and always gives a sense of the lived moment rather than the dry facts. She achieves, in fact, that balance between sense and sensibility which friends appreciated in Gérin's own work. This is a thrilling book to read, a page-turner, offering through specific vignettes important glimpses into the social history of the twentieth century. It will appeal to an audience well beyond Brontë devotees."

PATSY STONEMAN is Emeritus Reader in English, University of Hull, and Acting President of the Brontë Society. She is the author of *Charlotte Brontë* in the *Writers and their Work* series, Northcote House Publishers

Winifred Gérin
Biographer of the Brontës

Helen MacEwan

sussex
ACADEMIC
PRESS
Brighton • Chicago • Toronto

2 4 6 8 10 9 7 5 3 1

First published in paperback 2016 in Great Britain by
SUSSEX ACADEMIC PRESS
PO Box 139, Eastbourne BN24 9BP

and in the United States of America by
SUSSEX ACADEMIC PRESS
Independent Publishers Group
814 N. Franklin Street, Chicago, IL 60610

and in Canada by
SUSSEX ACADEMIC PRESS (CANADA)

British Library Cataloguing in Publication Data
A CIP catalogue record for this book is available from the British Library.

Library of Congress Cataloging-in-Publication Data
MacEwan, Helen.
Winifred Gérin : biographer of the Brontës / Helen MacEwan.
pages cm
Includes bibliographical references and index.
ISBN 978-1-84519-743-8 (paperback : acid-free paper)
  1. Gérin, Winifred. 2. Women biographers—Great Britain—Biography.
3. Brontë family. 4. Biography as a literary form. I. Title.
CT788.G44M33 2016
809′.93592—dc23

2015028866

Typeset & designed by Sussex Academic Press, Brighton & Eastbourne.
Printed by TJ International, Padstow, Cornwall.

Contents

List of Illustrations

The colour and mono plates are after page 96. Unless otherwise stated in plate captions, all pictures are owned by Irene Lock or Paul Gérin and reproduced here with their kind permission.

Preface

Why write a biography of a biographer? It is a question I have been asked more than once since embarking on this project. My last book was about the Brontës, a subject whose appeal is evident. But why write about someone who wrote about the Brontës?

It is many years now since I first read Winifred Gérin's biography of Charlotte Brontë. Together with Mrs Gaskell's *Life*, it brought its subject alive for me and, more generally, sparked an interest in authors' lives and a passion for literary biography. Later I went on to read Winifred's other biographies.

Her books were on my shelves for a long time before I became curious about their author, though I had wondered about the origin of her foreign surname. It was not until I moved to Belgium and first began to research the Brontës myself, after becoming fascinated by their time in Brussels, that I learned something about Winifred and her own association with Belgium. The entries in the *Dictionary of National Biography* outlined an enthralling story: marriage to a Belgian cellist, years living in Paris in the 1930s, and a series of exciting war adventures. At the time of the German invasion of Belgium, the Gérins were working for the British Embassy in Brussels. Having fled to Vichy France, they found themselves trapped for two years in Nice, finally escaping through Spain and Portugal to England, where they worked for Political Intelligence. Then, ten years after Eugène Gérin's death in 1945, there was Winifred's romantic meeting on the Haworth moors with her second husband, John Lock, and their decision to buy a house within sight of the Parsonage and devote themselves to researching the Brontës. Winifred Gérin, who wrote lives of all four siblings, was long known as *the* Brontë biographer.

I wanted to know more, though at this stage all I envisaged was an article about Winifred's Belgian links. I needed to trace the family of her Belgian first husband. There was a clue in the acknowledgements in her Charlotte Brontë biography, which mentioned the help given in her Brussels research by her nephew Paul Eugène Gérin, a lecturer at the University of Liège.

Paul Gérin's telephone number was in an online directory. I called him and a week later was sitting in his apartment in Liège, drinking tea and listening to him talk about his godmother Winny, the wife of his uncle Eugène. *Marraine Winny* was a formative influence and an important part of his life for nearly fifty years.

Professor Gérin generously placed at my disposal hundreds of letters in impeccable French written by Winifred to him and other members of his family. Most date from after Eugène's death and give a wealth of information on her activities in the post-war years – first trying to make her way in London as a playwright, and later gaining recognition as a biographer after her marriage to John Lock and their move to Haworth.

From the DNB entries I knew that Winifred had left an unpublished autobiography called *The Years that Count*. Thanks to contacts in the Brontë Society and Haworth I succeeded in tracking down this memoir. I met John Lock's second wife, who had owned it since he died in 1998. John was Winifred's heir and literary executor. After his death, many of her papers were sold to a private collector but Mrs Lock kept the autobiography, written in the last year of Winifred's life at the suggestion of her editor at Oxford University Press. To John Lock's disappointment, OUP eventually decided against publication, and he never found another publisher for it.

By this time I was eager to write a biography of Winifred, and Mrs Lock agreed that with the autobiography still unpublished 35 years after it was written, this would be the best way of making Winifred's life story known. She kindly allowed me access to the memoir. Winifred herself described this memoir as a 'partial' one, and while it filled in many gaps in my knowledge of her early years – her childhood, time in Paris with Eugène and wartime adventures – the years after the War are hurried through in a mere twenty pages, which is where Paul Gérin's letters became so invaluable.

The third main source of information was sitting in three large boxes in the attic of a house near Winchester. They belong to Robin Greenwood (related to the Haworth Greenwoods who knew the Brontës), a local history researcher who bought the bulk of Winifred's papers when they were sold in 2000. On visits to Robin and his wife Gilly's beautiful house I was given access to a treasure trove. The boxes contained letters written by Winifred to her family when she was a student at Cambridge and a newly-wed in Paris, and these give a fresher and more vivid impression of her than the memoir written in old age. They also contained typescripts of three of her plays, and manuscript poems written after Eugène's death. A collection of her early poems was published in 1930, but her plays and most of this moving later verse are unpublished.

I now had many of the essential jigsaw puzzle pieces of Winifred's life. Further pieces were revealed when I read the papers of hers owned by the Brontë Parsonage Museum, the files in the archives of her publisher OUP, and letters to her friends G.E. and Dorothy Moore held at Cambridge University Library.

Inevitably, some gaps remain. Some of her papers, including her diaries, were destroyed when her flat was flooded shortly after her death. The people she was closest to, with the exception of her nephew Paul – people who might have provided information and correspondence – are no longer living. Happily, the material salvaged provides a substantial portrait of her.

Research was needed in order to obtain the necessary detail that is the hallmark of Winifred's own biographical work but is lacking in her autobiography. She told her publisher it was intended to be 'selective and relating only to vivid memories' rather than a detailed and documented account, and death overtook her before she had time to revise it thoroughly. In the final pages of the memoir she wrote that one of life's greatest blessings is that we cannot see the future or know when our end will be (in the course of her life, this inability to know when the end will come for those we love, as well as for ourselves, was something for which she often had reason to be grateful).

Wherever possible I have checked the accuracy of Winifred's narrative and carried out research to establish the full facts. For example, her brief description of Eugène Gérin's clandestine broadcasts for the Resistance movement in occupied Belgium does not give such details as the name of the radio station he was working for. Thanks to much detective work, and help from specialised researchers, I found information on these broadcasting activities in Foreign Office files and in the log book of the studio where I discovered that Eugène recorded his programmes.

One of the aims of *Winifred Gérin: Biographer of the Brontës* has been to trace how Winifred became a biographer, how she set about the task, how well she met the challenge of writing about such iconic figures as the Brontës. It is my hope that readers will find it interesting to see a biographer at work. My primary aim, however, has been to tell Winifred's personal life story. I can only hope that she would not have been too averse to being the subject of a biography – as two of her own subjects, Emily Brontë and Elizabeth Gaskell, almost certainly would have been. She was initially reluctant to write her autobiography, for while she hoped to live on after death as a writer, through her biographies, she was convinced that other people's lives were much more interesting than her own. But despite these reservations she did decide to make her story known, and the autobiography was written – only to lie dormant for 35 years. Now, for the first time, that story can be read, supplemented with a great deal of additional material.

Winifred always wrote about people with whom she felt an emotional connection and affinity. Her empathy with her subjects brought them into a close relation with the reader. I trust that this book will bring Winifred herself close to its readers by conveying her enthusiasms, emotions and responses to experience as well as the events of her life.

HELEN MACEWAN
Brussels, 2015

Acknowledgements

I could not have written this book without Irene Lock, Paul Gérin and Robin Greenwood. My thanks are due first and foremost to them.

I would also like to thank the following:

Paul Gérin's children (Marthe, Hubert, Eugène, Vincent and Emmanuel) for sharing memories of Winifred and scanning family photos for this book.

Barbara Mitchell, for her help when I was embarking on the research for this book. Barbara wrote the entries for Winifred Gérin in the *Dictionary of Literary Biography* (1995) and the *Dictionary of National Biography* (2004). She also examined Gérin's biographical approach in her university thesis, *The biographical process: writing the lives of Charlotte Brontë* (1995).

The genealogist Alexander Poole, for research into the Bourne and Hill families.

Katy Stenhouse, granddaughter of Winifred's cousin Cuthbert Pearce, for supplying recollections, family history information and photos.

John Hickman, South Norwood historian, for answering queries and finding time in his busy schedule to meet me at Croydon Museum to search out old photos of Norwood.

Alun and Barbara Thomas of the Norwood Society for information. Barbara also did useful initial research on the Bourne and Hill families.

Jan Piggott, author of *Palace of the People: The Crystal Palace at Sydenham*, for information on the Palace in the early years of the century.

Elizabeth Cooper, the librarian at Sydenham High School, for her helpfulness in looking out information on the school during the First World War.

William Wood, the archivist at Whitgift School, for information on Charles Philip Bourne and Dennis Ely in the school registers.

Anne Thompson, the archivist at Newnham College, Cambridge, for documentation on Winifred's time there.

Frank Bowles, Superintendent of the Manuscripts Reading Room at Cambridge University Library, which holds Winifred's letters to G.E. and Dorothy Moore and also her correspondence with the Royal Society of Literature. Quotations appear by permission of the Syndics of Cambridge University Library.

Prof. Thomas Baldwin, G.E. Moore's literary executor, and Moore's grandson Peregrine Moore, for permission to reproduce a photo of G.E. and Dorothy Moore in the Moore papers at Cambridge University Library.

Eleanor Ward, the archivist at Keble College, Oxford, for information on Roger Bourne in the college registers.

The archivists at the Surrey History Centre for their helpfulness in giving me access to Holloway Sanatorium's records on Roger Bourne.

Staff at the tourist office of Plombières-les-Bains, and Mme Monique de Buyer of the local *Société d'Art et d'Histoire*, for information and pictures.

Robert Kanigel, author of *High Season in Nice*, for information about the diary of Elizabeth Foster, a resident of Nice during the Second World War.

Céline Rase, a PhD student at the University of Namur, Belgium, for valuable help with my research into Eugène Gérin's broadcasts to the Resistance in occupied Belgium.

John Taylor, author of *Bletchley Park's Secret Sisters*, for information and contacts.

Ingram Murray, whose father Ralph Murray was involved in the Political Warfare Executive's black propaganda campaign, for information on wartime activities in the Aspley Guise area, where he lived as a child during the War, and for giving me a guided tour of it!

Ann Dinsdale, Collections Manager at the Brontë Parsonge Museum, for her help with various matters, including access to the papers of Winifred Gérin owned by the Museum.

Sarah Laycock, Collections and Library Officer at the Brontë Parsonge Museum, for help in obtaining an image of the portrait of Winifred by Helen Bourne owned by the Museum.

Haworth historian Steven Wood, who has an encylopaedic knowledge of both past- and present-day Haworth and its inhabitants, for patiently answering numerous queries and for contacts in Haworth. To cite just two examples, thanks to him I was able to meet people in the village who knew Winifred and John Lock, and visit 'Gimmerton', the house where they lived.

Edith Petty and Margaret Hamer for taking the time to talk to me about their memories of Winifred and John Lock and of Haworth in the 1950s.

Ian Palmer, Haworth photographer, who supplied the stunning photograph for the cover of this book.

Martin Maw, the archivist at OUP, who kindly let me examine the Winifred Gérin files in the archives. Quotations from these files appear by permission of the Secretary to the Delegates of Oxford University Press.

And finally, Paul Gretton and Brian Bracken for reading the manuscript and making comments.

HAWORTH MOOR

The moors above Haworth are perpetually clothed in splendour, no matter at what season of the year. In summer their texture is of a sombre richness that recalls the vast canvasses of Veronese. The heavy, velvet green of moss half covers the rocky structure of the earth; the amber and topaz of the bilberry clumps stretches, hummock upon hummock, over every hill; the heaving, breathing, swaying mass of heather (the colour of plum-bloom, umber and of vine) that ruffles like a fur in the low breeze, sweeps on all sides to the horizon's verge; the emerald green of bracken and the silver green of the bent, lithe swathes of the grasses; the smoke-blue of the harebells and the pink of clover-flowers and the butter yellow of Emily's 'yellow-star of the mountains' enamel the ground at one's feet, while the sky is resonant with the cries of the lapwing and the song of the late and early lark. From the grey, far-flung farmsteads blue smoke arises, cocks crow, young cattle low, sheep-dogs bark and, far away on the hillsides, the bleating of sheep answers the bleating of lambs . . . Above all, skies of an illimitable vastness illumine and fleck, with their ever-passing procession of high clouds, the rolling stretches of moorland, vale and hill, evoking a wealth of colour from the ground that is as varied as it is beautiful.

From Winifred Gérin's *Anne Brontë*, Chapter 7.

Winifred Gérin regarded the labours of the scholars respectfully, and with some wonder, but that was not her way. She herself became passionately fond of her subjects, and cherished them as friends or daughters. Warmth, compassion, and enthusiasm characterize her work. A more academic biographer might have thought it unnecessary to get quite so weather-beaten in the course of research, but Winifred Gérin needed 'atmosphere'.

Entry for Winifred Gérin in the *Dictionary of National Biography* by Peter Sutcliffe, Winifred's editor at Oxford University Press.

To José Miguel

1
Norwood
Childhood and the End of Childhood

Winifred Gérin's childhood in the first years of the twentieth century, in an affluent London suburb amid the rolling Surrey Hills, seems in many ways far removed from that of the young Brontës growing up in Haworth Parsonage on the Yorkshire moors. In later life, however, when she became their biographer, she was struck by certain parallels between the two. These went beyond the fact that she was one of four siblings bound together by affection and affinities. There were similarities with the Brontës both in the cultural and imaginative richness of her family environment, and the family tragedies that gave her early experiences of loss.

Her first ten years, as the child of loving, highly cultured and well-to-do parents, could not have been happier. She was born in 1901 at the start of the Edwardian era, that golden age for being a child in which so many of our favourite children's books seem to have been set; Winifred's account of her early years in her unpublished memoir evokes family life as described in the opening paragraphs of *The Railway Children* and in many another tale of the period.

Until their sky darkened over them, which happened some time before the more general darkening of the skies in 1914, the four Bourne children led a carefree existence in the suburb of Norwood, in that Edwardian world of ladies in hour-glass dresses and very large hats, nursery governesses pushing perambulators and little boys in sailor suits. It was a world in which some of the streets were still lit by gas lamps requiring an army of lamplighters, and the first motor buses and cars had not yet banished horse-drawn omnibuses and carriages. A world where, in middle-class households like the Bournes', Mother had plenty of time to play the piano and sing in the drawing-room, leaving much of the children's education to a governess.

Life at Oak Tree House, South Norwood Hill, conformed in many respects to the stereotypes. The houses became grander the further up the hill you went, towards the Crystal Palace; the half-way point of

South Norwood hill marked the start of Upper Norwood, a name that indicated social as well as geographical elevation. With sixteen rooms, Oak Tree House at No. 216, which stood at that half-way point, was fairly grand, and there were always three or four servants, as well as a governess, to look after the family of six.

Winifred was the spoiled youngest of the children. All four were born in Germany, where their father, Frederick Charles Bourne, was a manager at the Hamburg branch of Nobel, a chemicals company later amalgamated with ICI. In Hamburg he met Katharine Hill, who was working as a governess and studying music and German.

Frederick had worked his way up to a management position from his first job as a shipowner's clerk. He was the youngest of four sons, with three half-brothers much older than him who also started out as clerks in south London. Little is known about his family. His father, Thomas, worked at a life insurance company in Southwark. He married a Maria Wheeler from Henley in 1839 and had three sons with her, the eldest of whom, Thomas James, was 20 years older than Frederick. After Maria's death Thomas married her younger sister, Jane, in 1858; Frederick was the only son of this second marriage. In her memoir Winifred states that she met no relations on her father's side apart from one niece who lived abroad. Frederick's middle half-brother, Josiah, died long before Winifred was born, and the youngest, John, vanishes early from the records. Thomas James, the eldest, had children and it was one of his daughters, Louisa, whom Winifred met in Paris when she was in her teens. Thomas James also had grandchildren of the same age as Frederick's children, but apparently the two families never met. Winifred gives no explanation for the lack of contact with her father's family, merely commenting that he seemed to be singularly short of relatives.

On her mother's side there was no such shortage of relations, though some of them Winifred, as a child, could happily have dispensed with. These were her 'maiden aunts', her mother's unmarried sisters, of which she considered there was a superfluity. Three of these – Aunts Fanny, Annie and Jessie – were Katharine's half-sisters, the offspring of her father's first marriage.

Katharine grew up in Brixton. Her father, Orsmby John Hill, was born in 1816 in Londonderry, the son of a navy captain who fell on hard times and died in the King's Bench Debtors Prison in Southwark – presumably finding nobody to bail him out. Ironically, the year his father died in penury was the same year that the teenage Ormsby John joined the Bank of England as a clerk. He was to remain for 45 years. Left a widower at the age of thirty, by the time of his second marriage some years later to Mary Ann Phillips, a butcher's daughter, he was rising steadily through the ranks. In the Hill dynasty founded by him and Mary Ann, both the name Ormsby and the choice of a career in Threadneedle Street, with members of the family in each generation entering the Bank as young clerks, recur with some regularity.

Katharine was Orsmby's and Mary Ann's third child. Her elder brother Ormsby Topham followed their father into the Bank, as did Cuthbert, the son of her elder sister Lily. Her younger sisters, Amy and Marian, were destined to join the ranks of the 'maiden aunts'.

In her twenties and thirties Katharine worked as a governess, taking the same path as several of her sisters: Fanny started up a school, Jessie was at one stage a governess in Paris and Marian taught the piano. In 1881, aged 21, Katharine was employed in the home of a Kensington solicitor with five daughters. Meanwhile, the young Frederick was living with his widowed mother a few streets away from the Hill family home in Brixton. He joined Nobel in the early 1890s; his work for the firm involved frequent business trips on the Continent even before he took up the post in Hamburg.

Frederick and Katharine had much in common. Despite differences in temperament – she was vivacious, he reserved, with a wry sense of humour - they were both cultured, well-read, unusually good linguists; both spoke fluent French as well as German. Their children were to inherit their passion for the arts and languages to a degree that made them an anomaly in the Hill family, successive generations of which produced city gentlemen rather than writers and painters.

The couple were married in Hamburg in January 1896, both aged thirty-six. Their first child, Charles Philip, was born at the end of that year, followed by Katharine Helen on 1 January 1898 and Roger Hereward on 25 December of the same year. Winifred Eveleen, the last child, made her appearance on 7 October 1901. Winifred is unlikely to have had any recollections of Germany, since in the year after her birth her parents returned to London, where Frederick continued to work for Nobel. By the time she was three or four the family was installed in the house in Norwood.

In those days Upper Norwood, today marred by drab post-war housing, still retained much of the quasi-rural charm of the Victorian period when it was first developed on the wooded slopes below the ridge of Beulah Hill. Until the early nineteenth century Norwood was a wilderness on the southern edge of London, known chiefly as the haunt of the gypsies who lived on the common and told the fortunes of day trippers from the city. But when the Beulah Spa Hotel opened in 1831 by a spring of mineral water just off Beulah Hill, the first villas started to appear on the high ground. When the Crystal Palace was re-erected on nearby Sydenham Hill in the 1850s its superior attractions led to the decline of the spa but its advent also accelerated development of the area, which offered superb views towards London to the north and the Surrey Downs to the south.

The most impressive villas in Norwood were at the top of the hill, for example in Church Road along which the carriages of the gentry rolled to functions at the Queen's Hotel, and the smartest shops were in nearby Westow Hill. The Bournes' house, one of a row no longer standing – the site is today occupied by the nondescript Howden Court – stood roughly opposite the junction of South Norwood Hill with Whitehorse Lane, a road in those days still rural in character. The house was built on two levels on sloping terrain, with a long garden at the back descending towards South Norwood Lake and Penge. In later life Winifred's sharpest memories of this home was of the drawing room, which was located on the ground floor at the front of the house and the first floor at the back. A balcony supported on pillars, leading off one of the tall back windows, commanded views of the Crystal Palace to the north.

Life in Norwood was very happy for the four children who romped boisterously through the spacious rooms and garden of Oak Tree House. They were self-sufficient in their imaginative and riotous games, and the main cloud on their horizon was the presence of successive German and Swiss *Fraüleins* employed to talk German and French with them. These unfortunates were loathed by Winifred in particular. She was a self-willed, rebellious child who identified with the young Jane Eyre when their mother read the novel to them, and was sometimes rude to her aunts. Phil, the eldest boy, was the perfect older brother, responsible and mature for his years, and particularly protective towards little Winny. Helen, 'Nell', who was timid with people outside the family circle, was similarly protective of the younger siblings. Roger, the second boy, was the problem child of the family. Clever but highly-strung, he was prone to uncontrollable rages and 'night terrors', for which he was dosed with bromide. (Could Winifred's observation of this brilliant but unbalanced brother have deepened her understanding of Branwell Brontë when she came to write about him?) Nell and Roger, being close in age, often played together as children, which caused Winny jealousy as she adored her sister.

The children were avid readers, particularly of stories from history, with a preference for those involving monarchs and a particular allegiance to the Stuarts first sparked by G.A. Henty's historical novel *Bonnie Prince Charlie*. They invented and acted out tales about fictional or historical characters drawn from their reading; these sagas, serial-like, went on for weeks, months, sometimes years. They called these characters their 'Night Friends'. When, much later in life, Winifred came to immerse herself in the Brontës' juvenilia, she immediately understood the obsessive nature of the imaginary world of the young Brontës, who acted out what they called 'night plays'. Another obsession that the two families had in common was drawing. From an early age the Brontës were artists as well as writers, drawing compulsively on every available scrap of paper. The young Bournes were almost as obsessive, making copies of the illustrations in whichever book they were reading or having read aloud to them (*Barnaby Rudge*, *A Tale of Two Cities* . . .) almost as meticulous as those of Charlotte Brontë, who strained her eyesight copying engravings.

The children's early love of literature was imbibed from their parents, both of whom read novels aloud to them in those pre-television, pre-wireless days. Their father read them Dickens in the evenings after work. His return home was eagerly anticipated by the children on winter evenings in particular. 'Damn the dog!' the short-sighted Frederick would exclaim on the way to his favourite armchair as he tripped over the black spaniel, Prince, stretched out near the hearth. Prince would then receive a conciliatory pat with the folded-up copy of *The Times* that Frederick was about to read. The children would wait impatiently while their father read his paper, drank his tea (to Winifred's wonder he always took it without milk) and ate slices of bread and butter. If he was more tired than usual after his day at the office and the evening's reading should be slow in coming, they would start to drop broad hints, loudly discussing the previous day's episode and wondering how the plot would develop, until Frederick, resignedly, would stretch out his hand to take up the current book. On those foggy Edwardian London evenings by the fireside he worked his way through much of Dickens. He was a marvellous reader, acting out the characters, some of whom became the children's constant companions in their games. They repeated snatches of Dicken's dialogues *ad nauseam*, and Sairey Gamp and Betsey Prig and Mrs 'Arris from *Martin Chuzzlewit* became so popular in the Bourne household that their father wearied of them; at one stage a specific ban was put on any further references to Mrs 'Arris.

A family so well versed in Dickens would have been aware that Dora Spenlow in *David Copperfield* lived in Norwood, and that at the height of his infatuation with Dora, when he thought nothing of tramping the ten miles to her house to catch a glimpse of her, the young David was 'well known on the Norwood road'. The Bournes may also have known that the young Dickens was himself familiar with the district in his youth, as he sometimes visited an uncle who lived in Thornton High Street.

As a boy of ten Frederick had been taken by his own father in 1870, the year Dickens died, to hear the great author reading from his books. The children were somewhat dismayed to learn that Dickens had, in Frederick's opinion, been florid and very vulgarly dressed, in a loud blue frock-coat edged with red, although this did not lessen the relish with which they listened to his works.

Their mother also read the nineteenth-century classics aloud to them. These readings, however, were associated not with the fireside but with summer evenings in the drawing room, and often took place on the balcony with its views of the Crystal Palace. Like Frederick, Katharine exposed the children early to grown-up novels; Winny, who was much younger than the others, was exposed to them very early indeed. She was only seven when her mother read *Jane Eyre* to them, but even at that tender age she was enamoured of Mr Rochester. *Jane Eyre* was followed by *The Mill on the Floss*; Winifred identified with the rebellious Maggie Tulliver, who was always getting into trouble as a child, as much as she had with the young Jane.

From their earliest years, however, the English classics were not the only literary influence on the children's imagination. The Bournes were perhaps unusual, even among the highly cultured middle class of their time, in the extent of their interest in foreign languages and literature – particularly French. The children's favourite toys were French ones, bought back by their father from business trips to Paris. There were cut-out paper dolls with whole wardrobes of different costumes and there were wonderful transfers to glue into their scrapbooks, and these things seemed more glamorous than anything in the shops in Westow Hill where they spent their pocket money each Saturday. Frederick also brought them French children's comic books such as the *Le Jeudi de la Jeunesse* annuals. From these they learned about the French way of life as well as absorbing the language. They learned about French food, and the role of *concierges* in French homes. They learned that French houses had parquet floors that were polished by valets and *bonnes* dancing over them with brushes on their feet, and became familiar with *gendarmes* and Parisian parks. They followed the adventures of juvenile heroes who were always playing some prank on an uncle or aunt – French families, much like the Bourne children themselves, seemed to be afflicted with armies of elderly relatives – only to pay the price, literally, for their naughtiness, as an aunt or uncle always had a legacy to leave which could be withdrawn when their displeasure was incurred.

The French books they read, or that their parents read aloud to them, made an indelible impression on Winny, steeping her in the history of the country in which she was to have many of her most intense experiences as an adult. The book that made the deepest impression of all was the memoirs of Jean-Baptiste Cléry, valet to Louis XVI and Marie Antoinette, the ill-fated monarchs who were swept off their throne by the French Revolution. Cléry was the only servant to accompany them and their two children, Marie Thérèse and Louis Charles, when the family was imprisoned by the revolutionaries in 1792. The King and Queen were guillotined in 1793; the young princess was released but the little Dauphin remained a prisoner and died under mysterious circumstances in 1795, aged ten. Winny, from her earliest years a stalwart royalist, was particularly drawn towards royal prisoners. Among English monarchs she was attracted above all to Charles I and his children, Henry, Duke of Gloucester, and Elizabeth, kept captives during the English Civil War. But Louis XVI was her special hero, and had become an obsession even before Mr Rochester first enthralled her at the age of seven. The French king and his family joined the 'Night Friends' whose adventures the young Bournes told each other endlessly not just at night but on their walks, characters from history alternating with those of Dickens or fraternising with them happily, effortlessly transcending the boundaries of time, space and language.

Cléry's *Journal de ce qui s'est passé à la Tour du Temple pendant la captivité de Louis XVI, Roi de France*,[1] published in 1798, may seem an odd choice of book for children, and stout Louis XVI, overfond of his meals even in captivity, an unexciting choice of historical hero. Perusal of a few pages of Cléry's journal, however, reveals him to be a born story-teller. Moreover, there was plenty in the tale of the royal family's five months' captivity in the Temple prison in Paris to appeal to children.

Cléry's story begins on 10 August 1792 with the storming of the Tuileries Palace, where the royal family had been kept under guard since being forced to leave Versailles at the outbreak of the Revolution by a pike-wielding mob. From the Tuileries they were taken to much stricter confinement in the Temple Tower, a grim medieval fortress. Cléry records the placid routine maintained by the family under the gaze of their guards. A fearsome-looking jailer with 'long moustaches, a long sabre, a great bunch of keys jangling from his belt and a long pipe in his mouth' would blow smoke into the King's face as he let the family out for their daily walk in the grounds, where they provided entertainment for a jeering mob.

---

[1] 'Journal of what took place in the Tower of the Temple during the captivity of Louis XVI'.

Clèry's narrative contained stuff grisly enough to thrill the most bloodthirsty of children, and the Bourne children appear to have been very bloodthirsty indeed. Members of the royal household were liable to have their meals in the Tower enlivened by the sudden appearance, at the window, of the head of one of their friends on a pike, with her heart impaled on another. This was how the Princess Lamballe, the Queen's confidante, was displayed outside the Tower by the mob, her blond curly hair bobbing around her face, after meeting her death in the massacres of September 1792.

The children must also have relished the intricate system of codes and signs developed by the prisoners to communicate among themselves and obtain news from the outside world under their jailers' noses. When the King was separated from the rest of the family and confined on a different floor, the twine used to tie bundles of candles served for lowering notes from one window to another. When pens and ink were confiscated by the guards, messages were sent, via Cléry, pricked out with pins. Folded in one way, a handkerchief placed by Clery in a pile of clothes back from the wash might inform the King that the Dauphin was ill; folded in another, it could convey news of the latest movements of the Austrian army.

Louis emerges from Cléry's chronicle as a sympathetic and lovable character, unfailingly courteous even to his jailers. It is hardly surprising that this account of his final months turned Winifred into a fervent royalist. She felt a passionate devotion to him and his family that amounted to frenzy and was unshaken by her father's attempts to provide balance by explaining the grievances that had led to the Revolution. Nell and Roger, however, became Republicans, and the nursery and garden became the setting for some sanguinary scenes.

In her memoir Winifred vividly remembers one Sunday when their parents were expecting a visit from one of Frederick's business acquaintances and his wife. The children were told that the couple were elderly and rather stuffy and were instructed to be on their best behaviour. Unfortunately, the date was 14 July and 'it needed no more to turn us into savages.' Their favourite game that summer involved regularly parading the heads of various dolls (sacrificed by Nell and Winny for the purpose) on top of the wooden poles used for their weekly sessions of 'remedial exercises' with a drill-sergeant. Red ink served as blood. On that Sunday afternoon on 14 July 1907 the children were marching the heads of their decapitated victims through the front garden, red ink streaming in abundance down the poles, belting out the words of the Marseillaise, 'Allons enfants de la patrie',[2] at

---

[2] 'Arise, children of the Fatherland'.

precisely the moment the visitors' carriage drew up at the front gate. Despite Frederick's explanations of the significance of the date for Francophiles, the startled visitors were unamused by this choice of a Sunday-afternoon pastime, confining themselves, however, to remarking that 'the children seemed extraordinarily bloodthirsty'.

Similarly, the little Brontës acted out events from the lives of their favourite monarchs (Emily broke a branch off a tree in the Parsonage garden when she was pretending to be King Charles II hiding in the oak tree) or battles between characters in their imaginary countries. Winifred wrote in one of her biographies of an occasion when the wild frenzy of the Brontë children's play-acting sent the family's old servant, Tabby, running out of the house in terror to summon her nephew to the Parsonage in the absence of the children's father.

'William! William! Yah mun goa up to Mr Brontë's for aw'm sure yon childrer's all goo'in mad, and aw darn't stop ith 'house any longer wi' em . . . '

Winifred records that William, plodding up to the parsonage, was greeted with 'a great crack o' laughing' from the children. Imagining the scene on a summer's day – 'the house-door is open and the screaming, gesticulating children are tearing about the parsonage garden'[3] – Winifred can have had no trouble in entering into the wild elation of an all-absorbing imaginary world that made the young Brontës' childhood an essentially joyous one despite the sorrows that also formed a part of it.

Another major source of nourishment for the children's imaginations was the Crystal Palace, a constant presence in their childhood, living as they were within sight of its soaring south tower. The Palace was their 'stately pleasure dome', their paradise, the source of many of their keenest delights.

Constructed for the Great Exhibition of 1851 and rebuilt the following year on its permanent site on Sydenham Hill, the massive iron and glass edifice was an emblem of Victorian pride in Britain's culture, industry and, above all, Empire. Dominating the visual world of Winifred's childhood, it embodied the national self-confidence inherited by the Edwardian world into which she was born.

---

[3] Gérin, *Anne Brontë*, Chapter 6.

The Palace was of course about more than mere patriotism and self-aggrandisement. The 'People's Palace' was conceived as a means of instruction through entertainment. The splendid grounds with their terraces, fountains and statuary, rivalling those of Chatsworth and Versailles, first sparked Winifred's love of fine houses and formal gardens, classical elegance and symmetry. The grounds provided instruction in the form of the 'antediluvian creatures' still to be found in Crystal Palace Park today: giant replicas of dinosaurs and other extinct animals, frightening in their brooding immobility, placed around lakes in a kind of theme park. They also offered pure entertainment of the fun fair variety in the shape of the 'Water Chute' (a boat that was hoisted up and then shot into the largest lake), Maxim's Flying Machine, which whirled you round in the air in gondolas, and the Human Laundry, in which you were 'mangled' by rollers.

Indoors, you could explore the history of great civilisations by wandering through the 'architectural courts' – Egyptian, Assyrian, Byzantine – which made the Palace a kind of visual encyclopaedia. In the south nave were the delights of the crystal fountain and, at the end, the great clock suspended over effigies of the kings and queens of England. Among the exhibits, you could marvel at a stuffed elephant from a circus. No wonder Dickens called the Palace 'fairyland'.

There was a great organ and there were concerts of the rousing and patriotic variety, with Handel and Elgar featuring prominently in the programmes. There was theatre, and the children were taken to Shakespeare productions performed by the company of the actor-manager Frank Benson.

Best of all were the fireworks, the Thursday evening 'Brock's benefits' named after the fireworks manufacturer, which they were often taken to see. These included great set-pieces depicting momentous battles and disasters of history – the Battle of Trafalgar, the destruction of Pompei – and 'living fireworks', men in asbestos suits with frames attached to their bodies; while the lancework covering these was burning, the men's movements were outlined in fire.

Although all these delights seemed very splendid to Winifred and her siblings, the Palace was already in decline, a victim of the over-grandiose vision that had conceived it. It was simply too big to maintain. The fountains were disused and rusty, the roof leaked, the building looked dilapidated and cobwebs festooned some of the exhibits and statuaries. It had come to be viewed by many as a tawdry and costly white elephant. It was, however, given a lick of paint and smartened up for one final blaze of glory. This was the great Festival of Empire, which opened in May 1911, the month before George V's coronation.

Edward VII had died in May 1910. It was a hot summer and in later life Winifred remembered being sent with the other children to Westow Hill to buy black hair-ribbons for the girls and black arm-bands for the boys. Ladies wore black dresses, gentlemen black ties. The cabbies and carters tied black ribbon to their whips or stuck a bit of black crepe in their caps.

Although the Bourne family went into mourning like everyone else, theirs was a Liberal household which had felt no particular affection for fat Edward VII. But Winny developed a fixation with the six children of the new King, George V, who were contemporary with her and her siblings: David, as he was known (the future ill-fated Edward VIII), Albert (the future George VI), Mary, who was about the same age as Nell, Henry, George and John. Until now the children's imaginations had been stirred by characters in books and by historical events and monarchs long dead. The Coronation marked the beginning of an interest in their own time.

Winifred's ambition was to see these marvellous children in the flesh, and her chance came when the royal family visited the Crystal Palace on 12 May 1911 to open the Festival. Wildly excited, Winifred was waiting with her mother on Dulwich Hill as the royal carriages came slowly up towards Crystal Palace Parade, and she had a full view of David and Princess Mary in their parents' carriage, Mary with white plumes in her hat, David solemnly saluting in his naval cadet's uniform (she thought they both looked nervous and ill at ease). The music and pageantry that followed were like something out of a fairy tale to ten-year-old Winny. She saw the royal family again more than once on that enchanted day – on the front balcony of the Palace, and in the grounds at dusk during the grand firework display that rounded off the proceedings.

The Festival continued for five months that year, 1911, which, little as they could have guessed it at the time, was to be the last of the unclouded years of childhood. One of the highlights was the Pageant of London, in which thousands of players participated from boroughs all over London to enact the historical scenes the children knew and loved from Lady Callcott's *Little Arthur's History of England*. Each day it was the turn of a different period: the young king Richard II on horseback confronting Wat Tyler, Queen Elizabeth's speech at Tilbury, Charles I on his way to execution. Local children, roped in to participate, could often be seen walking around the streets of Norwood in their costumes.

Another highlight was the All Red Route, showcasing the Empire which was coloured red on schoolroom maps the world over. On a twenty-minute ride on an electric railway you went past a Jamaican sugar plantation, Australian pioneers building log cabins and a Maori village with a real chief and members of his tribe who sang and danced.

A 'Masque Imperial' staged at the Festival showed the 'Genius of the World' summoning Britannia to lead her people to the Temple of Achievement, with representatives of her Empire laying their riches at her feet. Sadly, the state of Crystal Palace itself was rather less prosperous than the Empire as depicted in the pageantry. The Festival incurred major losses and that same year the Palace was placed on the market. The Earl of Plymouth rescued it by buying it for the nation, but its subsequent history was one of continued decline.

From Winifred's early childhood, visits to the theatre and to concert halls supplemented the entertainment provided at the Crystal Palace. With so many of their childhood games consisting of story-telling and play-acting, drama was bound to appeal to the young Bournes. Winifred's love of the theatre dated from the thrill of her first Christmas pantomimes at Drury Lane: *Jack and the Beanstalk*, *The Babes in the Wood*, *Sinbad the Sailor*. She always remembered the pre-war Drury Lane pantomimes as something completely out of this world. Even the music of the overture was almost unbearably exciting, building up to the moment when the curtains were swished apart by two bewigged and powdered gentlemen in knee-breeches and white stockings. Special effects such as the giant's hand descending from the battlements of his castle and bearing the heroine aloft to be devoured alive had her on the edge of her seat in the front row of the dress circle, where Frederick always booked their places well in advance.

Her love of music was acquired early in life from her mother, who was a competent pianist and had a repertoire of German romantic music. After the family hymn-singing session on Sunday evenings, Katharine would play Schubert and Schumann and Mendelssohn for the children's father; although not particularly discerning about music when he and Katharine first met, he widened his knowledge and taste by regular concert-going over the years. Both Nell and Winifred were given piano lessons by Aunt Marian, who had studied at the Royal Academy of Music, but from the start Winifred was the only really musical one of the children. She would stay behind in the drawing-room to listen when the others went off to play. Katharine had a pleasant mezzo soprano voice and one day she discovered that Winny, too, liked to sing. The result was that Winny soon had a little repertoire of songs: *Die Lorelei*, which became her father's favourite, and other party pieces such as Thomas Moore's *The Ministrel Boy* and *The*

Harp that once through Tara's Halls. Frederick was delighted by her new accomplishment. Nell and Roger, however, would express their opinion of her peformance by creeping downstairs from the nursery and hammering on the drawing-room door. Frederick would dart out just too late to catch them, and this became a weekly Sunday evening ritual until he decided instead to ignore the miscreants, with the result that this form of protest was soon abandoned.

It was Winny who, from the age of seven or eight, accompanied her father to Sunday afternoon concerts at the Royal Albert Hall. Generally a restless child, at concerts she sat still and spellbound. She heard some of the stars of the day: the violinist Fritz Kreisler, the immensely tall contralto Clara Butt, a well-known figure at Crystal Palace galas, and the pianist Vladimir von Pachmann, who wore his white hair to his shoulders like Liszt and would keep up a running commentary for the audience as he played. Winifred's love of Liszt's music dated from hearing Pachmann play the Hungarian Rhapsody No 2.

Music was to be important to her throughout her life, particularly in times of trouble. Another source of joy and consolation was the love of nature she inherited from her father. A city boy, brought up in Bloomsbury, he was always drawn to the countryside, and at that period Norwood still offered some of the pleasures of country life. Whitehorse Lane opposite their house, leading to Thornton Heath, where there was a villa reputed by local tradition (or so Winifred recalled in her memoir) to be the one that inspired Mr Carker's house in *Dombey and Son*, was one of the ancient lanes that had crossed the heath in the old days. The bench and horse trough on the corner of the lane turning from South Norwood Hill, a peaceful spot to rest half-way up the hill on a hot day, offered as tranquil a prospect as a village street. Opposite their house there were fields that had not yet been built on, with high overhanging hawthorn hedges. At weekends their father led them into the Surrey hills that rolled around Norwood for mammoth walks from which they returned with aching legs. He was a quiet man, and to those who did not know him well appeared withdrawn. He had eccentricities such as a habit of talking to himself as he walked, muttering and groaning, unaware at times of the children's company. And yet he was an inventive and imaginative companion for them.

He would endeavour to expand their young minds by refusing to give a simple answer to any question. In Socratic mode, he would challenge everything they said, trying to make them aware of the many shades of grey between black and white. If, for example, Nell asked, 'Was Nelson a good man?' Frederick would answer with another question. 'What do you call good?' 'Well, he was very brave.' 'Yes, but what do you call hanging Caraccioli just to please Lady Hamilton? Was that good?' (The young Bournes had heroes in common with the Brontë children born almost a century earlier, Nelson and Wellington being two cases in point.)

In between teasing his children and questioning their every utterance, Frederick passed on to them his knowledge and love of trees and flowers and birdsong. The deepest and most joyful contact with nature, though, was on summer holidays in the country. Winifred's earliest memories were of two long summers on a farm near the Suffolk village of Dunwich, the first of them when she was only four, where she first grew to love the countryside as she always loved, with passion. The farm was at the bottom of a deep rutted lane overhung with trees. They went for evening walks on heathland covered in bracken, through which the rabbits scudded away at their approach. When Winifred moved to the moorland landscape of Haworth in middle age after a life spent in cities, she was reminded of the walks on Dunwich Heath, during which her short legs could hardly keep up with her older siblings. When she first read Emily Brontë's poetry she had an instinctive empathy with Emily's ecstatic feeling of oneness with nature – both the natural universe in general and and the particular landscape around her native village.

For Winifred, as for Emily, the Brontë with whom she always felt a special affinity, animals were all-important players in the natural world of which humans are merely a part. There was always a family dog at Norwood, but it was at Dunwich that Winifred really discovered what animals meant to her, from her first ride in the farm cart in which the farmer, Mr Clarke, collected them from Saxmundham station, pulled by two horses called Bonnie and Dapper, and the thrill of waking next morning to the crowing of cocks and all the other animal noises in the yard outside. It was only when she moved to Haworth that she rediscovered the delight of being surrounded by sheep and horses, but most of her life was shared with pets. Her love for her animal companions always verged on the obsessive, for example when she refused to abandon a beloved cat while fleeing from the German invasion of Belgium and France in the Second World War.

After Dunwich, summer holidays were generally spent in Sandown on the Isle of Wight, where the children would be left for part of the time with the governess of the moment while their parents went to Switzerland.

From an early age Winifred was sensitive to the historical associations of the places where she was taken. For her, history was about people; the personages she had read about were real people to her, and this early interest in historical lives was clearly part of what made her a biographer in later life. For a staunch supporter of the Stuarts, the interest of Carisbrooke Castle near Newport in the Isle of Wight lay in the fact that Charles I had been imprisoned there in the months before his trial, and that after his death his daughter Princess Elizabeth had been brought to the castle and died there of pneumonia at the age of fourteen. Winifred's interest in this brother and sister had been awakened by Grace Whitham's *Captive Royal Children*, whose richly illustrated pages were among the most well-thumbed of those pored over by the Bourne children. She shed tears when she saw the sculptor Marochetti's monument to Elizabeth in St Thomas's Church near the Castle, in which the romantically idealised teenage princess lies with her head on the Bible given to her by her father on the night before his execution, her long hair flowing over its open pages.

Phil was the first of the four to be considered old enough to accompany Frederick and Katharine on their Swiss holidays, as a reward for doing well at school. In the event he missed the swimming and boating of Sandown, and in later years their mother recounted an odd incident involving him that took on significance with hindsight. Katharine, who loved country graveyards, had asked him to accompany her to the little Alpine cemetery of Zermatt containing the graves of climbers who had lost their lives on Matterhorn. After they had strolled around for a time, Katharine sat down to rest – she was already suffering from the arthritis that was to cripple her – and it was only then that she noticed that Phil had gone deathly pale and was shivering. 'Let's get out of here,' he said. She obeyed immediately. Neither of them ever spoke to each other of this incident, but Katharine never forgot it.

Like the young Brontës, the young Bournes received so much intellectual stimulation from their parents and one another that there hardly seemed a need for governesses, let alone formal schooling. The Swiss and German *Fraüleins* who replaced one another at regular intervals throughout Winny's childhood she saw simply as a nuisance. She derived a far better knowledge of French language and culture from books than from Swiss nannies. But happy as she was at home, she was eager to go to school. She envied Phil, who was sent to Whitgift School in Croydon, following in the steps of his cousins George Orsmby and Cuthbert Pearce, the sons of Katharine's sister Lily. Until her teens, however, she was educated at home with just one interlude of schooling.

One reason for this was that since both Nell and Roger were taught at home it was convenient for Winny to join them. During Nell's one experience of schooling, at Croydon High School, she suffered as much as Emily Brontë did on forays outside the family nest, while Roger was for a long time considered, rather like Branwell Brontë, too highly-strung for the attempt to be made.

Another reason why Winifred's first experience of school was delayed was the advice of the family doctor. She was a boisterous child with a lot of excess energy and after witnessing her, at the age of six or so, hurling herself down the stairs when summoned to see him in the drawing room, the doctor advised against sending so excitable a child to school too early. Winny herself, unhurt by her precipitate descent, considered the advice 'stupid'. She chafed irritably at morning lessons with the 'stupid' *fräuleins* and was wild with rapture when she was finally sent for a time at a local preparatory school; she would rush to the garden gate ahead of the fräulein deputed to walk her there and shake and kick it in her impatience. The school was run by a Miss Lemon or Miss Lulham. In old age Winifred recalled the name as Lemon – oddly, the superior Rosamund Vincy in *Middlemarch* attends a school run by a lady of that name – but according to one record, the school where Winifred first learned her letters, opposite the Queen's Hotel in genteel Church Road, was actually presided over by a Miss Lulham.[4] Winifred's most vivid memory of her time there was of writing her first compositions. Just the physical sensation of putting pen to paper was a joy, and from then on, despite the erratic spelling she retained even in adulthood, writing of any kind was such a pleasure that she even volunteered to write letters to the hated aunts.

Although attendance at Miss Lulham's channelled some of her energy, she remained a wilful child. She was defiant towards her aunts, one or other of whom was often present at the family's Sunday lunch, and in later life she recalled her reprehensible behaviour towards low-church Aunt Jessie one Sunday. Having spent the meal constantly correcting her niece's manners, chatter and 'forwardness', her aunt exhorted her to 'Say "*thank* you, Aunt Jessie"'. When Winifred, in a rage, retorted, 'I've nothing to thank you for! You've spoiled my whole lunch!' she observed her father, despite his unfailing courtesy to his wife's sisters, convulsed with silent laughter.

After her spell at Miss Lulham's, Winifred was back at home again, being taught with Roger and Nell. There was a single exception to the procession of unremarkable governesses. For a period in 1910–11 the three children were taught by a Miss Hodges who was a great improve-

---

4 Records of Sydenham High School, later attended by Winifred.

ment on her predecessors. Like the elderly Miss Jones in *Jeremy*, Hugh Walpole's novel of late-Victorian childhood, Miss Hodges must have appeared unprepossessing at first appearance – white-haired and suffering from arthritis – but she turned out to be a success, an important educational influence for the year and a half of her stay. As a prize for good work, she gave Winifred Thackeray's *The Rose and the Ring*. The rhymed page headings ('Here begins the pantomime/Royal folks at breakfast time', etc.) were soon being repeated by the three children as obsessively as the sayings of Sairey Gamp and her fictional friend Mrs 'Arris.

Maria Louisa Hodges talked interestingly about everything, particularly history and poetry. Despite her Victorian appearance she was a feminist for her time, and advanced and critical in her thinking. She tried to make Winifred question some of her assumptions about historical characters such as Louis XVI, getting her to read Harriet Martineau's *The Peasant and the Prince* in which the French king is depicted as a sluggard and glutton, but did not succeed in shaking Winifred's loyalty to the stout monarch. In introducing her to poets such as Wordsworth, however, and ensuring that she learned their verse by heart, Miss Hodges had a lasting influence and provided her with a resource that was to serve her well.

And then at the end of 1911 came what Winifred and Nell always called 'the end of childhood' – or at least of the childhood idyll they had known so far, with nothing to shake their absorption in their world of make-believe.

The tenth of December of that year was Phil's fifteenth birthday. He was mature beyond his years, physically as well as mentally. For this birthday he was given a gold sovereign, a dinner jacket, and a walking cane, almost as though it were a coming of age. He was now considered a young man and old enough to go to the theatre with his best friend, Dennis Ely. This was a friendship that was to bring significant connections for other members of the family too. Dennis – the son of George Herbert Ely, who, under the name of 'Herbert Strang', was the co-author of boys' adventure stories rather in the style of G.A. Henty – and his sister Dorothy were destined to be important in the lives of both Nell and Winifred.

Although school life took Phil away for much of the time and he did not share in most of the games of the three younger ones, who were as childish for their years as he was mature for his, he was a much-loved and essential member of the quartet. He showed great kindness to his youngest sister. Winifred was ashamed, at the age of ten, of not yet being able to tell the time. One evening that year, on return from school, Phil undertook to teach her between tea and dinner. He sat her down at the dining-room table before the mantel-piece clock, a handsome one with Westminster chimes, and turned the hands to every possible position. It took two hours, but Phil never once lost patience with her, and by dinner-time he was able to announce triumphantly that she had 'got it'.

She remembered him, too, as having a merry heart that made him universally popular. It found expression in song. He had been with Dennis to see *The Arcadians*, the hit musical comedy of that year and one of the longest-running ever staged in London. Phil was particularly taken with Peter Doody's song from Act III, 'Always merry and bright'. He had a good voice and sang it at the school concert.

> I've always been, since quite a lad,
> Cheery and gay when things were bad –
> That is a way I've always 'ad –
> I look on the bright side!
> I've gotter motter –
> Always merry and bright!
> Look around and you will find
> Every cloud is silver lined . . .

In the weeks leading up to Christmas Phil could often be heard singing Doody's little Cockney ditty around the house.

> I've often said to meself, I've said,
> 'Cheer up, Cully, you'll soon be dead!
> A short life and a gay one!'
> I've often said to meself, I've said,
> 'Cheer up, Cully, you'll soon be dead!
> A short life and a gay one!'

The days before Christmas were always particularly exciting for the Bourne children. Their mother incorporated elements of the season learned in her years in Germany, such as a spectacularly decorated tree; in those days Christmas trees were not as ubiquitous in Britain as they are today. Another German custom Katharine had imported was that of giving presents on Christmas Eve rather than Christmas Day. On 24 December the nursery would be out of bounds to the children for hours while their mother slaved within to transform it. Before the door was finally flung open she would put records on the gramophone, and the children would enter to the joyous accompaniment of carols and the scent of pine needles to find that the familiar room had become fairyland – the candles lighted on the tree, the presents piled below. Many years later, Nell wrote about that Christmas of 1911 in a little reminiscence called *The Threshold*, dedicated to the memory of her parents.

When I was a little girl, long before the first World War, the happiest memory of my happy year was invariably the one in which, on Christmas Eve, our mother opened the nursery door – which had been locked upon her for several hours – and admitted us to what was, to my infant mind, a veritable foretaste of Heaven . . .

There were lights shining from the Christmas Tree and reflected in all the tinsel and stars with which we had helped to deck it; there was solemn music issuing from the gramophone; there were lovely gifts such as Kings and Wisemen might have travelled far to bring and, above all, there was a mysterious radiance within ourselves, such as never illuminated our own delightful birthdays and which was associated in our minds with a starry night . . . shepherds . . . angels and, more friendly and accessible . . . an ox and an ass breathing heavily and solicitously (as our own dear dog always did) into a manger where lay a child . . .

All this intense happiness, a happiness to which we looked forward for many weeks, we owed to our mother alone, for our father, an enchanting companion for the rest of the year, hated festivities and always contrived to be in a bad temper for Christmas. It was for her, therefore, that our hearts thrilled with gratitude as we rushed over the threshold, it was towards her that our cries of rapture rose in the warm, bright room . . .

Then, one Christmas, a blow fell from which my parents never really recovered and which, to those of us who survived, brought the end of Childhood. For, that winter, the lights of our Christmas tree went out for ever.

Then followed the disappointing, disillusioning years reserved for those who have had a too happy childhood and I soon came to regard Christmas as a meaningless interruption to the few interests and occupations which made adult life worthwhile.[5]

A few days before Christmas, Phil woke in the night with a sore throat, calling out for water and saying he felt 'rotten'. The doctor was

---

[5] In the Gérin papers held by the Brontë Parsonage Museum [hereafter BPM papers].

slow to respond to the note sent to him – the household did not yet have a telephone – and, once he had called and taken a swab for analysis, did not return for a couple of days; the children's parents suspected him of putting the pleasures of the festive season before duty. On the day before the doctor re-appeared, Winnie crept into Phil's bedroom for a few minutes. She remembered afterwards that he was wearing his dressing-gown with blue and cream stripes. It was 23 December. Her mother came in and told her she had better not stay any longer in case Phil's illness was infectious. On the 24th the doctor returned in some alarm. The anaysis had shown that Phil had diptheria.

Despite the development of an antidote (antitoxin) in the 1890s, the disease was still dreaded, claiming many victims among children and in the slums of the period just as it had in Victorian times. For the safety of the other children, Katharine was persuaded by the doctor to leave Phil in the care of professional nurses summoned in haste from Croydon Hospital, and to move into the nearby Queen's Hotel with Nell, Roger and Winifred. As they drove there in the dark that afternoon Winifred clutched a book that Katharine had bought her for Christmas, picked out in haste from the pile of presents to keep her occupied. Called *True Stories of Girl Heroines* by Evelyn Everett-Green, it included the story of a heroine of Winifred's, Elizabeth Stuart, Charles I's daughter. It provided some comfort over the next few days of that miserable Christmas at the hotel with her mother and brother and sister, while their father remained behind at home with Phil.

Winifred woke on the night of the 27th in the hotel room she was sharing with Nell to find the lights on and Nell sobbing on the next bed. It took her some time to realise that the still more terrible cries she could hear were coming from their mother in the adjoining room. Frederick had just arrived at the hotel, so stunned by the news he had to bring it had taken him an hour and a half to walk the mile or so up the road from their house.

Phil had died earlier that evening. From the account given later by the nurses it appeared that he might very possibly have been saved but for the incompetence of the doctor, who had given him the antitoxin too late and, to compensate for the delay, in too great a quantity – a triple dose that proved too much for his heart.

Because she had been with him shortly before he died Winifred was given the antidote too. It had a disastrous effect on her metabolism and it was months before she felt normal again. But nothing ever did return to normal again, not even once the terrible days at the Queen's Hotel were over, days of being served festive meals in their rooms while everyone else was celebrating, and seeing their father break down when the waiter handed him a dessert iced with the words 'Happy New Year'; not even when she and Roger and Nell were allowed to return home from Hastings, where they were sent to stay with some of the aunts while the house was fumigated. They arrived back to find that their soft toys had had to be destroyed; their books were deemed safe once they had been baked in the oven. Winkie, the orange Persian cat, who had been sent to board with the vet, never returned home. She had been left out in a blizzard, caught pneumonia and had to be put to sleep.

Of the children, only Nell was taken to Phil's funeral in West Norwood Cemetery, where Katharine's parents were buried. It was attended by crowds of schoolfriends as well as relatives. But both girls often accompanied their mother afterwards on her weekly visits to Phil's grave. Katharine and Frederick found a suitable inscription for the headstone in some lines of Longfellow's.

How sweet a life was his!
Living, to wing with mirth the weary hours,
Dying, to leave a memory like the breath
Of summers full of sunshine and of flowers.[6]

Frederick proved to be even more inconsolable than Katharine, who found some comfort in visiting the grave. For the children it was an awakening from their dream world. When Winifred came to write about the four surviving Brontë children, this early experience of the death of a sibling must have given her empathy with Charlotte, Branwell, Emily and Anne, who in early childhood lost their two eldest sisters, Maria and Elizabeth, to tuberculosis at the respective ages of eleven and ten.

---

[6] From *In the Churchyard at Tarrytown.*

2
Paris 1913
'The most splendid adventure'

It was to be a long time before the children saw their parents looking happy again. Much as she had loved her eldest brother, Winny herself was still too young to realise fully how deeply his death was to mark her – in her memoir she called it 'an irreversible calamity affecting my whole life'. In the first months of the miserable year of 1912 it was just one of several calamities affecting her, which included the loss of Winkie and her toy rabbits.

But Phil's disappearance did have the immediate effect of altering the remaining siblings' relations among themselves and with their parents. Nell, at fourteen, had to step into Phil's place as the responsible eldest. Since, with the exception of one brief and unhappy experiment, she never went to school, she became increasingly her parents' favoured companion, needed by both to cheer them even after the first few months of mourning. It was she who often accompanied her mother – and her father when he could escape from the office – on the holidays abroad which brought Katharine some relief from mental and physical suffering.

At the end of January Nell went with her parents to Nice, where Katharine suffered a virtual breakdown, compounded by sciatica. She took to her bed for some weeks while Nell accompanied her father on excursions along the coast. His behaviour on these outings was even more eccentric than usual, long silences alternating with muttered remarks to himself and samples of his choice interjections, 'Brickbats!' being a particular favourite. Afterwards, however, Frederick said that Nell's company and her response to the natural beauty around them had acted on him like a balm. Nell seemed to grow up suddenly into a young woman on that holiday. returning from it with a tan and a French striped linen dress in which she looked like the 'Kodak girls' in the popular posters of the time. This sophistication was only skin-deep. Under it, she remained the timid girl she had always been.

Winifred still looked up to Nell as her confidante and guide, but after Phil's death Winifred and Roger became closer. While the rest of the family were in Nice the two of them were left at home for most of that spring in the care of Aunt Amy – the most dreaded of the aunts – and one of the succession of governesses whom Winifred viewed simply as an affliction. (When in later life she became familiar with the Brontë sisters' tribulations in this walk of life, did she perhaps have a revelation of the frequent unsatisfactoriness of things from the governess's point of view as well?) Happily, neither Winny nor Roger required much external motivation to immerse themselves in their favourite subjects. Although Roger was always well ahead of Winifred intellectually as well as in years, and was deep in Macaulay's History of England while she was still engrossed in Henty's tales, they shared an interest in history and old buildings. His thoughts were already turning to the possibility of becoming a clergyman, which he fondly believed was the next best thing to actually living in his beloved Middle Ages.

Frederick, while dearly loving all his children, had been particularly close to Phil. Now, although he still saw the three youngest as childish and 'feckless' in comparison with Phil at the same age, he had to invest all his hopes and expectations in his remaining children. Around that time, the 'nursery' became the 'study', and for the Christmas of 1912 Frederick bought them a splendid mahogany bookcase to mark the transition.

One effect of Phil's death was that for the first time Frederick really got to know his younger son, who turned fourteen at the end of 1912 and was fast growing to his final height of well over six feet. Because of his nervous problems, Roger had been too much in the care of women, with only his sisters for companions. Knowing his love for *Ivanhoe* and Scottish history, Frederick took him off on a Highland tour and was so impressed by his knowledge and also his physical resilience that from then on Roger's life became more normal; he was sent to a local prep school, where he took happily to Latin.

The children's summer holiday in Sandown the year after Phil's death was a dismal one. It rained constantly and they were accompanied by a particularly unsympathetic successor to Miss Hodges. As for Christmas, it was an occasion to dread, and was spent in a hotel near some of the aunts who lived in Hastings. There were none of the usual rituals; even present-giving was deferred until after they returned home.

But by May 1913 their mother felt sufficiently recovered to take the children on a holiday that Winifred was to describe as the 'most splendid adventure' and 'inspiring experience' of her youth. Katharine took them to spend a month in Paris, a city for which she had a particular fondness; she and Frederick had spent their honeymoon there.

It was the start of Winifred's romance with the city. Since early childhood she had been steeped in the history of France and the world of *Le Jeudi de la Jeunesse*. Now, for the first time, she made the acquaintance of the Paris of her own times.

In that last year before the outbreak of the First World War, in the spring of 1913, Paris seemed very beguiling indeed. Winifred's impressions were of a joyful, elegant city of chestnut trees in flower, white buildings, glittering fountains and the *fiacres*, drawn by jaunty little horses, that trotted along every boulevard in those pre-war days. It was the first really happy family time since Phil's death, and any intimations of war were far from the children's minds in that delightful month.

They stayed at a *pension* in Rue Galilée, close to the Arc de Triomphe and just off the Champs Elysées. Every unfamiliar detail of its 'Frenchness' interested Winny: the window-shutters, and the formal garden with flowers in tubs and paths covered in pebbles, quite unlike the gardens at home; Adrienne the chamber-maid, who wore a white cap with long streamers that floated out behind her when she brought the coffee, croissants and rolls to their bedrooms each morning; the table d'hôte – the single long dining-table at which everyone sat at dinner – where the children had the opportunity to listen to the general conversation in French and observe guests of various nationalities, such as a distinguished, aristocratic Russian couple with exquisite manners, probably fallen on hard times. The bearded Russian gentleman, who looked like the Tsar, always treated Winny with courtesy when she sat next to him, pouring out her wine and conversing with her kindly. It was her first experience of being treated like an adult and of taking part in grown-up conversation, and was one of the great thrills of the month in Paris. Another thrill for the two girls was wearing their new pale blue and cream striped evening frocks. They had only recently cast off their mourning clothes for Phil, and their day dresses were still 'half-mourning': black and white checked gingham.

Post-1914, post-1917, after the shattering of the old order all across Europe, Winny sometimes wondered about the fate of that Russian couple with old-world manners encountered at the table d'hôte of their Parisian *Pension*.

The best opportunity for fascinated observation of foreign ways was provided by a niece of their father's who lived just round the corner from the Pension Galilée, Louisa ('Louie'), and her husband Enrico. Louie, then in her mid-forties, was the daughter of their father's eldest half-brother and, although the children's cousin, was much closer in age to their parents. She was the only one of their father's relatives to figure in their life, but she and Enrico made up for this dearth of relations on the paternal side by being particularly colourful. Although English, Louie had acquired foreign mannerisms as well as several foreign languages, while Enrico Beltrán (despite his adopted Italian first name) was Spanish. This alone would have made him an object of fascination for the children, but as if that were not enough, he was – or had been – an opera singer. The pair had met in Milan, where Louie was studying music and Enrico was a soloist at La Scala – according to his admiring wife he triumphed in particular in the role of *Don José* in Carmen. After a botched nose operation that deepened his tenor voice to a less sought-after baritone, he turned instead to teaching singers.

The couple had now lived for some years in Paris, sharing their flat – crammed with photos of celebrities from Enrico's days of stardom – with two dogs, a 'Pom' called Lou-Lou and a toy spaniel called Chrissy. These pets were a major attraction, but the children would have warmed to Enrico and Louie even without them. They were an ebullient couple. The gay hubbub of the first meeting at their flat, where the 'bambini', as Enrico called them, were warmly and volubly greeted with continental embracings and kissings amid the excited barking of the dogs, set the tone for the delightful and very un-English 'foreignness' which Winifred found so bewitching. Plump Louie, with her auburn hair piece, low contralto voice and dramatic gestures, looked like an opera-singer herself and was fully as exotic as her husband despite her English origins.

In the course of their Paris holiday they grew very fond of Enrico, in particular. This hitherto unknown relative-by-marriage became their chaperone for the month and proved a delightful guide, kind and jolly as well as knowledgeable, with a love of history as ardent as their own. He was fluent in Spanish, French and Italian, but spoke no English. The children had understood French since early childhood, but despite, or perhaps because of, the Swiss nursery governesses, they did not speak the language fluently. Although Winny was in time to become a proficient French speaker she never lost her English accent. But with Enrico they chattered away without inhibition, and learnt much more with him than with the stiff French governess who gave them conversation lessons in the *pension* garden in the morning.

Afternoons were dedicated to sight-seeing. They saw the gardens of the Tuileries palace where the royal prisoners of Cléry's memoir were confined after the outbreak of the Revolution; the massive Conciergerie prison from which so many were sent to the guillotine;

Versailles, the scene of happier days for French monarchs; Napoleon's tomb. Winny, still a confirmed royalist, was moved by the monuments to Louis XVI and Marie Antoinette in the Chapelle Expiatoire and the graves of the victims of the Terror in the chapel garden (Nell, who had by now read Carlyle's *French Revolution*, remained as confirmed a Republican). Seeing with her own eyes the places where the human dramas that gripped her imagination had taken place was as important to Winifred then as years later when she became a a biographer.

The children were of course taken to the Louvre, where Winifred discovered that her taste was for Watteau and the Rococo rather than the earlier Old Masters. At that age paintings did not excite her as much as buildings and monuments and her interest was in the people depicted rather than the paintings in themselves. Nell, in view of the style of painting she adopted when she became an artist later in life, would probably have derived more enjoyment from the work of the French Impressionists while, conversely, Roger, the medievalist of the family, despised all manifestations of art after the fourteenth century. They found it hard to drag him away from the medieval wonders of the Sainte-Chapelle, Notre-Dame and the Cluny museum, but among the Old Masters of the Louvre he was indifferent and sat with his straw boater over his eyes pretending to sleep. Enrico was amused when Roger confided to him that the trial of his life was 'les girls', meaning his sisters, unaware of the word's association with chorus girls for French speakers.

Roger was also less receptive than his sisters to the romantic allure of the opera, where their mother took them for the first time. Hitherto their only comparable experience had been the annual pantomimes at Drury Lane, and those had been matinees. They felt very grown-up and sophisticated attending evening performances, at the Opéra Comique or the Gaieté Lyrique, of operas Katharine thought they would enjoy, such as *Carmen* and *Rigoletto*. Some of their happiest hours in Paris were spent in the *Pension* garden in the afternoons before these outings, their mother reading through the libretti for them and humming the main arias. When Frederick joined them at the end of their stay he took Katharine to see Gounod's *Faust*. It was the first time since Phil's death that the children had seen their mother decked out in her evening finery of lace and jewellery, and both their parents going out together looking cheerful.

Katharine was too delicate for their more intensive sight-seeing jaunts, but took them for drives in *fiacres* in the Bois de Boulogne and joined them and Enrico on trips down the river to beauty spots such as St-Cloud which were to acquire a romantic significance for Winifred in a later period of her life.

Winifred could not have imagined that this stay in Paris heralded the most intensely-lived period of her adult life. Not only would her happiest years be spent in Paris, but, like her cousin Louie, she was to experience the ultimate attraction of the exotic and the foreign when she fell in love with a dark, lively foreigner. And her Paris initiation would be put to good use when she became the biographer of Charlotte Brontë. Winifred's first contact with 'abroad' gave her an understanding of the impact on Charlotte of the continental, Catholic world of Brussels, just as her subsequent romance with a Belgian gave her a special interest in the spell cast on Charlotte by her Brussels teacher Constantin Heger.

3

Sydenham

The Great War Years

Back in Norwood on their return from that magical Paris trip, everything seemed very dull; Winifred compared it to the darkness succeeding the finale of a particularly splendid fireworks display on a gala night at the Crystal Palace. Happily, their father, whose inquiring mind was always open to new ideas and inventions, discovered a new source of pleasure for them all. Until then he had hired carriages from a local 'livery-stable' for special occasions; although the first motor cars were already appearing on the roads in the Edwardian world of Winny's early childhood, the moneyed classes were still conveyed chiefly in landaus and broughams. But a new age of transport was dawning. For George V's coronation in 1911, Frederick had hired a chauffeur-driven car to take him, Katharine and Nell to see the royal procession pass by in Whitehall (Winny had been left at home to eat her heart out on the occasion). The livery stable was replaced with a garage which hired out 'motors' bought from royal stables when discarded in favour of newer models. In 1913 Frederick first hired one of these to take the family on an outing. Since he was too unmechanical to learn to drive himself, he also hired a chauffeur.

In later life, what Winifred remembered most of the year leading up to the start of the First World War were these family motor tours, at first to nearby places of interest such as the Dickens country around Rochester but very soon as far afield as the Lake District and Scotland, and the West Country all the way to Land's End.

Speed was not the prime object of these early cars, and the Bournes' excursions took place at the leisurely pace characteristic of life for their class in these last days of the old order. Naturally, Frederick and Katharine were concerned about the threat of war; they could not but be aware of the mood in Germany, particularly through the German contacts they had kept up since their Hamburg days. Katharine had been upset by the anti-British comments of old friends there when she visited them in 1913, while Frederick was a natural pessimist who always expected the worst to happen. But intimations of the approaching crisis were pushed aside during those unhurried tours in 1913 and 1914. The aim was not to arrive as quickly as possible at their final destination but to stop as often as possible in order to enjoy each beauty spot, and to arrive at the next staging-post early enough to have plenty of time to explore before moving on. They always put up at some wonderfully-named old hostelry where you seemed to be stepping straight into the world of Dickens.

Needless to say, Bourne family tours were very much cultural ones. Roger was never so happy as when exploring the architecture of a cathedral. At the age of fifteen his vague thoughts of entering the the church were becoming more defined, and his reading included the writings of early churchmen like the Venerable Bede as well as medieval chroniclers such as Froissart. For Winny, what arrested her most was the beauty of the landscape as they cruised along between fields in all their summer glory and once, when the others were animatedly arguing some point, she enjoined them impatiently to 'be quiet and listen to the scenery'.

Yet these jaunts also brought glimpses of the poverty and hardship rampant in the country. They would often pass one of the tramps who walked the dusty roads from town to town. They were visions of another world that saddened their mother. She hit on the idea of preparing little pellets of 'coppers' in screws of paper before they set out each morning, to be tossed from the car as it rolled slowly past one of the dusty wanderers: the price, at least, of a meal. They would see, on the road behind, a hat being raised in startled acknowledgement. Apart from these moments of troubled conscience, everything was unclouded enjoyment and in later years Winifred could hardly credit the insouciance of her family and so many others like them in the lead-up to the Great War.

Back home, the two girls continued to be educated at home while Roger was sent for a time to a 'crammer's' in Eastbourne. The girls also attended oil painting classes at the Crystal Palace Art School, an experience that was to prove a defining one for Nell. But the start of the War marked the end of the art classes and for its duration the Crystal Palace was used as a naval training centre. The classes, to which Winifred was indifferent, were a joyful revelation to Nell of her own aptitude, which was soon spotted by the art master. Nell thus discovered her vocation in life much earlier than Winifred, who did not even consider writing biographies until she was in her fifties. Yet Nell's creative fulfilment, too, was, for different reasons, to be delayed for decades.

Winifred always remembered a warm day in early August when she and the other children sat up later than usual because they were all waiting for a special edition of the paper to be borne up South Norwood Hill by the newsboys. They were in the drawing-room, always associated in her mind with summer evenings when the high balcony window was wide open to the view of the Palace. Almost every day that particular summer they had heard their neighbour Mr Thompson singing his favourite song, *Cherry Ripe*, in the garden adjoining theirs.

The cries of the newsboys could be heard advancing up the hill and the children rushed out to buy the paper. That evening they all knew they would be at war with Germany the next day. It was 3 August, the day Germany declared war on France and invaded Belgium, the day before Britain declared war on Germany; the evening on which Edward Grey, the Foreign Secretary, saw the lamps going out all over Europe. In later life, whenever Winifred recalled the last days before the War, she saw the open window and the balcony and heard the strains of *Cherry Ripe* wafting from the Thompsons' garden in the balmy evening air.

With Phil dead (he would have turned eighteen at the end of that year) and Roger still only fifteen, there were no menfolk in the immediate family circle who could be called upon to fight, though in their extended family on the Hill side they had male cousins of military age. The early months of the conflict, when those who had gone to war were still 'expected home by Christmas', was an exciting time for Winifred. Katharine could remember rolling lint with her sisters to make bandages for the French wounded during the Franco-German war when she was eleven, and she soon had Nell and Winifred knitting mittens, scarves and socks for men in the regiments of their friends and relatives, sending them cakes and cigarettes, writing letters in French to the members of a French gun crew at the instigation of their current governess, a Mlle Bocquet. King Albert of 'gallant little Belgium' was now one of Winifred's heroes, and she put his picture in a frame, little imagining that she was destined one day to become one of his subjects through her marriage to a Belgian.

But her excitement gave way to more sombre sentiments as young acquaintances, distant relatives, men in their father's firm, were killed or returned home wounded or shell-shocked. The deaths of practically all Phil's former schoolfellows in the course of the conflict brought home the realisation of Phil's likely fate had he survived diphtheria.

Nell was the one most closely affected by the War, when in 1916 a young man she was close to, possibly engaged to, was killed on the Somme. The young man in question, though not named in Winifred's memoir, was almost certainly Phil's great friend Dennis Ely, who was at Whitgift School with him. At the time of Dennis's death in July 1916 he was twenty and about to go to Cambridge. The Ely family, who lived on South Norwood Hill for a time, were among the Bournes' best friends. During Nell's brief sojourn at Croydon High School she had made friends with Dennis's sister Dorothy, who was to remain close to both Nell and Winifred throughout their lives. From the start, Nell renounced any thought of replacing her first love. Home-loving and deeply attached to her family, she was to become more and more necessary to her parents in the coming years as they grew frailer in body. Her mother would have been bereft if Nell had disappeared from the nest along with the others. Her father, even before the onset of illness in his last years, was often low in spirits. As long as her parents lived her home was with them. Her dedication to the artistic vocation that was to provide her with her deepest fulfilment was postponed until she could devote herself to it wholeheartedly.

Because of the fear of bombardments on the coast, Roger had been brought home from his school in Eastbourne and a new tutor found for him. Mr Simpson, a retired classics master, proved highly congenial despite a ferocious squint, and over the next few years prepared his pupil for the entrance examinations to Oxford, on which Roger had set his sights. For Winifred, too, there was a change. In the spring of 1915, at the age of thirteen and a half, she finally – discounting her brief stay at Miss Lulham's – achieved her ambition of being sent to school. Her parents opted for Sydenham High School, one of the Girls' Public Day School Trust foundations, which had a good academic record. It was a short cycle ride from South Norwood Hill to the pseudo-Gothic school buildings on Westwood Hill. Winifred was to remain there until she was eighteen.

Her five years there were contented ones. Unlike Nell, Winifred was an outgoing teenager who took well to school life. She found Sydenham a kind and happy place, and made a lifelong friend there in Wilhelmina ('Mina') Breed, a plain, studious and kind-hearted girl who was later, like Winifred, to go to Cambridge. Winifred liked the teachers, many of whom were young and friendly. 'Crushes' on mistresses were very much in the air, a facet of life at girls' schools chronicled in the novel *Regiment of Women* by a former pupil, Clemence Dane, who was believed to have Sydenham in mind for the highly-charged emotional atmosphere of her fictional school[7] (footnote overleaf). In Dane's words, 'adoration was in the air' at

Sydenham. Winifred's own devotion was to a young history teacher called Dora Pennycuick; at this period of her life history had more appeal for her than English literature.

When Winifred started at the school the headmistress was the impressively energetic Helen Maud Sheldon, a former maths lecturer at Girton College, Cambridge, who had introduced the house and prefect system so successful at boys' independent schools. Given her aura of authority, her initials, H.M.S., were felt to be apt.[8]

Adèle Sanders, a classics graduate, who succeeded her in 1917, was also an impressive figure, renowned for her oratory and wit, wearing flowing black skirts that were long even for a period when girls still played hockey in ankle-length skirts. She was part-Swiss, and her francophone cultural background and love of the arts were very much in tune with Winifred's own. Miss Sanders instilled in the girls an appreciation of beauty. She also stressed the importance of the classics in a rounded liberal education for girls, teaching Latin herself by the direct method with a greeting of 'Salvete puellae' as she swept into the classroom.[9]

Winifred was just one of the many bright girls at the school. She did well in English, French, German, History and Art, was awarded some prizes and became a prefect in the sixth form. Despite the rigour of the curriculum under Miss Sanders, she never felt under undue pressure, and the friendliness of the teachers made Cambridge – whose dons were not in general remarkable for their youth or friendliness – all the more of a shock when she arrived there.

Her years at Sydenham were of course dominated by the War. The girls were expected to contribute to the war effort and the headmistress's exhortations emphasised the extra demands made of them. They must prove themselves worthy – through self-discipline, unselfishness, energetic dedication to duty – of the sacrifice being made by their brothers at the Front. There was also a growing emphasis on the need for girls to train for some kind of work so that they could replace the men who had gone to war, but it is uncertain whether at this stage Winifred herself contemplated a profession such as teaching. From early in life her ambition was to become a writer. Meanwhile, she and her classmates helped to issue ration books at Lewisham Town

---

[7] Incidentally, both Winifred and Clemence Dane wrote plays about the Brontës: Dane's *Wild Decembers* was published in 1932, Winifred's play about Charlotte Brontë and the Hegers, *My Dear Master*, was performed in 1955.

[8] A.E.L. Davis, entry in Oxford Dictionary of National Biography9

[9] These and other details of Sydenham are taken from Yardley, *Sydenham High School: Centenary Reminiscences*.

Hall and rolled bandages at the local Red Cross Hospital. They made clothes for Belgian refugees, sent food parcels to prisoners of war and collected money for military hospitals and the St Dunstan's homes for blinded soldiers.

Winifred had just turned seventeen at the time of the Armistice in 1918. The War over, she spent her last year at Sydenham (1919–20) working towards the Cambridge entrance examination.

Although she enjoyed school and did well academically, with one exception Winifred did not owe her most formative influences to the classrooms of Sydenham High School. By the time she reached the school most of her tastes had already been formed – through her parents, reading, foreign holidays. But Sydenham did develop what was to be one of the passions of her life: Shakespeare. She had seen some of the productions of Frank Benson's company at the Crystal Palace, but they had come to an end with the War, and it was at Sydenham that she first actually read the plays. Her initiation was completed when in March 1918 the Upper Fifth were taken to see *King Lear* at the 'Old Vic'.

Her parents were apprehensive about this excursion on two counts: the danger from air raids and the Old Vic's reputation at that time, when it was seen, in Winifred's words, as a 'bug-infested slum, frequented only by barrow-boys and barmaids'. Those were the early days of the Shakespeare productions at the Royal Victoria Hall in the Waterloo Road under the management of the colourful Lilian Baylis. Until the War, the Hall, under her aegis, had merely aimed to provide a more elevated kind of entertainment for the working classes than was to be found in the 'low' music halls of the time, not to speak of the gin-palaces and alehouses. Recreation was combined with education, 'temperance lectures' with variety shows. In the first year of the War, Lilian Baylis initiated a new and more ambitious departure. She hired the director Ben Greet to stage Shakespeare. It was the first step in the meteoric transformation of the Old Vic into 'the home of Shakespeare'.

For the evangelical Lilian, who maintained an ongoing and intimate dialogue with God and consulted Him on every detail of theatre management, seeking His guidance, for example, when her actors asked for pay rises, and who once said to Sybil Thorndike, 'Church and stage – same thing – should be!',[10] bringing Shakespeare to the barrow-boys in the gallery (where the cheapest seats still cost only tuppence, as in the theatre's early days in the 1830s) had a deeply

---

[10] Findlater, *Lilian Baylis: The Lady of the Old Vic*, p. 122.

moral purpose; he provided moral inspiration, taught you how life should be lived.

The Crystal Palace, with its mission to instruct as well as entertain, was the 'people's palace'; the Old Vic was the people's playhouse. Everything was done on a shoe-string. When Winifred was taken to see *King Lear* with her classmates, the Old Vic was still a theatre of hard seats (wooden benches covered in red oil-cloth) and sawdust on the floor. It was still lit by gas. The lavatories were almost medieval. Her parents' reservations about her visit were perhaps understandable given that these were the years when a theatre critic once discovered a rat gnawing his boot during a performance.[11]

And yet many of the leading Shakespearian actors were eager to work there, including the two Thorndikes, Sybil and her brother Russell, then in their thirties, who took many of the leading parts. The attraction was certainly not the salaries offered – after due consultation with the Almighty – by the notoriously stingy Lilian. What drew actors to the Waterloo Road was the quality of the productions and the electrifying immediacy of the contact with the audience. The horse-shoe design of the theatre brought the seats into as intimate a connection with the stage as in Shakespeare's own day. And there was a kind of Elizabethan authenticity in Ben Greet's unpretentious, almost rough and ready productions, in complete contrast to the lavish productions of Herbert Beerbohm Tree in the Edwardian era. The equally rough and ready audience responded with vociferous spontaneity and an ardour to match the actors' own.

The War, far from impeding Baylis's Shakespearian venture, proved to be the making of it. With male actors thin on the ground, other theatres either closed down or opted for light entertainment to keep up Londoners' morale; the Old Vic was thus able to attract good actors and became practically the only forum for Shakespeare in those years. Ben Greet viewed his productions there as a kind of war work. Lilian addressed the audience with rousing speeches during air raids, and never let a raid interrupt a performance. Lines such as 'This England never did, nor never shall/Lie at the proud foot of a conqueror' prompted patriotic fervour from the public.

To help raise the funds needed to keep the venture going, special matinees for schoolchildren were put on in the war years. They provided an introduction to Shakespeare for a new generation of Londoners, of whom Winifred was fortunate to be one on that school outing. She was particularly fortunate to see the Thorndikes in that production. As male actors were so scarce, the female ones took male

---

[11] *Ibid.*, p. 115.

parts when required, and Sybil Thorndike said she was happy to do so given that the men had so many of the best parts. On this occasion she was the Fool to Russell's Lear, playing him with sorrowful pathos. In future years Winifred was to see Sybil Thorndike in many of the roles in which she triumphed, but this was the one she always remembered as the most moving.

For a long time afterwards Winifred could talk of nothing but Shakespeare and the Old Vic. Like all her enthusiasms, it became a passion, an obsession. Around the same time, Roger was taken to see one of its productions by his tutor and came home almost as excited as Winny. Frederick, always willing to try something new, was curious enough to want to experience a performance himself, and returned home a convert, preferring the Old Vic's 'straight' acting style to the declamatory one of Henry Irving and Ellen Terry, the actors of his youth. In the ensuing years, when the Old Vic's success was drawing an increasingly middle-class audience, he and the three young people never missed a Shakespeare production, and Katharine in time became a fan in her turn.

In 1920 Winny wrote a light-hearted ditty expressing the affection for the theatre that had made 'Old Vicites' of the entire family:

When the Waterloo Rd begins
My cockney heart with melodies rings;
As the 'barrers',[12] one by one
File past us in the midday sun
As does seem so jolly and gay
On this blissful morning in May.
When the 'Old Vic' looms in sight
My heart doth dance with sheer delight;
When within the entrance halls
We give up tickets for the stalls
We are ready to shout and sing
And make the building above us ring;
When the well-loved curtain rises
We feel quite ready for all surprises![13]

That year, 1920, the year Winifred went up to Cambridge, Katharine took the two girls to Stratford for a week. It was a blissful

---

[12] The barrows of the 'barrow-boys', costermongers, selling their wares in the streets.
[13] Poem in a letter to her family, June 1920, in the papers held by Robin Greenwood [hereafter Greenwood papers].

experience for the stage-struck Winifred, who knew the names of all the actors and could reel off long passages of the plays by heart; she would get up early to learn Hamlet's and Richard II's speeches and declaim them in her bedroom, trying to imitate the inimitable voice of her favourite actor, Ernest Milton. Her teenage passion for Shakespeare was one of the things that led her to try her own hand at writing plays in later years, first in her twenties and then in the most difficult period of her life, immediately after the Second World War.

4

Cambridge
'Bill' and 'Q'

Winifred arrived at Newnham College, Cambridge, at a time of change and optimism following the end of the War. Normal university life had been resumed. The men's colleges – which during the war years had been almost emptied of undergraduates, filling up instead with army cadets – were once again teeming with students, cheerfully flaunting the colourful waistcoats then in vogue. In the reaction against the privations of the long war years, despite the losses that had left almost every family in the land bereaved, Winifred and her contemporaries at Cambridge had a keen appetite for all the pleasures the university could provide.

At Newnham and Girton, one change in the air was the women students' demand for equal status with the men. They were not yet full members of the university. They sat the same Tripos exams as the male students but did not have the right to wear caps and gowns or to attend the degree certificate ceremony at the Senate House, receiving instead 'titular degrees' through the post, predictably nicknamed 'B.A. tits'.

There had been protests against this state of affairs since the 1890s, but in 1897 the university had voted against changing the status quo. At the time Winifred arrived, the issue was shortly to be put to the vote once again. Women had grown used to replacing men in the workforce in the war years and were increasingly demanding equality with them, although on the whole less stridently than the previous generation, the Suffragettes.

These concerns, however, were not uppermost in Winifred's mind on her arrival at Newnham. She took up residence in October 1920 just before her nineteenth birthday but she had already had a foretaste of Cambridge life earlier in the year, when she stayed at Newnham for a week in March to sit the entrance examination. During that week she sent daily bulletins to her anxious family, reporting that her Latin translation exam 'was simply blissful and I enjoyed every moment of it and didn't feel a bit worried'[14] (footnote overleaf). Roger, though almost three years older, was taking his Oxford entrance exam at the same time: 'I haven't had any news from the poor old Cleric – I wonder what his papers have been like – mine have so far been so unhoped-for that I can't believe it will last.'

As for Cambridge, it was 'the most beautiful place in the world.' She was in raptures over St John's College, dear to her as the college of Wordsworth, and its Bridge of Sighs, and 'Nell, I have discovered that at Jesus College there are lots of Burne-Jones windows and I'm longing to go – Oh! Everything is simply too glorious.'

During the week of the entrance exams she delighted in the quaint shops in town, where, living up to the reputation she had for always being hungry, she soon discovered a 'tuck-shop' extremely popular with students. She was not without friends with whom to partake of tuck-shop and other Cambridge treats. Her school-fellow Mina Breed was taking her own entrance exam at Girton, the older of the two women's colleges, four miles out of town. And in town, in Magdalene Street, opposite the Pepys library, there were George and Dorothy Moore and their two-year-old son, Nicky.

Winifred was lucky to have these Norwood friends at Cambridge. Dorothy was the sister of Dennis Ely, Phil's friend who was killed on the Somme. She was several years older than Nell but the two had become friends during Nell's brief time at Croydon High School and Winifred was soon included in the friendship. In 1916 Dorothy had married the philosopher George Edward Moore, twenty years older than herself, who had also grown up in Norwood. A fellow of Trinity College, he was highly influential in his day and his *Principia Ethica*, published in 1903, was required reading for philosophy students. He was one of the trio of Cambridge philosophers – the other two being Bertrand Russell, and Wittgenstein who joined them at Trinity in 1929 – regarded as the founders of 'analytic philosophy'.

Moore had been particularly admired by the Bloomsbury writers, who had embraced his creed that the prime objects in life were love, the creation and enjoyment of aesthetic experience and the pursuit of knowledge.[15] The Bloomsbury chronicler Frances Partridge, who went up to Cambridge a couple of years before Winifred, left a little pen portrait of the middle-aged philosopher as she glimpsed him at a meeting of the 'Moral Sciences' club, sitting on the hearthrug holding both ankles and 'tying himself in knots' as he earnestly considered the

---

[14] All the correspondence with Winifred's family cited in this chapter is in the Greenwood papers.
[15] J.M. Keynes, *Two Memoirs: Dr. Melchior: A Defeated Enemy, and My Early Beliefs* (London: Rupert Hart-Davis, 1949), p. 83.

question 'what one *exactly* meant when one said one was going to Madingley that afternoon'.[16]

Frances evidently felt that too much time and energy could be devoted to such investigations, while not doubting that these apparently trifling issues led to 'profitable molelike tunnelling in all directions'. Winifred's reaction to Moore was rather different. For her the mild-mannered, pipe-smoking professor soon became simply 'Bill', Dorothy's name for him (for some reason he disliked his real first names). He became a friend as well as the husband of her friend. She said later that the Moores, both of whom remained friends for life, were one of the greatest educative influences of her life, certainly more so than her Cambridge tutors. Moore's Socratic approach and dialectical methods made him challenge everything you said and forced you to justify your every statement. Your most innocent remarks would be greeted by a gasp of incredulity and a look of astonishment: 'Do you *really* think *that*?' he would ask.[17] With his benevolent air and remarkably bright eyes, he was always asking you 'what exactly' you meant by something – a useful exercise for a future writer like Winifred.

Bill had more to give his friends than intellectual rigour alone. After his death in 1958 Dorothy wrote to Winifred: 'I have been pleased to discover that so many people realised that Bill was good as well as great, and that many who scarcely knew him spoke of his kindness and helpfulness with appreciation, and of his moral, as well as his philosophical, influence upon them . . . Of course I knew that he was beloved by his friends, but I had not realised how widespread his influence was.'[18]

Like her husband, the forthright Dorothy questioned everything and had intellectual rigour. Like him, too, she was kind, in a matter-of-fact, unsentimental way. As hosts the Moores were utterly unpretentious and informal. Visitors were set down without ceremony at their kitchen table, where the food was often unusual and the talk always interesting, and plunged straight into whatever stimulating discussion they happened to be engaged in at the time; everyone was made to feel completely at home without being bidden to do so. There was never constraint of any kind in the Moores' house, and it was always open to Winifred.

Dorothy was curious and open to new ideas, and at their kitchen table Winifred gained many new notions. It was there that she first

---

[16] Partridge, *Love in Bloomsbury: Memories,* p. 67.
[17] Keynes, *Two Memoirs,* p. 83.
[18] Letter of 1 November 1958 (Greenwood papers).

heard the ideas of Freud discussed – in this instance, in relation to the education of little Nicky. On the basis of certain Freudian beliefs about infant sexuality, the Moores harboured the conviction that it was wrong to kiss a small child. Despite this interdiction they both doted on Nicky, and Moore shared in the care of his son. Each afternoon, in his free hours between lectures and tutorials, Dorothy would be given a break from parental duties as her husband, gown flying and mortar-board perilously perched on his head, charged around Cambridge pushing Nicky in his pram, a familiar sight in those years; a couple of years later, Nicky's younger brother Tim would be whisked around town in the same way.

Dorothy, and sometimes Bill, would pop into Winifred's room at Newnham with Nicky in tow. Their company and that of their little boy were one of the main attractions of Cambridge for her.

In the summer before she went up to Newnham, a few months after taking her entrance exam, she was back in Cambridge for another stay, this time staying in lodgings with Nell. As well as coaching Winifred for a maths entrance exam, Dorothy steered the two girls round more of the sights. They were invited to accompany the Moores to a degree ceremony at the Senate House, Bill resplendent in his doctor's robes and the girls in their smartest coats, posted to them in haste by Katharine when she heard of the invitation, and, at her insistence, wearing white gloves. Best of all was one perfect day when Dorothy took them up the river for lunch at the Orchard Tea Garden in Grantchester immortalised by Rupert Brooke, who lodged there in his undergraduate days. After that it was on to Byron's pool, all three young women delighting in the sight of Nicky as he dabbled his arms and legs over the side of the boat. And back to The Orchard for tea under the spreading boughs of the apple trees, by the riverbank garden full of larkspur and poppies. Winny described every detail of the outing in a letter to her mother.

Once installed in her room in Peile Hall at Newnham at the start of the Michaelmas Term, Winny continued to write almost daily letters to Katharine and Nell and less frequent but equally affectionate ones to 'Roddy', who had gone up to Oxford, and her father. Her missives to Frederick dealt with weightier subjects than those to the rest of the family, matters financial and intellectual. A recurring issue was her regular need for fresh funds, and justification thereof, with apologies for sometimes overrunning her allowance (chiefly on tea parties and books). She also discussed with him aspects of her studies that she knew would interest the literary-minded Frederick.

Katharine was in particular need of the comfort of Winifred's letters. Despite her own period of study in Germany before her marriage, she was oddly hostile to the idea of Winifred going away to university. By now in her sixties and in chronically bad health, she was not reconciled to her children leaving the nest and was never happy unless she had them all around her – always with the empty space left by Phil, of course. She had Nell's companionship, but she counted down the days until Winifred's and Roger's vacations.

Winifred does not seem to have resented or felt oppressed by the rather clinging nature of her mother's affection. If Katharine often worried about her student daughter, Winny – despite the cosseting she received as the spoiled baby of the family – sometimes sounds like a concerned mother herself. Her letters home were written for pleasure as much as out of duty, dashed off effortlessly in the quiet half-hour after lunch, but they continually express her concern lest her mother should be missing her. She condoled with Katharine over every headache and toothache and hoped she was having visits and theatre outings to keep up her spirits. She felt some guilt at leaving home against her mother's wishes. 'I do worry a lot about deserting my family and I am always very thankful when you write cheerfully'. She herself missed the loving family circle and was delirious with delight whenever Nell and her mother announced a visit to Cambridge, but she was finding too much to enjoy in her new life to have much time for homesickness.

Newnham, founded in 1871 shortly after Girton, was in Winfred's time in the charge of Blanche Athena Clough (1861–1960), nicknamed 'B.A.' by her charges. She was the daughter of the poet Arthur Hugh Clough and the niece of the college's formidable founder, Anne Jemima Clough. With her 'deep chuckle, twinkling eyes and shrewdly humorous features', she was a popular figure.[19]

In 1920, Newnham was still in some respects an old-fashioned place by the standards of the time. The rules on chaperones, for example, though chafed against and increasingly challenged, were still in force. No woman student could visit an undergraduate in his room or receive one in her own without the presence of a female companion. In one letter Winny tells her parents that her services as chaperone were required by a friend, Edie, whose cousin Hubert was coming to tea. 'Poplico [her name for her father] always said my elderly appearance would serve for such a purpose and he is quite right. The poor youth is terrified of all girls and has only come because Edie has promised him to get an alarming chaperone.' Edie had to fill in a 'ridiculous' form with her own name and Winifred's, Hubert's name and the day and hour he was expected. Once the timid youth arrived, 'We had a

---

19 Phillips, *A Newnham Anthology*, p. 122.

very happy time. He enjoyed himself so much he stayed 3 hours, 3.30–6.30, when all men are cleared out of college.' The hour of the 'dressing-bell' was 6.30 p.m. – in those days you still 'dressed' for dinner. Another dress code rule was the requirement for women students to wear a hat in town.

Like most of the students, Winny mocked some of the college's traditions and restrictions, but she enjoyed its routines and rites. The routine was work in the morning, games – often hockey – in the afternoon and work again from tea to 10 p.m. with an interval for dinner. The rites included after-dinner 'coffee' parties and late-evening 'cocoa' parties, there being unwritten rules about whom you could invite for either depending on whether you were a first-, second- or third-year student. In the colder months, such gatherings took place round the fires in the girls' rooms. Keeping warm in the chill fogs of winter, in those days of unheated lecture rooms and daily coal allowances, was a constant concern. The amount of coal placed in the scuttles each day by a man pushing a trolley, although more generous than in the war years, was not enough to keep the fires burning all day long. But when it was too cold or foggy for hockey there was enough coal for Winifred to spend happy afternoons reading in front of the fire, with a tabby cat who belonged to the college and had become her particular friend curled up in her lap.

Keeping biscuit and cake tins well-replenished was another important concern in the women's colleges where the food – even after the end of wartime rationing – was notoriously inferior to the men's in both quantity and quality. Winifred noted that 'the men seem much better fed than we are, and even in lodgings they have a good many courses to each meal'. The contrast drawn in Virginia Woolf's *A Room of One's Own* between the roast partridges served at a male college and the thin soup, uninspiring greens and prunes and custard served up at a fictional women's college called 'Fernham' was based on a visit to Newnham in 1928. Winifred was perpetually hungry, and in this she was not alone. The misogynous college porter, known as 'Ignatius' ('a terrible old boy who treats us all as children naturally imbued with vice – we are all in dread of him and though we treat him with the greatest affability he scolds us upon every possible opportunity'), when asked by a visitor how the young ladies spent their days, replied, 'They eats and eats, with intervals for meals'.[20]

Winny relied on food parcels from home containing cakes which were brought out for the tea parties she gave for Mina, for Dorothy and Nicky, or for her new Newnham friends. She quickly made

---

[20] *Ibid.*, p. 141.

friends. Jean Stewart, who went up to Newnham in 1921, wrote later of Winifred's 'warm friendliness', charm, kindness and vitality.[21] A student called Olga Walters in her own year was a close friend despite being very different in personality. A doctor's daughter, she was intellectual and introspective. 'People as a whole don't care for her as she is difficult to know, and very shy outwardly – she says it is always her fate that people at first don't like her!' Although Winifred often found Olga too intense and liked to relax with her more extrovert friends, she learned much from her intellectually and enjoyed their quiet, reflective times together. She described one November evening they spent together. 'We had a happy evening, Olga and I, by my fire – she mended her clothes and I read Aeshylus' *Prometheus* aloud and we were both intensely thrilled.

Although college life had its privations, Winifred seems always to have been in high spirits. Despite the cold lecture halls she got much enjoyment out of the lecturers. She was reading History and English and had the privilege of attending lectures by the legendary Arthur Quiller-Couch, editor of the first *Oxford Book of English Verse*. As Professor of English Literature he had founded the new school of English in 1917 and it was thanks to him that Winifred was able to take English as a tripos in its own right rather than as part of 'Medieval and Modern Languages'. His elegant lectures on style and literary criticism, published in the collections *On the Art of Writing* and *On the Art of Reading* under the pen name of 'Q' by which he was generally known, were to influence generations.

Q's weekly lectures were at 12 o'clock on Wednesdays at the Arts Theatre and Winifred was soon a worshipper, despite the fact that he appeared to disapprove of women students. This at least was the impression given by his invariable habit of starting lectures with the greeting 'Good morning, gentlemen', a practice he had kept up even in the war years when, on occasion, every student in the room was female. According to his first biographer, Q actually had no personal objection to the women students of Girton and Newnham attending his lectures, and in fact admitted them against the wishes of the university administration. He addressed them as 'Gentlemen' simply because in theory he was lecturing only to members of the University, and women did not officially hold that status. '[H]e believed in being strictly correct on formal occasions . . . The women . . . understood all this and, far from resenting his manner of beginning his lectures, rather enjoyed it'[22] (footnote overleaf). Another biographer, A.L.

---

[21] Winifred's obituary in Newnham College Roll Letter (1982) by Jean Pace (née Stewart).

Rowse, claims that his 'Gentlemen' was just a joke – an in-joke – and was actually intended as a form of protest at the women students' status.[23]

Be this as it may, the form of address does not seem to have lessened his popularity with his female listeners, who arrived early at his lectures, occupied most of the available seats, leaving many of the men to stand at the back, and presumably participated in the enthusiastic stamping that denoted approval of the speaker.

> 'Q's lecture came off this morning, and all I can say is that all, undergrads and students, fell in love with him. He is the sweetest old boy, with a way of putting his head on one side and smiling in an all-conquering, provoking way – he is *so* comical that we howl with laughter and stampede through the greater part of the lecture . . . He is also very emotional and *shook* when he read anything particularly beautiful – He read bits of *Prometheus*, *Hellas* and *Epipsychidion* . . . – as it was an open lecture all the townfolk came too, so you can imagine there was some scrum – Undergrads literally sat at Q's feet in a circle and we only got seats by going early – Dons and undergrads, students and townsfolk all sat jumbled up and everybody kicked up the Devil's own shindy when the dear man desisted. He has a passion for Shelley, but tried to be unbiased and first said all he could against him – but by the end he had to speak his real mind and simply glowed with enthusiasm – he says that Shelley is far and away the most popular poet with all undergrads, as he can judge from his own experience and tremendous stamping and cheering seemed to show that he was right . . . It is like going to a particularly delightful play, a Shakespeare or a Barrie, to hear him.

Apart from his performing skills, Winifred appreciated the grace and old-world elegance of his lectures. In tutorials – she was one of six women students to have the luck or ill luck, as she joked in later days, to be tutored by him; she claimed that he expressed contempt of women's intellectual powers – he would pounce on 'purple passages' in essays, 'extraneous ornamentation'. He had denounced such prose in his lecture *On Style* with the exhortation 'Murder your darlings': 'Whenever you feel an impulse to perpetrate a piece of exceptionally fine writing, obey it – whole-heartedly – and delete it before sending your manuscript to press. *Murder your darlings*'[24] (footnote opposite).

---

22 Brittain, *Arthur Quiller-Couch: A Biographical Study of Q*, p. 65.
23 Rowse, *Quiller Couch: A Portrait of 'Q'*, p. 117.

He was similarly enraged by anything he regarded as a sloppy use of words – particularly 'jargon', ready-made phrases. He would swoop down on a seemingly innocuous phrase such as 'in the case of': 'What case? A case of champagne? a coffin?' It is fortunate for him that he did not live to see the ascendancy gained by 'jargon' today. Like Moore's stringent challenging of the content of what Winifred said, this continual challenging of the words she used was good training for a future writer.

Winifred enjoyed what Moore and 'Q' each had to give her, possibly not reflecting how opposed they were in many of their values – 'Q' a traditionalist and Victorian to his fingertips, Moore a guru of the often anti-Victorian Bloomsbury writers.

She was less enamoured of the tutors at Newnham than of the lively male lecturers, finding them dry in the extreme – a dryness that had a dampening effect on her enthusiasm. Her reaction to these Newnham women was somewhat similar to that of Vera Brittain in 1913 in her first encounter with the principal of Somerville College, Oxford.[25] Winifred's most chilling encounter was with a Miss Firth who was, briefly, her history tutor. Winifred's special subject for the entrance exam had been her beloved Stuarts and the Glorious Revolution. But Miss Firth, a colourless, shrunken-looking little woman, set her to write on 'early Norman legislature'. It was a topic on which Winifred knew nothing. This first essay was handed back to her by the tutor in silence, with the comment 'I note that you can neither read nor write' written across it.

Winifred's choice of history as one of her university subjects had seemed a natural one. It was born of the love of the drama and human stories of the past, dating back to her childhood craze for Louis XVI and the French Revolution and Charles I. Her liking for Miss Pennycuick, the history teacher at Sydenham, also had something to do with it. Confronted with history as she was required to approach it by the Cambridge syllabus and by Miss Firth, she felt, in her own words, 'blighted'.

Reading for the History Tripos suddenly seemed much less attractive. At nineteen Winifred had seldom been prepared to do anything she didn't want to do, and she took action. She wrote to her parents asking to be allowed to switch to reading French rather than History, marshalling as many arguments as she could think of.

---

[24] Arthur Quiller-Couch, *On the Art of Writing* (Cambridge: Cambridge University Press, 1916).

[25] Vera Brittain, *Testament of Youth* (London: Victor Gollancz, 1933), Chapter 2.

I want to know whether you would object if I took French instead of History. There are two (or more) reasons why I think French will be better. Firstly all the dons here say that I shall never get a post at any school for history (although of course English will be the subject I shall principally teach). They say headmistresses far prefer an English mistress who can at a push, teach another language and help out the language mistress.

Old Firth herself says she does not think me at all suited to study history! and the English don would greatly prefer me to take French. I shall much more enjoy doing French as 'Streak' is the Mods don and is awfully nice, very different from old Firth. Moreover, as Roddy will be taking Mods next year I think it would be extremely interesting if we both did so. Streak says she expects her French students once during their three years at college to spend part of the holiday in France! and I don't think you would be very averse to that plan!! I am sure Roddy will have to do ditto so wouldn't it be gorgeous? Of course if you and Poplico disapprove I shall do as you wish, but I would much rather do *French* and English, instead of *History* and English.

Winifred's tone is rather reminiscent of that of the subject of her most celebrated biography, Charlotte Brontë, a similarly forceful, persevering and persuasive character, writing, at the age of twenty-five, to her aunt in a bid to be allowed to study French in Brussels in order to improve her employment prospects as a teacher.

Winifred's request was a serious enough matter to warrant a reply from 'Poplico'.

> MY DEAR WIN,
> Your mother and I have talked over your letter and want further information before giving you a definite answer. My quotations are from your letter: 'All the dons here say that I shall never get a post at any school for history.' Who are 'all the dons'? You showed me a letter from Cambridge – I suppose from the English don – stating it was a common thing to combine History with literature, and suggesting to you to do this very thing.
> 'The English don would greatly prefer me to take French.' Is this the same lady as wrote you before you went to Cambridge?
> 'Miss Firth does not think me at all suited to study History.' This may be because of your strong likes and dislikes. To be suited may mean the possession of an impartial mind. But does she say that your deficiencies in that respect are such as to make it improbable you will take your degree?

I should like answers to all the foregoing questions, but still more to the following:

Which subject (History or French) will ensure with greater certainty your taking a degree in the shortest possible time?

Subject to your answers to these questions I regard as *Hauptsache*[26] that you take your degree as soon as possible and that it is only *nebensächlich*[27] whether History or French will best serve your employment. A livelier subject is better suited to correspondence, but we must take account of the fact (framed in pink if grey is distasteful) that my life may be quite short, and that Mother will then be hard-pushed to find money for two university students. If the change of subject delays the date at which you can take your degree you would certainly regret it if my death intervenes, for the extra time required for taking the degree might stint Mother too much.

On the other hand once you get your degree you have that safe and it will ensure you some amount of earning power, which if need be (and if we shall have the means) you can afterwards add to by further study – be it French or whatnot.

We all enjoyed yesterday's theatre very much, but I have no time today to write about it. Talintyre [the family dentist] soon managed Mum's bridge today with no pain.

We all send our fondest love to our darling,

FROM DAD.

This exchange of letters reveals that at this stage of her life Winifred, like the young Charlotte Brontë, seems to have been contemplating a career as a teacher, though like Charlotte she is certain to have viewed it as a poor second best to a career as a writer. It also shows that Frederick was worried about his health. He may already have been suffering from the kidney disorder that was to kill him, Bright's disease. Given that he died a wealthy man, his reference to concerns about the family's financial security after his death seem to have been motivated both by his habitual pessimism – tempered though it was by his whimsical humour – and by the wish to encourage Winny to qualify for some kind of occupation.

Charlotte Brontë got her way, persuading her father to let her study in Brussels and her aunt to fund the trip, and Winifred got hers. Miss Clough, when consulted, consented to the ditching of

---

[26] German: 'the main consideration'.
[27] German: 'immaterial'.

History, and 'old Firth', in favour of French and 'Streak'. Winifred was to take French for Part I of the Tripos and English for Part II. Presumably, faced with 'B.A.'s approval, Poplico's doubts were soon beaten down.

'Streak' or 'the Streak', the Director of Studies in Modern Languages at Newnham, was Pernel Strachey, at that time in her midforties. She was a sister of Lytton, and, like Moore, friendly with many of the Bloomsbury set. Tall and thin like her brother, with a small head and a timid manner – her friend Virginia Woolf compared her to a 'delicately stepping fawn in a wood',[28] Frances Partridge rather less flatteringly to a 'shy, faintly amused giraffe'[29] – she was described by a student in Winifred's year as having 'an humorous, quizzical and wholly endearing personality.' One of her endearing traits was to come out with totally unexpected sallies, as on the occasion when, addressing a gathering of Newnhamites, she informed them that 'the proper study for womankind is man.'[30] In 1923 she was to succeed 'B.A.' as principal, a post in which she remained for almost twenty years.

As a tutor Winifred did not find all her ways endearing and was put off by her perpetually startled expression, and her habit of discouraging initiatives such as Winifred's decision to produce verse rather than prose translations of Ronsard's poetry with the question 'Do you think it is a good plan?', uttered in a neutral tone. But once she was used to her, Winifred got on very much better with her than with Miss Firth, and 'Streak' gave her the run of her personal library of French books.

Frederick took an informed interest in Winifred's studies both French and English. They corresponded on the subject of Romanticism in literature, an exchange prompted by a reference of Winifred's to Theodore Watts-Dunton's treatise *The Renascence of Wonder*. Although Frederick was not a university man his letters indicate that he was familiar with literary movements and works of literature in English, French and German, with Chateaubriand's *René* and Goethe's *Werther* as well as Keats' *Endymion* and Shelley's *Prometheus Unbound*.

His letters display a mind that was inquiring and analytical, whimsical and idiosyncratic. 'My dear Win,' begins one, 'so you think the motive force of Romanticism to lie in Wonder, while I think it to be the conflict between subjectivity and objectivity with stressing of

---

[28] Cited in the biography of Pernel Strachey on the Newnham College website.
[29] Partridge, *Love in Bloomsbury*, p. 60.
[30] Phillips, *Newnham Anthology*, p. 149.

subjectivity. Wonder may serve to some extent to distinguish Romanticism from Realism, but not, I think, usefully, from Classicism. And even as regards Realism, bear in mind that its professors did not inveigh against Wonder, but against subjectivity. They said: put a stop to 'la mise en scène perpetuelle du moi'[31] and to authors' 'confidences'. 'Le grand art est scientifique et impersonelle'[32] and 'l'artiste ne doit pas plus apparaître dans son oeuvre que Dieu dans la nature.'[33] In the swing of the pendulum *away* from Romanticism, the denial of subjectivity was the cause . . .

'I have many more brickbats ready to throw at you, but not now when you are busy,' Frederick ends after discussing an excerpt from *Tintern Abbey*. 'Mum had a bad head this morning after yesterday's theatre. Nevertheless she is now playing cards with the Lundholmes. She and Nell send fondest love joined in by Dad.'

Winifred evidently enjoyed the intellectual exchanges with her father but shows scant deference for him in her letters, calling him a 'dear little Pedant' and confidently disputing his take on Romanticism.

Another exchange of letters with her father related to one of the cultural treats on offer in the Cambridge of her day: Sheppard's Greek plays. John Tresidder Sheppard was a classics lecturer at King's whose lectures and dramatic readings – he was a born actor – enjoyed great popularity. Even more popular were his productions of Greek plays at the New Theatre, the first of which, in 1921, was a four-hour version of Aeschylus' *Oresteia* trilogy in the original Greek, to which people flocked from far and wide. Following the Greek tradition, women's parts were taken by men and the huge cast notably included George Rylands as Electra. Rylands, then a first-year student at King's, with his bright blond hair and eye-catching blue suits, was as flamboyant a figure as Sheppard and was soon to be renowned for his own drama productions at Cambridge, which influenced generations of British actors.

Winifred had no Greek and could only follow the play in translation, but was required to study classical drama as part of her English tripos. A letter from Poplico reveals that she was eager to see Sheppard's *Oresteia* – and anxious to see it in relative comfort.

---

[31] 'Perpetually putting one's personality on stage'. Paraphrased from a letter from Gustave Flaubert to George Sand, 15 December 1866. Flaubert believed that the novelist should not 'mettre sa personnalité en scène'.

[32] 'Great art is scientific and impersonal'. *Ibid*.

[33] 'The artist should not appear in his work any more than God in nature'. Letter from Flaubert to George Sand, December 1875.

MY DARLING WIN,

I enclose money to cover your expenses until your return. Dear Mum's sweedling[34] tells me to add enough to enable you to *book* a seat for the three-in-one Shepparded Aeschylus, but memory and Mum alike fail me as to the amount, while clumsy fingers have mislaid your own carefully provisioned, but wrongly-added estimate. Not knowing the figure, I will make a shot at at it and enclose herewith £3.10/-, which with 10/- enclosed by Nell yesterday makes £4 altogether, receipt of which please acknowledge. – I cannot tell you my darling daughter how much we long to have you back, but it is quite by unpremeditated indiscretion that I tell you that in certain quarters the sum total of longing has been soared higher by the appalling size of cold legs of mutton, which require help for their consumption.

Mum's sweedling aforesaid re. booking versus queue was very deftly staged. Scene I: a *booked* daughterlet takes her seat with all belongings intact, and sandwich-sustained sits out the 5 hours eyeing tragedy with composure. Scene II: a *queued* daughterlet wakens to an earlier crow. In two hours' scrum and snow (or rain), her sandwich lost with hat and coat and pins for hair, she comes bedraggled to the scene (not seat). With cold and wetted feet, she's corkscrewed out of shape and from uncertain foothold peers through bobbing gaps of space with only fleeting glimpses of a much cut play and carrying nought but fractioned Aeschylus away. Scene III: the queued daughterlet, exhausted by 2 hours' scrum and 5 hours' disappointment, has to be doctored on her return home. Tableau: nurses and misery.

So book, book, book and charge the cost to
Your ever affectionate
DAD.

Winifred's attendance at the Greek play got her into trouble with Miss Steele-Smith, her Director of Studies in English at Newnham, the third of the trio of Newnham tutors she recalled in later life. The play was a triennial event; this was Winifred's only opportunity to see it while at Cambridge and she was determined not to miss it. The matinée performance she went to clashed with an afternoon coaching in Middle English by Miss Steele-Smith, but Winifred, assuming that the higher importance in the scheme of things of seeing a Sheppard production was so self-evident as to require no explanation even to

---

[34] 'Sweedle': amalgamation of 'swindle' and 'wheedle'.

'Steely', went off merrily to the play without giving Middle English a second thought. She was totally taken aback when she was summoned to the High Table at breakfast the following day and ordered by 'Streak' to apologise to Miss Steele-Smith for not asking permission to miss her class.

Dismissive of the donnish disapproval incurred, Winifred had no regrets. The play made an indelible impression on her, another landmark in her long-standing passion for the stage.

Other Cambridge recreations were of a lighter nature than Aeschylus. There were debates; the Newnham Debating Society had just become incorporated with those of the men's colleges and Winifred reported that the men speakers were more fun. 'The men try to turn a debate into a panto', abusing each other mercilessly to raise laughs. There was dancing in college on Saturday evenings, when games (musical chairs, tugs of war between the different halls) were followed by country dances, winding up with 'dear delightful Sir Roger'.[35] Around Bonfire Night there were student rags, but in these the women students did not participate. Instead, they were kept indoors, as Newnham was traditionally 'besieged' by male undergraduates – a 'lark' Winifred looked forward to.

The most dramatic besieging of the college, however, took place in the summer of 1921 after the vote on full membership for women, a right that had been granted at Oxford the previous year. At Cambridge, the women students' hopes were dashed when the motion in favour of the innovation was defeated, apparently largely owing to the numbers of non-resident M.A.s who turned up to vote against it. Women students at Cambridge were not to be granted equal status with men until a quarter of a century later, in 1947.

In the excited aftermath of the election at the Senate House, it was reputedly one of the non-resident, traditionalist M.A.s who, elated by the result, incited some of the undergraduates to march on Newnham. Once arrived at the main entrance the young men had the idea of battering down the gates with one of the trolleys used by the college porters to distribute coal.[36] Of course apologies from the university flowed in thick and fast after this feat, which provided Winifred and her friends with an exciting couple of days and became a landmark in the college annals.

Mostly, life at Cambridge passed very harmoniously, and relations between the sexes were perfectly amicable. Winifred, however, did not lose her heart to any of the male undergraduates in her circle of friends,

---

35 Sir Roger de Coverley, a country dance.
36 Phillips, *Newnham Anthology*, p. 150.

despite Katharine's fears that her daughter would attach herself to 'someone unsuitable' (many of their conservative Norwood neighbours thought it more likely that a university education would make her unmarriageable[37]). Olga Walters was already going out with the man she later married, a clever, left-wing older student called Kingsley Martin, who in 1930 was to become editor of the *New Statesman*. He had been a conscientious objector in the War, although he had served in an ambulance unit. Winifred disliked his incessant talk and did not take to any of the intellectual friends he brought along on boating excursions with her and Olga, finding them callow.

It is not surprising that Winifred found little in common with Olga's politically-minded friends. Her own responses to life were simple and emotional, springing from her enjoyment of the arts and nature rather than from any philosophical or political analysis. Music was one source of pleasure in her university years; she had her first taste of taking part in choral singing when she sang Bach's St John Passion with one of the men's college choirs. Her mother had been afraid that she would lose her faith as well as her heart at Cambridge, viewed by their Norwood acquaintances as a hot-bed of atheism. However, Winifred was in fact a more assiduous church-goer there than at any other period of her life. Admittedly, she was drawn by the music and the beauty of Holy Trinity Church and King's College Chapel rather than the sermons, rousing though she found some of them.

Apart from the attraction of church music, it was to nature rather than religious services, now and later in life, that she turned for spiritual sustenance. Like so many before and after her she responded with ecstasy to the beauty of Cambridge as she discovered it in each season of the year. Autumn was always a favourite time with her, and what better place to chart the changing colours of the trees than along the 'Backs', cycling to and from lectures on autumn mornings? In spring and summer she spent as much time as possible on the Cam. 'This morning I went as "ballast" with a rowing party who have still to pass their test – it is rather a delightful job as you just lie, curled up, in the stern of the boat and read, and all that is required of you is that you should be heavy, which requirement I fulfil. I read Henry V and found the river very conducive to the study of Willy S.' In her first year, like many another fresher, she herself took the rowing proficiency test.

In later life Winifred said that much as she had enjoyed her time at university, and glad though she was to have been there, for her it was not the life-changing epoch it is for some. Other influences and expe-

---

[37] The same opinion was expressed by Vera Brittain's mother's acquaintances in 1914. *Testament of Youth*, Chapter 2.

riences were much more important in shaping the person and writer she became. Her first two years in Cambridge were a time of gleeful enjoyment of its beauty and its social, artistic and intellectual pleasures. Her third year, however, was to be overshadowed by another family tragedy.

5
Holidays in France
'Plom' and 'Cannes'

Winifred, by her own admission, was an average rather than brilliant student. She had long wanted to be a writer; but she had no particular ambition to excel academically. In contrast, Roger was expected by his family to distinguish himself at Oxford. Studying had always been the one thing he wanted to do; Oxford had long been his mecca. He had imagined himself finding his spiritual home among its dreaming spires – and Roger's spirit was truly at home only in the Middle Ages.

Educated largely at home right up to the year he went to Oxford, the temperamental Roger had from earliest childhood been used to being handled with care and treated differently from his siblings. Despite his periods of schooling he had made scarcely any friends and had never mastered the social skills needed to mix with companions of his own sex and age. The person he had been closest to in his teenage years, his companion on brass-rubbing expeditions to old churches on family holidays, had been Winifred. As for romantic relations with the other sex, here he was in a state of innocence.

At the age of twenty-one he was plunged unprepared into life at an Oxford college. An early reference to him in one of Winifred's letters home seems to hold out hope that college would make Roger more sociable: 'I'm glad to hear the dear old cleric is becoming sporty – he will become quite humanised at Oxford.' Sport would have been one means of integrating with fellow students, and in fact he was a competent swimmer and rower, but for him these had always been solitary pursuits. He had no interest in games in themselves and no team spirit. To the other students he appeared arrogant. He was tall and good-looking and physically attractive to girls, but had no idea how to approach them. Cut adrift from the support of his family, he was isolated and remained so.

Just how isolated, Winifred did not realise until it was too late, for although they corresponded, 'Roddy' did not speak of his loneliness.

From her father she later heard an anecdote that gave her some insight into how her brother had fared in the rough and tumble of college life. He had been told to go to a tutor's house for some coaching and asked some fellow students for directions. When he arrived he found they had given him the address of a brothel. The shock was traumatic.

His tutors found him shy, awkward and 'odd' – 'a strange being with many oddities' was the comment of one – but were satisfied with his work. He was required to take a language as one of his degree subjects and chose German, an unusual choice at a time when most undergraduates opted for Latin or Greek. Mr Montgomery, the German tutor, was pleased with his progress. 'Shows promise . . . I look for him to do well later.' Mr Montgomery was Roger's favourite tutor, and the hours spent in his study at Lincoln College were among his happiest at Oxford. The positive reports continued until towards the end of the Trinity term of 1922, when tutors noted that Roger's behaviour was becoming increasingly bizarre.[38]

Around that time Roger announced to his family, out of the blue, that he was in love with a student, the daughter of one of his lecturers, and intended to marry her. Frederick pointed out that he had as yet no income to marry on. Even more pertinently, the girl in question viewed him as no more than an acquaintance. She was completely taken aback when Roger carried out his intention of proposing to her, and promptly turned him down. For the next week – it was the beginning of the long vacation of 1922, and Roger had come home – his family were witnesses to the terrifying breakdown of his mind, always fragile.

To his family it appeared to happen almost overnight. Sudenly he was charging about the Norwood house, raving. One moment he would be in the garden picking flowers to take to the girl he claimed to love; the next, tearing up to the attic threatening suicide. He viewed everyone around him as an enemy. He believed that his food was poisoned, and that an Oxford acquaintance was stalking him in Norwood in disguise. While the family doctor was dithering about what to do with him, on 6 July Roger took an action that precipitated the decision. He rushed off telling the family he was going to catch a train back to Oxford. Some hours later a policeman called at the house to say that Roger had been arrested at Windsor. He had taken the wrong train, and when the instruction 'All change' came at Windsor, the terminus, he had refused to leave the train, become aggressive and got into a tussle with the guards. It took four police constables to over-

---

38 Entry for Roger Bourne in Keble College ACA 1 A/6 Collection register (1920–1927). By permission of the Warden and Fellows of Keble College, Oxford.

power him. Frederick and the doctor drove to Windsor station, and Roger was certified insane there and then.

Winifred never ceased to regret that Roger had not been at Cambridge with her. She felt convinced that he would have been drawn into the circle of her friends and that with her companionship and support the balance of his mind could have been preserved.

Roger was committed to Holloway Sanatorium for the insane in Virginia Water. When first admitted he was violent. For the first year or so in the asylum he remained extremely agitated, and his madness was of the kind most distressing to witness as well as for the sufferer. He heard voices; he suffered from a variety of delusions and hallucinations, such as the belief that he was being tortured with red-hot needles. He was at times a danger to the other patients and at times to himself, and spent periods confined in a padded cell. On one occasion he put his head through a window pane, on another asked the attendants to kill him. He was convinced of his own unworthiness and, at one point, even believed he had committed a horrific crime. Two months after his admission to Holloway, at the time when he would have been preparing to return to Oxford for the Michaelmas term at the start of his third year, Roger wrote a letter to his German tutor.

> DEAR MR MONTGOMERY,
> You were good enough to ask me to write if I were to have a pleasant vac. I know now I am to die.
> I am deeply, deeply grateful to you for all you did for me.
> You must know I murdered my brother: so you see what manner of man I am. Only you knew me at my best, and Oxford is ever present to my mind: and Oxford to me is St Mary's[39] and your study.
> Yours very truly
> ROGER H. BOURNE[40]

At first his parents – or at least his mother, for Frederick from the start was pessimistic – lived in the hope that he could be cured. They sought advice from specialists and even brought a psychiatrist from Vienna to treat him. As the weeks and months went by, Roger became calmer, but he did not become sane. In March of the following year Frederick had his name removed from the university register. By that

---

[39] Presumably the University Church of St. Mary the Virgin.
[40] This letter and records relating to Roger from 1922 to 1926 are in the Holloway Sanatorium case files held by the Surrey History Centre. Ref. 3473/2/25 (Vol. 20). Quoted courtesy of Surrey History Centre.

time he had given up any hope that the son he had known would be restored to them.

Frederick was proved right, and Roger passed the rest of his life at Holloway. His family visited him often even though there could be no real communication with him, for as he grew less agitated, his speech deteriorated and became unintelligible, and after the first year or two he no longer spoke at all.

He had dreamed of a career of scholarship as a clergyman among the ecclesiastical splendours of the Church of England. He was destined instead to live out his remaining six decades in a building that had a splendour of its own; with its traceried windows, stepped gables and pinnacles, Holloway was an extraordinary, immense, red-brick neo-Gothic conception.

Its attractions went beyond the flamboyant beauty of its buildings. From its inception its patients had benefited from an enlightened and innovative regime. Intended for the 'genteel insane' and, originally, for curable cases, it provided an environment designed to cheer and stimulate the inmates instead of the blank walls of traditional asylums. The great hall was gorgeously decorated and gilded, the grounds laid out with shrubberies and winding walks. Surveillance was discreet in order to provide patients with the illusion of living in an Edwardian country house, with elegant furniture, freedom to wander from room to room, croquet on the lawn and concerts in the evenings. In its last years the asylum introduced an open-door policy, with some of the inmates being free to wander around the leafy village of Virginia Water.

In his *Notes from a Small Island* the American writer Bill Bryson describes working as an orderly in the sanatorium in his youth, shortly after arriving in England in the early 1970s. He found it a bizarre but delightful place and recounts having a long conversation on his first day, before he got used to the ways of the institution, with a 'dapper fellow in tweeds' who explained the mysteries of cricket to him. Not until his well-spoken interlocutor veered off the subject of cricket and claimed to have been involved in experiments at Porton Down in the 1940s, to be wanted by the Russians and to be living at Holloway incognito, did Bryson realise that he was an inmate and not a member of staff.[41]

Roger's 'genteel' fellow-patients included many clergymen and schoolmasters. His tall, distinguished figure could be seen daily striding about the lawns, kept immaculate by the patients themselves, with the rather arrogant demeanour that he retained in madness and

---

[41] Bill Bryson, *Notes from a Small Island* (London: Doubleday and Company, 1995), Chapter 5.

that may have contributed to his isolation at Oxford. At Holloway, though, Roger had his admirers among the other inmates. In her memoir Winifred wrote that some of them showed him a touching deference even though he ignored them and seemed heedless of his surroundings. She was moved by the strange loyalties and attachments she observed on visits to the Sanatorium. 'There is a sublimity, as well as a horror, in madness,' she wrote.

When not walking, Roger spent hours each day doing fiendishly complicated jigsaw puzzles, an occupation at which he was more skilled than many a sane person. Despite his apparent unresponsiveness, something in the expression of his eyes whenever she greeted him convinced Winifred that he still felt affection for his family and she fancied that his soul was in some unfathomable way in communion with theirs. He always remained her beloved brother, and as long as he lived, she paid regular visits to Holloway whenever she was able.

This new catastrophe was almost as devastating as Phil's death ten years earlier. It cast a pall over Winifred's last year at Cambridge. The consequences of Roger's madness went beyond the grief of losing him and the regret at the lost promise of his life; it had the effect of isolating the family. Frederick, in particular, wanted as few people as possible to know about it outside the family and their closest friends, and shrank from sympathy from anyone outside that close circle. As a result, Winifred was reluctant to invite her friends to stay in Norwood, and back at Cambridge felt as if she were concealing a shameful secret. One terrible shadow thrown by the tragedy was her father's dread that the seed of madness in the family might be passed on to the next generation should she or Nell have children. In Nell's case this already seemed unlikely given her resolution not to marry. Winifred had so far not met anyone she had any thoughts of marrying, but had certainly not ruled out the possibility, and her father's fears were appalling to confront.

Winifred appears to have been unaware of one cause of her father's anguish. One of his half-brothers, Josiah, spent the last months of his life in an asylum for the insane and died there at the age of thirty-seven while Frederick was still a teenager. The register recording Roger's admittance to Holloway states that the supposed cause of his madness was the history of insanity in the family, and makes reference to this uncle. Yet there is no mention of him in Winifred's memoir. Did her father deliberately keep their uncle Josiah's madness from his daughters?

Frederick had retired early because of health problems. As far as these allowed, he had been enjoying a placid and contented retirement, reading for hours in the London Library (much used by Winifred later in life when she became a writer), walking and permitting himself longer continental holidays. But after the onset of Roger's madness Winifred never saw her father completely happy again. One thing that brought him some consolation was music, and he would ask her to sing for him in the drawing room where the whole family had gathered in happier days. Katharine would play for him and Winifred would sing, and in later years she would remember one day in that summer of 1922 seeing her father, with his hand shading his eyes, weeping silently at the far end of the long room while she sang, and would reproach herself for not going to him and trying to comfort him, but she had not wanted to intrude upon his grief.

As they had done when reeling from the blow of Phil's death, the Bournes sought consolation across the Channel. A family holiday had already been planned that summer in a destination new to them, the spa town of Plombières-les-Bains in the Vosges mountains in eastern France, near the German border. Visits to Roger were forbidden until he had become calmer; the doctors were trying him with various treatments. Frederick stayed behind to be within call, but Katharine, Nell and Winifred made their way by train to the Vosges as planned.

Plombières was a delight from the moment they alighted at the pretty station by the park created by the Emperor Napoleon III and breathed in the mountain air. It is a long town winding along the bottom of a narrow valley. Tall sandstone houses in soft shades of beige, cream and pink nestle in the valley bottom and clamber some way up its lushly wooded sides, with numerous alleys and steps connecting the different street levels. The myriad balconies whose elegant arabesques adorn every facade have given Plombières the designation of 'the town of a thousand balconies'. In the eighteenth century, wrought-iron ones replaced most of the earlier wooden constructions, from one of which Josephine Bonaparte, taking the waters while Napoleon campaigned in Egypt, fell when it collapsed under her and some of her entourage as they leaned out to admire a dog in the street below. (She was not seriously hurt, and more damage was done to the passer-by she landed on, whose leg was broken.)

Katharine was hoping to find relief from her arthritis and sciatica in the splendid thermal baths, the *Thermes Napoléon*, built by Napoleon's nephew Napoleon III, who spent several summers in Plombières. The Emperor took to the little town very kindly but found it in need of improvement and set about transforming it, building an elegant new quarter by the park he had laid out, with an extremely grand hotel alongside the new baths. He also replaced the old church with a handsome neo-Gothic one whose slender soaring spire is the town's main landmark.

A popular summer resort since the Romans first discovered the properties of its hot springs, Plombières was particularly fashionable with the wealthy in the nineteenth century and the *Belle Époque*. Its thermal waters, notable for being among the hottest in Europe and for their radio-active qualities, have been sought over the centuries by sufferers from rheumatism, gynaecological problems (they were believed to be of assistance for sterility) and numerous other ills. They are supposed to be particularly efficacious for intestinal disorders, and the 'intestinal cleansings' mentioned in a guide book issued a few years before the Bournes started frequenting the town are still advertised today.

Katharine had come here to 'take the cure', but by the end of the summer all three felt that the place had healed them in a miraculous way. There was restorative power in its very air, balsamic from the surrounding pine and beech forests, and in the refreshing gurgle of the spring water to be heard on every path climbing into the mountains. The grandeur of the landscape, reminiscent of Switzerland, had been appreciated by many a romantic soul before it was discovered by the Bournes. Delacroix, Berlioz and Musset had raved about the water-falls, streams and dramatic rock formations to be seen on the walks near the town. Mme de Staël had written that she enjoyed the beau-ties of nature here as in no other place.[42] Winifred found a simplicity and timelessness about life in Plombières and on the farms around that appealed to the poet in her. She noted that the very implements used in daily life seemed to have changed little since medieval or indeed clas-sical times; the mowers still used scythes, oxen pulled rudimentary wooden carts and the postman blew a little horn.

For Winifred the holiday in Plombières marked the resumption of the love affair with France that had begun in Paris. The months at Cambridge reading Racine and Molière had taught her nothing about the contemporary culture of the country, and despite her exposure to the language as a child her grasp of conversational, idiomatic French was almost non-existent. Plombières started to change that. She and her family went to plays in the elegant casino which had entertained the fashionable pleasure-seekers of the *Belle Époque* and still laid on a very full programme. The nightly performances were of a higher standard than those of the average British touring company, for the

---

[42] Roland Conilleau, *Plombières-les-Bains: hier et aujourd'hui*.

actors were Parisians who were in the Vosges to 'take the air', and the productions were the recent theatrical hits of the capital. Thanks to the modern comedies they saw, Winifred started to pick up the French of her own day.

For the next nine years the Bournes spent part of every summer in Plombières or 'Plom' as it soon became in the family *argot*. They made friends there; to the end of their lives Winifred and Nell maintained a friendship with a Parisian family they met one summer, visiting them in their house in Normandy and being visited in turn over the decades by several generations of the family.

Plombières also provided an initiation in French music, and they became acquainted with some of the musicians who summered and performed there. In the casino the Bournes were able to hear the works of French composers, hitherto almost unknown to them, from Rameau and Gluck up to those of their own time. They struck up a friendship with a French violinist called Gabriel Willaume, who had played with Saint-Saëns. On a visit to him and his wife in Paris one year Winifred was present at a private performance of César Franck's violin sonata in his house.

Listening to music-making in the intimacy of a circle of professional musicians was a novel and delightful experience for Winifred. She could not have imagined then that the atmosphere she tasted briefly in the Willaumes' home in Paris would before too long be that in which her own day-to-day life was lived.

Winifred left Cambridge in 1923 with a second-class honours degree in English and French. Her friend Jean Stewart, who went on to become an academic, gained a first-class degree in French; Winifred had no such aspirations. But she did have one steadfast ambition, and that was to write.

She prepared herself for her chosen *métier* by reading voraciously and writing prolifically. She hinted later that family troubles – Roger's breakdown, her parents' poor health – were one reason why she did not seek paid employment of any kind after coming down from Cambridge, or consider living away from home, at a time when her university friends were embarking on further studies, acquiring practical training, venturing into the employment market and, in some cases, marrying. But doubtless her choice was dictated by inclination as well. Although her attachment to her family had made her uneasy lest she was neglecting them by going off to college, it is unlikely that it would have fettered her had she really longed to spread her wings and leave the nest, or at any rate find a job. The idea of becoming a teacher hinted at in letters home from college seems to have been dropped, office life is unlikely to have held many attractions for her, and as for marrying, in later life she never mentioned meeting anyone in this period with whom this prospect was even a remote possibility.

In the years after Cambridge, her old schoolfriend Mina Breed did post-graduate study at Mount Holyoke College in Massachusetts and, back in London, a course at Mrs Hoster's prestigious Secretarial Training College on Cromwell Road. Devoted to her parents, with whom she lived until their death apart from brief periods abroad, Mina was very career-minded. By the end of the twenties she had packed in a couple of years with the International Labour Organisation in Geneva and a spell as a lecturer with the Workers' Educational Association. It was an impressive record even by today's standards. Jean Stewart stayed on at Cambridge, and became a lecturer there. Even Olga, who Winifred always felt failed to live up to her potential, got herself some secretarial training and some temporary jobs, for example as an editorial assistant for the *Encyclopedia Britannica*, as well as marrying her Cambridge love Kingsley Martin in 1926.

Winifred, however, appears to have been content to remain in Norwood for the rest of the 1920s, learning her craft, as she saw it. Her English literature course at Cambridge had stopped short of the twentieth century. Now she read her way excitedly through the writers of her own time. Cambridge had given her, as she put it, a kind of 'guided tour of the established hierarchy of writers' from Chaucer to Matthew Arnold, after which reading these early twentieth-century writers was like a discovery of new and exotic countries, or, in Winifred's words, like 'learning a new language'. The imagery and fluidity, the fragmented vision of the new writers, made learning this language an exhilarating experience.

Notebooks of Winifred's from the 1920s list the books she read. They contain notes on her reading, transcriptions of passages, indexes to the contents of each notebook, showing the orderly, cataloguing habits that would stand the future biographer in good stead (when she became a professional writer, her note-taking was prodigious). As well as revisiting old favourites such as the Brontës, Fanny Burney, Jane Austen, Hardy and Meredith, she was devouring Virginia Woolf, Lytton Strachey, the Sitwells, Katherine Mansfield, D.H. Lawrence, Vita Sackville-West, Rosamund Lehmann. She read biography, and also some literary criticism such as Middleton Murray's *Keats and Shakespeare*.

The future biographer in the making is also seen in the number of pages taken up by notes on the life and works of the Brontës, with many transcriptions of Emily's poems. The Brontës did not form part of the canon covered by the Cambridge English tripos and, for the first time, she was studying their work critically and finding out about their lives. She read Mrs Gaskell's *Life of Charlotte Brontë* and three of the chief biographical and critical studies of the Brontës available at that period: Swinburne's study of Charlotte Brontë, Mary Robinson's of Emily, both written in the late nineteenth century, and, closer to Winifred's own time, May Sinclair's *The Three Brontës*. Brontë biography was not yet the veritable industry it became in the second half of the century, when Winifred herself was one of the first in the field.

Winifred was writing almost as fast as she read. Perhaps not surprisingly in view of her chosen literary genres at this period, though, it was a considerable time before she become a published writer. The novel never appealed to her as a literary form; she said that she could not invent plots. She wrote poetry and plays – plays in verse. They have not survived, but the titles of three of them – *Hector*, *Hamlet at Wittenburg* and *A Song of Roland* – indicate the kind of subject matter she favoured. She was inspired by dramatists of the period who have long fallen by the wayside, such as Gordon Bottomley, who wrote plays in blank verse, or Laurence Binyon, more remembered today for his poem *For the Fallen*. Thomas Sturge Moore, brother of Winifred's friend G.E., also wrote many verse dramas.

She later acknowledged with hindsight that in her haste to become a writer, and her excitement about literature and language and literary forms, she had failed to realise that before she could have something to say, she must first have *lived*, and 'listened to what life had to say'.

In the meantime, apart from reading and writing, there was the cultural life of London to enjoy. The Old Vic, although renovated in those years for its new middle-class clientele, still retained some of the charm of its early pioneer days, and the Bournes remained staunch supporters. There was ballet; Olga introduced her to Diaghilev's Ballets Russes. There were singing lessons with Enrico, their beloved cicerone of the magical Paris holiday ten years earlier. He and Louie were now living in London, and Winifred and Nell went regularly to their flat in Holland Park for voice coaching. Nell had no aptitude for singing, but as with the art classes at the Crystal Palace, their father wanted them both to have the same opportunities, and since the loss of Roger the two girls had become even closer than before. With Enrico they continued the discovery of French music begun in Plombières, for he was a devotee of the songs of French composers such as Fauré, Debussy and Chausson. Then there were the regular holidays in France, which included music-filled days in Paris.

Apart from Roger, one cause for concern to the family in those years was Frederick's poor health, and in March 1928 he died of uremia, after a short illness, at the age of sixty-eight. (His will, running to several pages, left anxiously detailed instructions for the constitution of a fund for Roger's care and maintenance, to be administered by Nell and Winifred as trustees.) In a brief and heartfelt tribute to him in her unpublished memoir, Winifred speaks of her difficulty in finding the words to express all that he had meant to her, wishing that she could have found those words and spoken them to him while he lived. He had been not just a delightful companion but an inspiration to her, 'the fountain-head of all good things in my first twenty years'.

Once again, after a family loss or tragedy the members remaining looked to the continent for alleviation from grief. In the winter after Frederick's death Katharine, Nell and Winifred headed for the shores of the Mediterranean, to Cannes. In the decade leading up to the Second World War, as arthritis tightened its grip, Katharine would often escape there from the fogs of London.

The Bournes' choice of the Riviera was hardly an original one. Hordes of well-off British sun-seekers made the same journey between November and April each year (in the hot summer months it was seen rather as a place to avoid). In the twenties, before the development of mass tourism, the Côte d'Azur was also a fashionable destination of the Parisian beau monde and leading figures of the avant-garde arts. The year 1924 had seen the première by Diaghilev's Ballets Russes of *Le Train Bleu*, a ballet about a group of thoroughly modern young people disporting themselves on the sands, its name a reference to the glamorous night express train that bore passengers to the Mediterranean from Calais and Paris. The scenario was by Jean Cocteau, who held court in Villefranche-sur-Mer as a leader of the avant-garde, and the costumes were by Coco Chanel, credited with having started the vogue for sunbathing when she appeared in Cannes in 1923 sporting a tan.

Agatha Christie's *The Mystery of the Blue Train* had been published earlier in the year the Bournes arrived in Cannes. Throughout the 1920s, British and American writers were excitedly discovering and settling on this part of the Mediterranean coast. They came in quest of adventure, inexpensive living, health, artistic inspiration and a life less bound by convention. Somerset Maugham and his male companion had made their home on Cap Ferrat in 1926. The same winter that the Bournes spent in Cannes, D.H. Lawrence, seeking respite from the consumption that was soon to kill him, was wintering along the coast in Bandol, whose benign climate Katherine Mansfield had sought some years earlier when dying of the same disease.

The Bournes are unlikely to have been wealthy enough to travel on Le Train Bleu, but whatever the price of their tickets, waking on the train after the overnight journey from Paris to find themselves in a completely different world was an invigorating sensation.

Cannes seemed magical to Winifred, who was viewing it through the medium of her recent reading. She had just finished Chapman's translations of Homer, and for her the pines and cypresses, twisted olive trees, golden sands and deep blue sea summoned up the landscape of classical Greek mythology. As she walked on the beach or on Île Sainte-Marguerite or Île Saint-Honorat, the little wooded islands a short boat-trip away, poems crowded into her head almost too fast for her to write them down. She did so feverishly, neatly copying selected ones into a notebook in preparation for a volume of verse that she hoped to publish. She already had a title for it: *The Invitation to Parnassus*.

The Bournes arrived in Cannes not long after Winifred's twenty-seventh birthday. She had never yet been in love, and as yet had no personal experience of the kind to put into her verse – it contains few direct references to her own experiences and emotions – but she was wildly enamoured of poetry and ancient Greece, Keats and Ovid, and the natural world around her. On solitary walks, she wandered about that winter as if intoxicated – drunk with verse and images of the seas and shores of antiquity, seeing around her the world of Dionysus and the Parnassian summits, Venus and the island of Cythera. She could hear sirens' voices in the waves, and the 'pad of sandalled feet' of ghosts of Grecians passing

> with jangle of pipes and horns and cymbals
> of drums and clarions and timbrels.[43]

Along the coast a greater poet than her, the dying D.H. Lawrence, by now too weak to take more than short strolls along the beach at Bandol, was drawing similar inspiration from the Mediterranean world – at once so old and so eternally young. It found expression in one of his *Last Poems*, 'Middle of the World':

---

[43] 'The Embarkation for Cythera'. From *The Invitation to Parnassus and Other Poems*, p. 39.

This sea will never die, neither will it ever grow old,
nor cease to be blue, nor in the dawn
cease to lift up its hills
and let the slim black ship of Dionysos come sailing in
with grape-vines up the mast, and dolphins leaping.

Many of Winifred's poems celebrated the joyousness of this Mediterranean world of mythology. Others delved into its darker side. She spared a thought for those who had been ferried across Acheron and, on the far side of its dark waters, turn to take a last look at the 'sights and sounds and shapes and softest scents' of life before sinking

into an underworld darkling and drear
Where nothing lovely ever shall appear.[44]

Winifred, who was ambitious to become a published writer, saw verse as one means of achieving immortality. In 'Envoi', the last poem in the collection *The Invitation to Parnassus*, she bids the bright images that she has evoked to fly

into the quenchless radiance of art
beyond the blight of my mortality
where change and death and sorrow have no part
where only you of all my world shall last
long after I who shaped you shall be past.

For the moment, the aspiring poet thus anticipating her own mortality was still unpublished but she was twenty-seven years old and very much alive. A poem called 'The Birth of Venus' seems to herald jubilantly the new phase of her existence that began as the result of an encounter in Cannes. She depicts Aphrodite, lifted by nereids from the brine, rising to a triumphant blare of conches accompanied by 'a symphony of sound': the drums of the sea reverberate with a muffled boom about a far reef, the spray clashes like cymbals, the winds flute and the waves 'trumpet their curly notes'.

Love, in her poem, is born to the accompaniment of music. The image proved apt. A concert that Winifred attended that winter in Cannes included an arrangement of Ravel's *Pavane pour une infante défunte* in which the solo cello part was played by a musician called Eugène Gérin. The music arrested Winifred's attention immediately – as did the musician.

---

[44] 'Across Acheron'. *Ibid.*, p. 63.

Exactly how she and Eugène Gérin got into conversation after the concert is not recorded, but once they did they found many things to talk about. Their first conversation – it was in French – was not about music but about poetry. It revealed that Eugène was not just well read in French verse, but a writer of verse himself. He told her that he was Belgian, though he was French on his mother's side and had spent the first years of his childhood in northern France.

Eugène Gérin was thirty-two, five years older than Winifred. If romantic heroes are supposed to be tall, dark and handsome, Eugène at any rate met two of the criteria. He was not a tall man but he was dark, with thick hair swept back from a high forehead, and his looks were striking, with deep-set eyes that had an intense gaze under prominent brows. In photos he rarely smiles, and his brooding, somewhat melancholy expression is almost worthy of a Brontëan hero. In the early days of their acquaintance Winifred felt that this melancholy expression was deceptive, for he had a puckish smile and in conversation was witty and entertaining.

She soon learned something of his life. Having graduated with distinction from the Brussels Conservatory, he had spent eight years as a cellist with the Monte Carlo opera orchestra, which had performed at the premières of some of Diaghilev's Ballets Russes productions. It was a secure post, a government appointment in what was often an insecure profession. However, at the time Winifred met Eugène he had grown dissatisfied with life as the second cellist in this orchestra and was taking a break from it while he considered what to do next. He disliked what he called its civil service mindset, and felt fettered. He wanted to make his own way as a soloist.

This and subsequent conversations with Eugène Gérin in Cannes convinced Winifred that he had a romantic and artistic soul to match her own and that he was an artist not just by profession but in every feeling, 'vibrant to his heart's core', in her words. She said later that he was 'the epitome of her every ideal'. Events proved that Eugène, for his part, was not unimpressed by this romantic, enthusiastic young woman who spoke quite good French, although with a marked English accent.

The acquaintance was continued, and deepened, over the next couple of years. They met again in Paris, where Eugène had settled after breaking definitively with the Monte Carlo orchestra and was seeking engagements both as a soloist and an orchestral player.

He had already made something of a name for himself as a solo cellist in Belgium and in various French towns where he had played regularly over the years. He had also toured North Africa. Reviews of recitals given by him in his native Belgium as a recent graduate of the

Brussels Conservatory testify to the impact of his playing and to his personal charisma. He was someone people noticed. And from an early age he wanted to be noticed as a poet as well as a musician; for him writing poetry was more than a hobby or sideline. He published verse in journals and newspapers from his teens onwards, and revelled in being known in some musical and literary circles as 'le violoncelliste poète'. A caricature in a French regional journal shows him sitting astride his cello, bow in one hand, pen in the other.[45] A book of his poems was published in 1922.

He had written verses about the suffering of war; as a young student at the Conservatoire in the years between 1914 and 1919 he had escaped involvement in the conflict but witnessed his elder brother, who was studying the violin, having to interrupt his studies to go and fight. (In the inter-war years Eugène performed at charity concerts for causes such as war orphans, *mutilés de la guerre, tuberculeux de la guerre*; so many that in 1939 he was to be awarded the *Médaille d'Or de l'Ordre de la Couronne* for his services.) Like Winifred's, though, most of his verse was lushly romantic. There were some love poems, suggesting he was not immune to the charms of women before he met her (women were not immune to his; his conquests had begun during his time at the Conservatory). But his poems celebrated above all the beauty of nature and music.

A pen portrait of him in a Belgian arts journal of 1924 paints a picture of his appearance, personality, musical talent and success with 'the ladies'.

His forehead is broad and high, his eyes keen and searching, revealing a will of iron; their look is piercing and perspicacious, both bold and caressing. His mouth is *gourmand*, sensuous, with just a touch of bitterness, and when he smiles his smile is often ironic. It is a physiognomy at once strange and sympathetic. You can tell that he is something out of the ordinary. 'A great artist!' cry the ladies, and when we have the ladies on our side, the battle is won. A virtuoso cellist, with a rare capacity, and what power of interpretation, what art, what technique, what finesse, what passion in his fingers! He explores every facet of his art tirelessly, seeking out all possible effects. He is highly cultured, a poet, but always with a joke at the ready to make you laugh.[46]

---

[45] *Le Nouveau Dijon*, 19 September 1925.
[46] Translation of part of an article in *Belgique-Spectacles*, 19 December 1924, reprinted from the journal *Perfils et Silhouettes*.

For Eugène, music and poetry belonged together. Music was a kind or poetry without words, while poetry, or poetic prose, could be used to express what music meant to him, as in this prose piece dedicated to his chosen instrument:

> With pathos and passionate eloquence, the cello expresses every human feeling. It sings in turn of love and pleasure, bitterness and sorrow, ecstasy and contemplation. Its warm sonority, noble and disquieting accents, gravity and majesty, its tenderness, convey the grandeur and profundity of its soul. The melancholy sweetness of its song penetrates us with its poetry and induces reverie.[47]

A sonnet addressed to Eugène by an admirer[48] suggests that under Eugène's fingers the cello did indeed express this full gamut of human emotions.

> Tous les sanglots humains, foi, ferveur et tourment,
> El la sublime joie et nos vagues alarmes,
> Les transports de la fièvre et la douceur des larmes,
> Peuvent-ils donc sortir d'un fragile instrument?[49]

It was a miracle wrought by Eugène's musicality and skill.

> De la boîte sonore où semble battre un cœur
> Pour qu'ardeur et mystère en nos âmes débordent,
> A vos longs doigts nerveux suffisent quatre cordes.[50]

Winifred and Eugène discovered a common sensibility in their response to music, poetry and nature. The flavour of that sensibility, and the rather high-flown tone of some of Eugène's literary productions, is conveyed by another little prose piece of his, 'La Nuit', which Winifred translated into English. Like many of Eugène's compositions it opens by evoking the magic and mystery of the hour of twilight, also a favourite time of day in Winifred's own.

---

[47] Translation of prose poem in *Annales Africaines*, 27 February 1925.
[48] Poem by Charles De Bussy written in 1922. Reproduced in *Belgique-Spectacles*, 19 November 1926.
[49] 'All human sobbing, faith, fervour and torment, sublime joy and vague fears, the transports of fever and the sweetness of tears – can they be produced by a fragile instrument?'
[50] 'Your long sensitive fingers need no more than four strings to make ardour and mystery overflow into our souls from the sounding box where a heart seems to beat.'

La nuit descendait, lente et sereine, déployant son vaste manteau sombre où quelques étoiles semblaient de petites quantités phosphorescentes sur un fond opaque. Pas un souffle dans l'air. Aucune feuille ne bougeait. Tout avait la fixité d'une nature morte.

Cependant j'écoutais, dans mon cœur, la voix mélodieuse d'un violoncelle pleurant ses notes de cristal sous l'archet persuasif du Rêve.

En l'entendant je me croyais dans un des enchantements de l'Au-delà.

Si quelqu'un m'avait, alors, adressé la parole, je ne doute pas de la réponse qu'il eût reçue:

'Laissez-moi, je me suis enfui hors du monde!'[51]

Night came down sedately and serene, shaking out her dark vast mantle with its stars, that showed like phosphorescent blots on the black ground. Not a breath on the air. Not a leaf moving. All things appeared as pictured in 'Still Life'. Nevertheless I heard in my heart the melodious chanting of a cello weeping out its crystal cadences beneath a dream-possessed bow. Hearing it I believed myself translated into one of the Enchanted Places of the Soul. Had anybody spoken to me in that hour I do not doubt I should have answered him: 'Let be, I have passed out beyond this mortal sphere.'

As Winifred's friendship with her 'poet-cellist' blossomed into courtship in this highly-charged atmosphere of music and verse, the pair, like a hero and heroine in a romantic novel, had some difficulties to overcome. The main obstacle was Katharine's disapproval, and Eugène's reluctance to cause a rift between mother and daughter. Katharine liked Eugène on their first meeting, but liked him as a friend of her daughter's, not as a prospective son-in-law. She saw marriage with him as imprudent on more counts than one: financially, and because he was 'a foreigner'. Katharine's addiction to foreign travel does not appear to have lessened her conventional disapproval of such a move. Perhaps her strongest objection, though, was the fear that marriage with Eugène would take Winifred far away from her.

For Winifred herself, of course, Eugène's foreignness was a strong part of the attraction. Her tastes and education seemed to have been long preparing her for marriage with a 'foreigner'. She was drawn both to Eugène's native language and the culture of France, his adopted country. Courtship in a foreign tongue, the exploration of a foreign

---

[51] *Annales Africaines*, 27 February 1925.

culture as part of the discovery of the other person, the sense of love triumphing over differences, are elements that heighten and add piquancy to romance. No wonder that one reason why Winifred felt a particular bond with two of the writers she explored later in life both as playwright and biographer, Fanny Burney and Charlotte Brontë, was that both fell in love with 'foreigners'.

It was no wonder, either, that Winifred had a particularly strong feeling for Charlotte Brontë's Brussels novel *Villette*. After her meeting with Eugène many things in the novel must have struck a chord, starting with M. Paul Emanuel's looks – the Spanish blood in his veins that gave his face the dark hue essential to a Brontë hero (Eugène was so dark he was often taken for a Spaniard), surprisingly combined with blue eyes (Winifred tells us that Eugène's eyes were 'intensely blue'). The foreign M. Paul is all vehemence and temperament and liveliness and volatility. He is mischievous; he torments and teases Lucy, for example about her English accent. Eugène was lively and often mischievous, and he teased Winifred about *her* English accent. M. Paul, Charlotte tells us, has none of the dullness and phlegm of his Belgian compatriots. The blood in *their* veins is 'too gluey to boil'; the blood in *his* flows much too fast to be solely Belgian in origin. Eugène was half French and he was witty, typically considered a Gallic rather than Belgian characteristic.

Throughout their courtship, poems about her and Eugène's love for each other poured from Winifred's pen. They record the difficulties of their courtship and tell of a love sometimes painful in its intensity. They hint that as his looks suggested, Eugène did indeed have a strain of Byronic melancholy, alongside the puckish humour. At times it verged on the morbid. She speaks of his disenchantment with his life, of the 'ravage of sad thoughts' she could trace on his brow. Their moments of passion were for him 'a delicious anguish'.

> How pale, my dear, this love is making,
> How pale and grave, your face. . . . [52]

She wonders why he speaks so often of wishing to die as she cradles him, her body his bier. She looks forward to a much happier outcome of their embraces:

> For you shall sleep, and you shall rest,
> – and dream of blisses too –

---

[52] 'The Beautiful Face', August 1931. One of a collection of unpublished poems called *The Promise to Psyche* (Greenwood papers).

And shed – like tears – upon my breast
The ills that anguished you.

There, as you will, still softly lie;
Take all I have to give;
– so you forget to doubt and die
And ask to love and live![53]

Yet she would not have wanted him otherwise, for his mysterious sadness was part of the man she loved.

If I could turn your heart from grief to gladness
I could transform your very semblance too!
I love your soul's unalterable sadness,
Since I love you![54]

Chronicling the raptures and torments of that uncertain courtship period, 'We go into love', she wrote,

. . . like schoolboys into battle, most happy to be killed;
the thunder breaks and we prefer its rattle
to that suspicious calm with which our days were filled
in pause before the storm. . . .

Despite family opposition, love prevailed, as so often in romantic novels and not infrequently in life, and she and Eugène were able to

. . . keep the faith the months cannot destroy
through the long torment of deferred joy.[55]

In her memoir Winifred does not specify exactly when Eugène told her he couldn't live without her and asked her to marry him, but she does say where his declaration took place. It was in Plombières, on a walk in one of the woods on the hills overlooking the town. Perhaps it was at their favourite hour of dusk; Eugène wrote a sonnet called *Soir à Plombières* that he dedicated to Winifred.[56] He told her that however uncertain his profession, he was sure of his feelings for her.

---

[53] 'Why will you always talk of dying?' *Ibid*.
[54] 'It Were Not You'. *Ibid*.
[55] 'Ode in Honour of Cupid and Psyche'. Published in *Poetry Review*, July–August 1933.
[56] Published in the journal *Vivre*, November 1932.

'As for mine,' Winifred writes in her memoir, 'I think I had loved him from the first time I heard him play the *Pavane*.'

These were exciting years for her artistically as well as emotionally, for she was seeing a collection of her poems through the press. *The Invitation to Parnassus and Other Poems* by 'W.E. Bourne' was published in 1930. The publisher was Erskine Macdonald, a pseudonym for Galloway Kyle, who had founded the Poetry Society shortly before the First World War. Over the years Winifred had several poems published in the Society's journal, *Poetry Review*. It would be interesting to have an account of her experiences in getting her book published, for Galloway Kyle's methods appear to have been less than scrupulous. He had specialised in publishing First World War poetry and in 1918 brought out a volume of Vera Brittain's verse inspired by her experiences as a wartime nurse. Vera found him slow and unbusinesslike, and her biographer describes Kyle as a publisher of 'distinctly dodgy credentials' and his publishing business as a 'racket'. He took advantage of amateur poets anxious to be published at all costs (and, in the case of war poets, to get their books out before they were killed), and was not scrupulous about paying out royalties.[57] His authors generally paid all or most of the publication costs; Katharine, like Vera Brittain's father, is likely to have subsidised the venture.

Winifred's volume of verse did not cause a major stir in the literary world but did have two or three mentions in the reviews. Like the Brontë sisters when they published under their pen names of Currer, Ellis and Acton Bell, 'W.E. Bourne' was assumed by reviewers to be a 'Mr'. An unnamed reviewer in the *Times Literary Supplement* advised 'Mr Bourne' to be less 'prodigal' and more restrained, but concluded with encouragement:

> In 'Pastoral Ode' he [i.e. 'Mr Bourne'] exclaims, 'how satisfying are your silences,/how gladly in your shades would I abide/for an eternity!' But within a score of lines the silence is shattered by 'fanfares and clarions of the dawn' and 'a very bacchanalia of birds'. Yet although his verse often deadens our response by a mere din of words, there is no denying the musical force of his impulse and an elemental expressiveness which only needs to be more disciplined to be really effective.[58]

There were also some kindly words from Austin Clarke in the *New Statesman and New Nation*. Reviewing Winifred's book along with

---

[57] Mark Bostridge, *Vera Brittain and the First World War: The Story of Testament of Youth* (London: Bloomsbury, 2014), Introduction and Chapter 4.
[58] *Times Literary Supplement*, 12 February 1931.

nine other volumes of poetry on 27 June 1931, he said: 'Mr Bourne's invitation to Parnassus is quite pressing.' Quoting with approval some lines from the long poem *The Embarkation for Cythera*, he accompanies this pat on the shoulder with a friendly recommendation for the future: 'If he can bit his runaway fancy he should do well.'

Having launched the sailors in her poem on their voyage to Cythera, Greek island of love and birthplace of Venus, and her book of verse on the literary waters of London, Winifred prepared to embark on her own great voyage of discovery: life with Eugène Gérin.

6
Paris Idyll
1932–1939

Winifred and Eugène were married at Croydon registry office on 28 September 1932 and caught the Paris boat train that afternoon. They had a good crossing and escaped seasickness. 'At Boulogne we were sensible enough to declare some English cigarettes we had put in one of the cases, and were the first through the Customs there, otherwise with our eight hand cases ! we might have had to put up with a long search. At the Gare du Nord mine was the first trunk to be brought into the Customs and we got through at once.' [59]

Winny was writing to her mother in bed on the morning of the 30th, from Eugène's rented flat in Rue des Batignolles. She described the street as 'romantic and tranquil'. It was in the 17th arrondissement in the northern outskirts of the city, in a quiet residential area half-way between the Montmartre cemetery and Parc Monceau, where she and Eugène were to spend many hours in their Paris years.

> My darling Phantom [one of a range of unexplained Bourne family nicknames, like 'Piggy' or 'Gui-Gui' for Nell and 'Weed' or 'Weedie' for Winifred herself],
> While the kettle boils on the electric cooker and Eugène is gone over the road to fetch croissants I am beginning my letter . . .
> We could not be more happily installed than we are here. It is really quiet: although the main entry is on a main street, our bedroom looks out on a street where nothing passes from 8 pm to 8 am. It is as utterly silent all night as Auteuil. [60] We are well supplied with towels, linen, etc.: incidentally the sheets are Vosges linen – unbleached – really magnificent . . . We are far happier than kings

---

[59] All the letters from Winifred quoted in this chapter are in the Greenwood papers.
[60] Borough in the 16th arrondissement of Paris, near the Bois de Bolougne.

and are convinced that no two other creatures in all Paris are so perfectly blissful. Believe what I tell you for your own happiness' sake as well as for the sake of justice: Eugène is an angel of tenderness, consideration and care: he had thought of everything before leaving Paris so as to receive me lovingly – if I go on allowing myself to be waited on and cared for as it is now I shall be no better than an American woman! He gets up and makes the coffee – and what coffee! – in our little kitchen and runs across for the croissants and serves me in bed – We had a very restful day yesterday though he expent [sic] himself for two hours playing his cello for me while I remained in bed – Some day you will hear him – he played Haydn and Chopin and Schumann – more Schumann and still more Schumann, Fauré, Saint-Saens – all the happiest music to give vent to his wild gaiety – of course everything by heart.'

In her unpublished memoir, Winifred also recounts how, on their first morning in Paris, Eugène told her on awakening, 'There's someone I want you to meet. Here is the only rival you'll ever have to fear.' He fetched his cello from the corner of the room and played her the joyful Rondo of Haydn's second cello concerto as the fittest expression of his feelings before rushing out to buy the breakfast *croissants* from the bakery opposite. As he made the coffee – a solemn and indeed sacred rite with him –he sang a little ditty that Winifred attributes to Paul Géraldy, a now largely forgotten poet and playwright popular in the early 20th century:

Reveilles-toi, ma chérie! Ne dors plus de la sorte!
Les deux petits croissants attendent à la porte![61]

The coffee and croissants were to be the habitual morning ritual during her life with Eugène in Paris. Throughout those years Winifred would regularly strive to allay Katharine's doubts about her marriage with a 'foreigner' and life abroad with assurances of their happiness together.

In his tiny handwriting, Eugène squeezed a little note for Katharine into the end of Winifred's first letter as a married woman:

CHÈRE MAMAN,
Encore toute ma gratitude pour tout ce que vous avez fait pour moi, mes remerciements également à Nelly. Si le mot Ange n'exis-

---

[61] 'Wake up, my darling! Don't sleep like that! The two little croissants are waiting at the door!'

tait pas on devrait le créer pour votre adorable et adorée fille. Je ne vous dirai qu'une chose, c'est que je suis très heureux et je m'efforcerai pour que Winny vous dise la même chose. Affectueuses pensées à toutes deux. Eugène.[62]

As for any young couple starting out in life, the early days were taken up with the practicalities of their new home. They had the briefest of honeymoons and it was spent in Paris, for Eugène was preparing for some forthcoming engagements. For Winifred, being with him in Paris and getting to know it for the first time as a resident rather than a visitor was honeymoon enough, even if one of their first concerns was to buy a towel rail. As the spoiled youngest who, apart from the years at college, had always lived at home with servants to take care of most household affairs, until now Winny had never had to concern herself with the kind of preoccupations that now filled up her days: the household 'linen', the daily food shopping. She was soon able to send a favourable report on her progress in cooking, though the young ménage apparently had some domestic help. 'I am really a quite recommendable cook. Although I never have to do anything unaided, I *could*, if need be.'

They soon moved to a bigger flat in a brand-new block just round the corner in Rue Dulong. The first few weeks passed in a flurry of expeditions to the Galeries Lafayette to buy furniture. Then came a stream of deliveries and of workmen. She was soon able to report to Nell that, 'The gas works, the windows open, the doors lock – all of which they didn't do before, as the paint had stuck and the gas leaked and the locks were blocked!'

Winny gloried in her new 'doll's house' and in all their purchases. Bohemian as her life with Eugène was to be in some respects, precarious as his profession must have been at times, there was little of the impoverished artists' life in a garret in the style in which they set up house together. Their taste in home furnishings, or at any rate Winny's taste, was for the classical and elegant. 'We are hoping that all our new furniture likes us as much as we like it! We have been very well treated by the Galeries Lafayette which made to order our arm-chairs, dining table and chairs and buffet: all beautiful copies, executed in their own workshops, of Louis XVI pieces.'

---

[62] 'Dear Mama, Once again, all my thanks for all that you have done for me, and thanks also to Nelly. If the word 'angel' did not exist, it would have to be created for your adorable and adored daughter. All I will say is that I'm very happy and I will do my best to make sure that Winny says the same. Affectionate thoughts to both of you.'

Winny's favourite monarch also dictated the style of their curtains, which were yellow and rose like the rest of the *salon*, so delighting her that she drew a sketch of them for Nell. 'My sweet little tulle curtains have ruches of the same material. The cretonne curtains are made exactly alike only their ruche is in a contrasting colour in *silk* – the proper Louis XVI style. All the household linen came today embroidered as only in France, with 'G.B.' [Gérin-Bourne)], even to the dusters! I have been able to get real *toile de Vosges* sheets which will last our lifetime.' In between more mundane tasks Winny would seat herself on one of the new chairs and do a little embroidery, raising her eyes frequently from her work to contemplate the Limoges coffee set displayed in the *vitrine*, next to some Rockingham cups Katharine had given her.

But more important to their life together than all these amenities was a little second-hand rosewood Pleyel piano they bought whose warm tone, Eugène said, was particularly suited to the cello. Though not a first-rate pianist by any means, Winifred wanted to be able to accompany him during his daily practices, and one of the first things Eugène did after their marriage was to order a sheaf of piano scores for pieces that they could play together. The daily music session was one of the new pleasures of life with Eugène. They worked on the repertoire of cello concertos – Haydn's, Schumann's, Dvorak's – and on some of Liszt's Hungarian rhapsodies, which had exciting and difficult time changes and syncopations. He taught her about harmony and went through each piece with her phrase by phrase. 'In these few days I have learnt as much as in twelve weeks' lessons, as I have, as it were, a three-hour lesson each day, each bar dissected and taken in turn. Certainly the artist's approach to a piece of music is as different and as superior to the layman's as cheese to chalk. In one glance everything is clear to him and the most embroiled passages tidied up and explained.'

Except when Eugène's concert engagements took them outside Paris, the pattern of their life in Rue Dulong was similar throughout their years there, until the events of 1939 put an end to the idyll. They were almost always together. His profession meant that when not on tour (and she always accompanied him when he was) he was often practising at home or free to spend time with her. When they were not making music or reading in their doll's house – Eugène too was a great reader – they were out exploring the city. Winifred was in love with Paris and French life as well as with Eugène. She loved the vitality of French life, the friendly, intelligent conversation of the shopkeepers, the plethora of produce sold from barrows in the narrow streets, where the vendors still 'cried' their wares; the abundance of traditional crafts and trades still plied in little workshops as in past centuries – book-binding, tapestry-restoration, chair-caning; the aesthetic sense that informed everything. On rambles through the old streets, she delighted in particular in the antique shops that seemed to be in every neighbourhood, overflowing with furniture that for her epitomised the grace and style of French living. She discovered the truth of the stereotype that the French turn living into an art. (Another common stereotype, the perception of Paris as the titillating capital of what she disapprovingly referred to as 'Montmartre nudist shows', she dismissed as a travesty of the respect for family values, work and education she perceived as the bedrock of French life as it was really lived.)

She particularly loved Paris in the autumn, always a favourite time of year with her and now associated with her honeymoon weeks in the city, especially October days when the leaves were turning yellow and the city seemed to be wrapped in a golden haze. In a letter to her mother she described a particularly lovely still, autumnal evening when she and Eugène dropped everything to walk in the Bois de Boulogne. The beech groves glowed in the light of the setting sun and the fallen leaves blazed orange and golden under their feet. They lingered by the lakesides after dark and continued their walk by moonlight. 'We were all aglow with walking and as there were few other enthusiasts we sang Haydn and ran to keep warm.'

They had their favourite beauty spots to which they made frequent excursions. Many of these were parks belonging to former royal residences, such as the gardens of the Château du Petit Trianon, Marie Antoinette's romantic rural retreat in the grounds of Versailles, where she created a little paradise with a *Jardin Anglais* and a model village of thatched cottages. Here Winifred and Eugène went each spring to see the magnolias in bloom. St-Cloud, to the west of Paris, was another favourite destination. Like the Trianon, St-Cloud was associated for Winifred with her first visit to Paris at the age of twelve, and here again they encountered the ghost of Marie Antoinette. The château loved by the Queen, where Napoleon later proclaimed himself emperor, was destroyed in the siege during the Franco-Prussian war, but the park remained. One of Winifred's happiest memories in later life was of afternoons in the Parc de Saint-Cloud, she working at her embroidery while Eugène read to her from Galsworthy, a favourite of his. At sunset they would linger at a vantage point overlooking the Seine, drinking in the view of the city.

Winifred and Eugène were sociable and made very good friends in Paris, but were contented when alone together, sufficient to each other. Eugène was good company. He made her laugh. He also laughed *at* her at times. Despite her years learning his language, Winny had what her Belgian in-laws called a 'délicieux accent britannique' and her grasp of idiomatic French was still incomplete. She had discovered this to her chagrin on her first visit to Plombières, where, having just spent two years reading French literature, she found herself unable to ask for the simplest item in a haberdashery shop. The gaps in her knowledge gave Eugène opportunities to have fun at her expense. He was an odd mixture. Tender and romantic as he was, he had a mischievous and positively Rabelaisian streak, and sometimes instructed his well-brought-up young English wife from the Surrey suburbs in Gallic terminology of a kind she had learned neither at Newnham nor in Plombières.

She innocently fell into the linguistic traps he set her. She would come out with some ribald expression he had taught her, but which she had not understood, in some wholly inappropriate context – asking for something in a shop, or in conversation with their friends. Winny didn't like being laughed at or made to look a fool, but somehow Eugène got away with it. She had a great capacity for hero-worship and he could do no wrong in her eyes. She was strong-willed, but Eugène, like a hero in a Brontë novel, was master of her. Perhaps he was the only person who ever was.

Eugène's concert tours took them to various European countries. Foreign musicians were not particularly well-paid in Paris and tours abroad were often more financially appealing.

One of these in particular was an adventure for them both. Katharine must have felt that her fears for the daughter who had attached herself to this foreign musician – fears that she would lead a thoroughly Bohemian existence – had been fully justified when in the autumn of 1933 Winifred gleefully announced that she and Eugène were about to go off with Alfred Rode and his 'gypsy orchestra' into the wilds of darkest Spain! Katharine was doubtless prepared to accept that life with a musician might necessitate a lot of travelling – but at this news of travels with a band of gypsy musicians in Spain, a country little known to tourists at the time, she probably concluded that Winifred was well on the way to becoming a gypsy herself.

Alfred Rode's orchestra of twenty or so musicians (needless to say, not real gypsies), then very much in vogue, played the gypsy music of Hungary, Romania and Greece whose rhythms had been incorporated by Liszt and Brahms. The musicians wore exotic costumes and the instruments included a cimbalom and pan pipes. Eugène had been playing with Rode's 'Orchestra of Tziganes' since 1931, when it performed at various venues in England, starting with an appearance at a special variety performance at the London Palladium attended by the King and Queen. Since then, the orchestra had been touring in France and other European countries. Eugène enjoyed the experience and made good friends among the other players, who found him very 'sympathique'.

Alfred Rode, born Alfred Spedaliere in Italy, was at that period still in his twenties. He was at various points of his career a film actor, producer and director as well as leader of the orchestra that was at the height of its popularity when Eugène joined it. In the 1931 British film *Carnival* with Matheson Lang and Chili Bouchier, a tale of jealousy inspired by *Othello* and set in Venice, Rode's musicians make a dramatic appearance playing at a masked ball in their embroidered, wide-sleeved shirts and waistcoats.

Rode commanded high prices for concerts and could afford generous pay for his musicians. In her letters home from the northern Spanish provincial towns they visited, Santander, Bilbao, Oviedo and Zaragoza among others, Winifred stressed the favourable terms of Eugène's contract. The two of them could afford to stay at good hotels. Though not as grand as the ones where Mr Rode went with his hispano-suiza car and glamorous American wife, their suites were luxurious for the price. Her observations on the strange country in which they found themselves were the typical ones of any English visitor at the time. In those days of the short-lived Second Republic, before the country was developed as a tourist destination and just a few years before the civil war that was to tear it apart, Spain's ways struck outsiders as quaint and puzzling but endearing, if exasperating at times.

Winifred savoured the art treasures and the medieval appearance of the towns and found the people unfailingly aimiable. She recounted, however, that reports of the country's spirit of *mañana* had been in no way exaggerated, with everyone walking at a leisurely pace or, where possible, saving their legs by making equally slow progress on a donkey (she adored these animals, which cluttered the narrow streets with their panniers, while, predictably, deprecating the bullfights). The hotel staff did not rise until late and the usual answer at railway stations to the question of what time the train arrived at its destination was 'in the course of the day'. They travelled between towns on trains which she described as being so low and narrow they were like a cross between hen coops and toy trains. The so-called Expresso, which was always late, stopped at every little station and people had time to get out to stretch their legs and discuss the *lotería* with the locals.

The gypsy orchestra played twice a day. The so-called 'matinee' was at seven in the evening, so they dined late, at nine, finding Spanish cuisine as mysterious as Spanish hours but generally very palatable. The evening performance was not until midnight and Winifred was in bed in their spacious hotel suite by the time Eugène returned.

Until the War put an end to this pleasant existence, such tours were a regular feature of their life. Of the European capitals they visited, Amsterdam held a particular place in their affections. They loved its dream-like silence and serenity, broken only by carillon chimes from the seventeenth-century church towers, with flower-laden barges gliding along the canals undisturbed by the noise of motor traffic. In those pre-war days, Winifred thought Dutch streets and canals still looked as they did in the paintings of the old masters. And it was in the Netherlands that she really came to appreciate painting for the first time. Eugène's tours gave her the opportunity to gain familiarity with the art collections of some of the great European galleries.

And between tours, there was always more of Paris to explore. For Winifred at least, viewing the city through the medium of her own happiness, the city of the 1930s retained much of the charm that had won her heart on her first visit in 1913, even if the *fiacres* of her youth had been replaced with honking motorcars. She called her memoir *The Years that Count* and in terms of emotional fulfilment – fulfilment as a writer and public recognition were to come much later – the seven years with Eugène in Paris were undoubtedly the ones that counted most for her. They were heady years for her personally, and the more general headiness of the cultural scene in 1930s Paris must have formed a vivid backdrop to her excitement in her new life.

Throughout the decade, those Parisians who could afford to do so continued to enjoy themselves as determinedly as in the twenties. There was jazz galore at the nightclubs and entertainment was provided by stars of the calibre of Maurice Chevalier and Josephine Baker. The jazz and nightclub scene had little appeal for Winifred, but there was much in the arts world to interest her. As in the twenties, the city was a hub of experimental movements in the arts, attracting some of their chief exponents. These were the years when James Joyce, who lived in the capital throughout both decades, was writing *Finnegans Wake*. Winifred and Eugène may have visited Sylvia Beach's famous bookshop in Rue de l'Odéon, *Shakespeare and Co.*, where Joyce and other writers hung out. Some of the new literature may well have left Winifred behind, but having been enthralled by Virginia

Woolf's stream of consciousness when she read Woolf's novels in the twenties, she would have been aware of the literary trends that continued to break new ground in the 1930s.

In painting, her tastes inclined towards Watteau rather than Miró and she is unlikely to have relished the disturbing work of the Surrealist painters like Max Ernst then working in Paris. In music, her preference was for classical rather than jazz, but here her tastes were less traditionalist. Since the days in Plombières she had been receptive to work by modern composers who had moved away from traditional melody, and to French composers in particular. She had ample opportunities in her Paris years to attend concerts of new works by such composers as Milhaud and Poulenc, as well as Stravinsky, who was living in the capital at the time.

As in London, theatre was an important part of her life. The Comédie Française was her Parisian substitute for the Old Vic, and she became as familiar with its stars as with those of the London stage. Cocteau, Gide and Giraudoux were all producing major works and Winifred must have particularly enjoyed those drawing on classical themes such as *La Machine Infernale*, Cocteau's reworking of the Oedipus myth, and Giraudoux's *La Guerre de Troie n'aura pas lieu*, a criticism of the attitudes that brought about the First World War and the lead-up to the Second.

She and Eugène also became familiar with the French film stars and directors of the period, particularly after discovering an intimate but surprisingly opulent *cinéma de quartier*, neighbourhood cinema, close to their flat. With talking movies still in their infancy (the first American talking motion picture was shown in Paris in 1930) the decade which produced Jean Renoir's *La Grande Illusion* and *La Règle du Jeu* was an exciting one for cinema.

From the mid-thirties Winifred gained more intimate acquaintance with the French film scene when Eugène became involved in it himself. These were the early years of film music; his services as a musician were well paid and he found it easy money. Winifred accompanied him into the studios and was able to watch the shooting. She got to know some of the directors and actors and saw at close quarters such French stars of the time as Harry Baur. Her foray into playwriting later in life was in part an attempt to recapture the thrill of being on the film set.

Eugène's early successes when a recent graduate of the Brussels Conservatory had seemed to be marking him out for a career playing the classical repertoire rather than the eclectic musical trajectory he took in Paris in the thirties. He was evidently always ready to try something new. However, from Winifred's account it seems likely that alongside the ventures that brought in 'easy money' he also gave some concert recitals in those years.

As the decade wore on, the effects of the Wall Street crash of 1929 kicked in and the mood in Paris changed. By the mid-thirties the scenario was one of economic depression and social unrest – workers' protests, the fascist-led riots of 6 February 1934 that led to the overthrow of the government – exacerbated by increasing concern about what Hitler's next move would be across the Rhine. Politically, things were looking increasingly grim in the second half of Winifred's time in Paris, and the threat of war overshadowed the brilliance of the enjoyments the city offered. The illuminated fountains of the Expo (World Fair) in 1937 lit it up each night, but the vast mural painted by Picasso for the Spanish pavilion, his response to the bombing of Guernica, was a reminder of the Spanish Civil War which many saw as the testing ground for a war that was soon to embroil the whole of Europe. By the time of the visit of George VI and Queen Elizabeth to Paris in the summer of the following year, opulently hosted by the city, it was no longer possible to forget for long the demands from Hitler coming thick and fast across the border. Earlier that year Germany had annexed Austria. Shortly afterwards came the Munich conference. Well before the Wehrmacht overran Czechoslovakia in the spring of 1939 it was clear to the Gérins and the many who thought as they did that the policy of appeasement of successive French governments, aimed at avoiding at all costs a repeat of the events of 1914–1918, had failed abjectly and that war had become inevitable.

Given that both Winifred and Eugène were opposed to the defeatist mood so rife both in France and Belgium, and given their staunch support for the Allied efforts once the War started, they and their friends must often have discussed the probability of war. But nothing could dim the radiance of Winifred's years in Paris with Eugène before the events that overturned both their lives. She was secure in a heaven of her own. The forewarnings of the approaching disaster certainly reached her from the world outside but could not destroy her personal happiness.

The only thing that dimmed their happiness apart from their growing conviction that war was coming was the non-appearance of children as the years passed and Winifred entered her mid- and late thirties. In the opinion of a doctor they consulted, the reason could have been the long-term effects of the antitoxin given to her by the incompetent doctor who overdosed Phil. The amount given to Winifred had also been too strong, upsetting her metabolism and hormones and triggering an early puberty.

Happily for her, in 1933 there was an event in the Gérin family in Brussels which, over the years, was to go some way towards compensating the lack of children of her own.

Winifred had had a cordial relationship with Eugène's family since her first introduction to them in the days of courtship. Like her, Eugène was the spoiled youngest and very family-minded, and whenever possible the two of them spent a few days with the Gérins in Brussels, usually as part of a round trip that also took in a visit to Katharine and Nell in Surrey.

The Gérin family home in Rue Georges Moreau, where Eugène had spent his teens and student days, was a much more modest establishment than Winifred's childhood home in Norwood. It was an unassuming three-storeyed terraced house, like most Brussels houses tall and rather narrow, located in a part of Anderlecht – a largely working- and lower-middle-class suburb – that was one of the city's Jewish quarters, close to the Gare du Midi.

Eugène's father had died some years before. His elder brother Maurice lived on the first floor of the family home with his wife Marthe, a primary school teacher; his mother, Eugénie, occupied the three rooms on the second. The ground floor was rented to a Jewish family who worked in the leather trade. In shops and workshops throughout the neighbourhood, Jewish artisans plied the trades traditional in their community. There were Jewish bakeries and Jewish butcher's shops. The Gérins' house was half-way between the local church and the synagogue. Maurice and Marthe worshipped at neither – neither Eugène nor his brother were church-goers – though Eugénie enjoyed putting on her best clothes to go to mass. Sundays therefore passed largely unmarked in the house, but on the Sabbath the tenants' floor filled up with guests and a pool in the yard with carp for the feast.

Eugène's mother was French. His father had met her while working at a factory in Maubeuge in northern France near the Belgian border, where Eugène's early childhood was spent. When the two boys were still small the family moved to Belgium, where their father found work as a fabric sales representative. After some years in the province of Namur in sourthern Belgium they settled in Brussels.

Eugénie, known as *Maman* or by the diminutive form '*Man*', was an intelligent, resourceful woman who ruled the roost in the household. She had always had social aspirations for the family and ambitions for her two boys, and had made sure they were given the opportunity to acquire musical training. Although not highly educated in a formal sense she was a great reader of the classics. She and

Winifred took to each other at once and Winny would send her translations of nineteenth-century English novels.

Maurice had studied violin at the Conservatory. The two brothers' musical gifts must have been inherited from their father, who played the horn in the brass band of the factory where he was employed; apparently he was recruited on the basis of his skill as a wind player as much as anything else! Once the family moved to Belgium the two boys were enrolled first at the conservatory in Namur and then at the Royal Conservatory of Brussels. Like Eugène, Maurice had envisaged a career as a classical musician. But while Eugène was just too young to be called up in 1914, Maurice was not so lucky, and when he was demobilised in 1919 it was too late to return to the Conservatoire. He earned a living playing in orchestras in Brussels restaurants and *salons de thé*. Jazz, imported by American troops, was all the rage. Maurice could play the trumpet and saxophone as well as the violin, and before his marriage had toured Europe with jazz orchestras. At the time Winifred first knew him, before health problems set in, he was earning good money.

One of the family stories about Eugène's young days in Brussels illustrated well the different destinies of the two brothers, and Eugénie's spoiling of her adored younger son. After the War, Eugène had to do his military service. He would arrive home in the evening and throw himself into an armchair complaining of exhaustion and tired feet, and his solicitous mother would hurry to bring a basin of warm salty water to bathe his 'poor' feet. Late one evening after these ablutions, Maurice was playing in the restaurant where he was employed at the time when a group of high-spirited young people entered in party mood and proceeded to enjoy themselves drinking, laughing and dancing. Maurice spotted his younger brother among the merriest of these carousers and noted that Eugène's 'poor' feet were not too tired to dance.

Maurice married in the same year as Eugène, 1932. Winny was very fond of both him and Marthe. In September 1933 their only child, Paul Eugène, was born, his second name being, of course, in honour of his uncle, and Eugène and Winifred were asked to be the godparents. For Paul, Winifred was not just 'la Tante Winny', Aunt Winny, but 'Marraine Winny', Godmother Winny, and in future years it was the latter appellation that was generally used by him and often by the rest of the family too.

She became something of a *fairy* godmother to him. She could not have foreseen how important he and she were going to be for each other, but she took an interest in him from the start. He grew into a shy, sensitive and affectionate child. She was concerned that loved though he was by those around him, as the only child in a household of adults with parents who were too busy to spend much time with him he lacked many of the pleasures that had made her own childhood so joyful. Until Paul was old enough to go to school, his days were spent with his grandmother. His mother did not return home from work until the evening and he saw little of his father, who would come home in the small hours from whichever establishment he was playing at, rise late and do his music practice before leaving for work again. Eugénie read to him and told him about history; she had numerous anecdotes of the French Revolution. What she did not do very much was take him out to play, and he looked forward to the regular visits of Uncle Eugène and Aunt Winny, when the house became more animated.

Paul was a highly observant child. In old age he, like Winifred herself, wrote his memoirs, in which he recorded his early impressions of *Marraine Winny* and traced what she came to mean in his life. *La Tante Winny* and *l'oncle Eugène* brought glamour and Parisian *chic* to the house in Anderlecht, tales of the French capital and of Eugène's concert engagements. During their visits the house seemed to fill up with laughter. Eugène's witty talk would light up the room and both he and Winny were great *raconteurs*, she speaking fluent French with the marked English accent about which Eugène sometimes teased her. Winny was always simply but elegantly dressed. Paul found her *très distinguée* and her manners very 'English'; he felt he had to be on his best behaviour in her presence. His uncle was the opposite; he was often outrageous, and he didn't scruple to make jokes at Winny's expense. Paul felt she would not have permitted anyone else to take such liberties.

They always brought 'Pussy', their white Persian cat. Love of animals was a strong bond between Winifred and Eugène – Winifred once said she could not have loved a man who could deliberately step on a beetle in his path – and even before their marriage Eugène had always kept a cat. The one member of the household who did not look forward to their visits was the house cat Radjah, also a Persian, a gift from Eugène to his mother, and to avoid conflict between the two animals they were quartered in separate rooms in the attic. Paul hated his grandmother's cat, which had a vicious temper, and much preferred the visitor. One of his treats was going up to the attic to feed him.

The visitors also brought their nephew wonderful toys from Paris and London such as a set of lead fox-hunting figures – horses and red-jacketed riders and hounds from the English shires. Paul played with the little figures incessantly until they were faded and broken. Between visits, letters and postcards for the whole family would arrive regularly from Winifred from the towns where Eugène's concert engagements took them, often on the Mediterranean coast.

Eugène always said that after a period under Mediterranean skies he would have a yen for a few days under the cloudy ones of Brussels, the city of his youth. It was a conservative and provincial place in those days, and perhaps Winifred found it sombre after Paris, with its overcast skies and narrow streets, closely-packed with tall brick houses. For her the city's main attraction was the presence of Eugène's family, but in time she doubtless discovered that the little capital, while lacking the sparkle of Paris, had its own quiet, understated charms. One special charm for her was that Brussels was the city that Charlotte Brontë called 'Villette'. On Winifred's first visits she was eager to seek out the Pensionnat Heger in Rue d'Isabelle, which inspired Madame Beck's school in the novel. It was a disappointment to learn that the school, and the quiet cobbled streets around it where Charlotte and Emily Brontë had walked, had disappeared in 1910 when the area was redeveloped. But in the eighteenth-century squares of the *Haute Ville* (Upper Town) and the winding medieval streets of the older *Basse Ville* below it, both evoked in obsessive detail in *Villette*, she discovered much of the setting of the novel. She had always had a special feeling for Charlotte Brontë's haunting last novel set in a continental school, full of French phrases and impressions of 'foreignness'. As she got to know Brussels over the years, the book became charged with her own personal associations. She came to feel that now she *knew* and understood Villette.

The city had other charms, of course, such as the Art Nouveau buildings in the newer parts of town, dating from the Belle Époque. The charms of Anderlecht, where her in-laws lived, were not so immediately apparent, though their house stood in a pleasant enough area near the town hall. Anderlecht was an industrial suburb of factories and businesses. Close to the Gare du Midi was the big Côte d'Or factory, from which emanated a scent of chocolate cheering to the nostrils of those trudging to work through on chill winter mornings. It was a fragrance that sometimes caught the nostrils of Winifred and Eugène as they walked the short distance from the station to Rue Georges Moreau, warm and nourishing as the welcome that awaited them in the family home.

Towards the end of the decade, though, a personal catastrophe in the household in Rue Georges Moreau combined with events on the world stage to make their visits there less happy. In March 1939, the month of Hitler's invasion of Czechoslovakia, Maurice had a stroke which left him, at first, practically paralysed. With the help of physiotherapy he gradually recovered enough to play the violin again, but not quite as he had before, and things were never the same again for the Gérin family. There were financial worries; throughout the three years or so of Maurice's convalescence, the family had to rely on Marthe's salary. The occasional holidays at Ostend, where Maurice used to get summer engagements with an orchestra, came to an end. Paul now saw a lot more of his father than before, but this father was no longer the one he had known. Maurice's self-confidence had gone, his infirmities made him irritable and he saw the War coming in a mood of pessimism and defeatism.

In the months leading up to the declaration of war on Germany by France and Britain, Paul noticed that though his uncle's and aunt's visits were no less welcome, the atmosphere at home during their stays had become less harmonious. Arguments would arise between Eugène and his elder brother, and Winny would take the same side as Eugène, arguing as hotly as the two men. The subject of dissension was the approaching war and whether or not Belgium should remain neutral.

As a veteran of the First World War who believed Belgium should avoid involvement in another devastating conflict, Maurice was loyal to King Leopold III and supported the policy of neutrality that he had announced in 1936. In 1937, Germany had undertaken to respect that neutrality. But Eugène and Winny had no faith in the neutrality of Belgium; they did not doubt that in the event of war, the country would inevitably become involved, and they were eloquent in pointing out the dangers posed by Hitler. Maurice, whose life had in many ways been blighted by the first war, felt that Eugène, the more fortunate younger brother who had never known combat, was in no position to lecture him.

In the last months of 1939 and the first ones of 1940 Paul noticed that his uncle's and aunt's appearances at the house were more frequent. They visited almost every weekend, but some mystery surrounded their activities at that period. They were present at the family party to celebrate his sixth birthday in September but some of the carefree, jolly atmosphere of former family reunions was missing. Although Paul was too young to understand the events that were triggered by Germany's invasion of Poland in September 1939, he was not too young to notice that everyone around him seemed preoccupied.

Winifred and Eugène spent the months leading up to September 1939 in Paris and London.

Afterwards, Winifred always remembered a lovely spring day in April 1939 which encapsulated her life in Paris with Eugène. The pervasive sense of an approaching catastrophe could not spoil their enjoyment of each moment of that day. They had taken a picnic to one of their favourite haunts, the gardens of the little Château de Bagatelle on the site of a former hunting lodge in the Bois de Boulogne. It was a favourite spot of Marie Antoinette; it cannot have been coincidence that the French queen Winifred loved was associated with so many of the places where she went with Eugène. It was a warm, cloudless day and they spent most of it lying under a chestnut tree and reading *Villette*. They had been preparing for the War by brushing up their languages, and Eugène had been working on his English by reading only English books. He had an instinctive love of the Brontës' writing quite independent of Winifred's devotion to them. The blissful day seemed to go on and on. Winifred recounts in her memoir that when the shadows lengthened and they at last got up to go they noticed that the leaves of the chestnut tree, which that morning had been closed, had opened out in those few hours. It was as if nature, too, sensed what was coming and had accelerated its pace in order to pack as much of life as possible into that one fleeting day.

They spent that summer in England with Katharine, Nell and Ellen Gilbert, always known simply as 'Gilbert', who alone remained of the live-in servants. She had joined the household twentier years earlier as a parlour-maid and had long been much more than a faithful retainer; she was also companion, friend and often adviser. Few believed in Chamberlain's 'peace in our time' and in 1938 Katharine had bought a bungalow in Virginia Water so that in the event of war she could move out of London and be near Roger. The house was a mere half-mile from Holloway, practically within sight of its gables. By now Katharine was too badly crippled by arthritis to visit Roger, but he was brought to have tea with her each week. It was in Virginia Water and not at the family home in Norwood that they all spent the last summer before the War.

At the end of August Winifred and Eugène returned to Paris, but only for a few days. Eugène was a reservist in the Belgian army and could be called up at any time. After the German invasion of Poland on 1 September, Belgium, though still officially neutral, started to mobilise, and Eugène was instructed to report to the Brussels HQ. They shut up their flat, took leave of their friends, who were also waiting to be called up and also packing their belongings, and set off for Brussels. The Paris idyll and the days in Rue Dulong were at an end. Most of their treasured possessions had to be left behind in the flat. But Pussy went with them on the train to Brussels.

7
Flight from Brussels
The Summer of 1940

In the months following September 1939 when his aunt and uncle appeared so preoccupied on their brief visits to Rue Georges Moreau, Paul did not realise that they were living in Brussels, in a rented flat in another part of town. It was not until after the War that he learned they had spent those months doing secret work for the British Embassy.

On arrival in Belgium, Winifred and Eugène found that reservists had merely been told to await further orders. In view of this, given Eugène's opposition to Belgian 'neutrality' he considered that his loyalty was to Britain rather than Belgium. On 3 September he and Winifred went to offer their services to the British Embassy in the elegant Leopold Quarter, which in later years came to be dominated by the buildings of the European Union institutions. There they were received by the Press Attaché, Mr De Sausmarez, and his aide, a Major Ackroyd.

In the years ahead, Cecil De Sausmarez – the aristocratic name was that of his family's Norman fiefdom in Guernsey – was to reappear in their lives with some regularity. He was a cultured man who loved Montaigne and had until recently taught classics and modern languages at Wellington College; the War changed the direction of his life, as it did that of Eugène and Winifred. A Churchillian rather than Chamberlainite from the outset, he had left his teaching post for one in which he could contribute to preparations for the coming conflict.[63] Winifred found him a highly volatile character; when in good spirits he was extremely ebullient, and extremely talkative.

---

[63] Much of the information on De Sausmarez in this chapter and in Chapter 9 is taken from interviews with him recorded in 1975 and 1977 by CEGESOMA (Centre d'Études et de Documentation Guerre et Sociétés contemporaines – Centre for Historical Research and Documentation on War and Contemporary Society, Belgium). Catalogue ref. nos. AA 851, AA 2268/182 and AA 2268/183.

The Gérins were required to produce credentials to prove they were not German agents. A military friend of Eugène's, later active in the resistance, acted as his guarantor, while as her own guarantor Winifred gave the name of her cousin Cuthbert, who worked in the Bank of England. Major Ackroyd then took them to an office he had set up in what Winifred describes in her memoir as the fashionable part of the city – probably the area round Avenue Louise. It advertised itself as a travel agency. The only other person working there was Ackroyd's secretary, Simone Van Maele, a young Belgian woman. The 'travel agency' turned out to be simply a cover to conceal the office's real purpose. From nine in the morning to six each evening Winifred's and Eugène's task, a humble but valuable one, was to put circulars into envelopes as quickly as they could – Ministry of Information propaganda bulletins to counter the German propaganda machine. The envelopes had to be addressed by hand and posted from various locations in the city to Belgians who were known to be opposed to neutrality and to have been involved with British Intelligence in the First World War. The aim was to have a resistance movement in place when war arrived, which De Sausmarez saw as an important part of his role as press attaché; he was also using his position in order to contact anti-Hitlerite Belgian politicians and journalists. The Belgian 'agents' to whom the circulars were addressed distributed them in turn to other trusted recipients. The British Embassy could not openly breach the terms of the neutrality, although in fact both the British and German embassies were engaged in such propaganda work, and the work, therefore, had to be kept secret. Eugène's family thought that he and Winifred were working for the Red Cross and discreetly asked no questions. As a contribution to the war effort, Eugène and Winifred refused a salary for their work, an altruistic gesture they had cause to regret later when unable to draw on their funds.

This was their routine for the eight months of the 'Phoney War'. It was brought to an abrupt end on 10 May 1940 when they were woken at dawn by the noise of gunfire. Pussy, who always slept on their bed, slipped under it as they jumped out and ran to the window. The sky was full of aircraft, glinting silver in the rays of the rising sun. For the first few moments Winifred thought they were on their way to invade Britain, but Eugène said, 'No, it's for us.' The news on the radio soon confirmed this. Germany had invaded the Netherlands and Belgium that morning and both were now at war with Germany. Eugène and Winifred rejoiced to hear that the Foreign Minister, Paul-Henri Spaak, had insisted on being heard first when the German ambassador was about to read his country's declaration, and had voiced a strong protest at Germany's second act of aggression in 25 years against a neutral Belgium.

They made their way to the British Embassy. An incident they witnessed on their journey brought home dramatically the change in their world announced by those dawn planes. Waiting for a tram, they saw several German parachutists descending from the skies and a Belgian officer, not far from where they were standing, shooting one of them with his revolver, to general cheers. At the Embassy they found Cecil in ebullient mode and a mood of euphoria that the so-called neutrality was over. There was a joyful reception of the British tanks that had been waiting at the border and had reached the city that morning. Air raids began that very day and on their way home Winifred and Eugène found themselves having to take refuge in doorways, no shelters having been built because of the Belgian neutrality.

The euphoria evaporated over the next three days as the news from the front became worse, and on 13 May the Embassy staff decided to move to Ostend. The Germans were expected to enter Brussels at any moment and the Gérins were among the staff who spent the whole of that last day in Brussels in the Embassy courtyard, burning all the records that had been created in the past months. Before they left they had just time to say goodbye to Eugène's mother, at a tram stop outside the Gare du Nord. For the time being the family were going to stay with Marthe's father on the outskirts of Brussels.

Winifred and Eugène caught a train to Ostend that evening. Most of their clothes were left behind with the concierge of their Brussels flat, but Pussy accompanied them on the train in his basket, complete with his litter tray and supplies of food. They arrived in Ostend to find the town plunged in the darkness of a complete blackout and the streets deserted. Under these circumstances the addresses of hotels Major Ackroyd had given them were of little use. They had to take pot-luck, and because of the suspicions of fifth-columnists had to rouse several hotel owners before they found one willing to take them.

A scene of chaos awaited them the next morning when they reported to the British Consulate, which was besieged by Jewish refugees seeking visas to Britain before the Germans arrived. Some of them had crossed Europe from as far away as Bulgaria. The Gérins were set to work dealing with their applications, with instructions to issue visas only to applicants with a specified amount of English currency or a guarantor in Britain. Hardly any of the refugees were able to meet the latter requirement, and the Gérins found themselves obliged to turn down most of the applicants, leaving them to escape as they could through France. It was a heartbreaking task.

Eugène and Winifred had expected to spend some months in Ostend while the German advance was halted. Instead, the following day they heard that the British ambassador had been captured on his way to Ostend – fortunately Cecil took a different route – and that the Netherlands had surrendered. On 15 May the remaining staff were told to get out as quickly as they could. The Gérins were offered visas for England and places on one of two cross-Channel ships waiting in the harbour for British nationals and legitimate refugees. But at that very moment Belgian reservists were being told by loudspeaker that they were about to be mobilised, and to report at La Panne or Ypres. Eugène therefore felt bound to remain, and Winifred turned down her place on the ship in order to stay with him in Belgium, where they both believed the War would be continuing for some time.

'You're a wonderful woman,' Cecil said to her as he took leave of them and thanked them for their work, impressed by her courage. Winifred never forgot the compliment although she felt it was unde-served. If she and Eugène had known how events were going to evolve they would certainly have been among those piling onto one of those waiting ships. Indeed, if they had had the benefit of foresight they would never have left London in August 1939.

They hired one of the last available cars in Ostend with two British couples who lived in Belgium and were now among the hordes trying to get across the border to France. The idea was to drive to La Panne, where Eugène had been summoned to report, but at the last moment there was a change of plan. One of the couples were just lamenting the fact that they were unable to say goodbye to their son, who was in the Belgian army, when that very son, at the head of his platoon, marched into the square where they were waiting for their car on a café terrace. He told them La Panne was cut off and the Germans were advancing on all the ports. They asked the driver to take them to Ypres instead, only to learn from loudspeaker announcements once they arrived that reservists were now being instructed to make their way to Paris. Clearly the Belgian army was in retreat and was hoping to regroup in Paris and hold back the German advance from there. Their driver could take them no further than Abbeville, which was the HQ of the British Command and full of refugees. When they inquired about accommodation they were directed to a café where they found the British Commander, who issued orders for them to be found lodgings for the night.

By now, every town and station was teeming with refugees. The following morning the Gérins fought their way onto a train to Paris. Because of air raids it made only halting progress, and they saw empty trains with their windows machine-gunned. They stopped near

Dunkirk and saw the sky glowing red over the town; soldiers scrambling on board said it was on fire. The Gérins could guess little of the drama that was beginning to unfold there, with the evacuation of the port only a few days away. The train got as far as Armentières, where they were given a bed for the night in the first house at whose door they knocked, by a young mother whose husband was at the front. She insisted on giving up her bedroom to them.

During the night the town's station was bombarded. They heard the din but were too weary to stir. The next morning, thanks to a lift from a farmer, they got on a train to Paris from Béthune, a town some miles away. Like every train they had been on, it was full of French troops; they seemed unconcerned by the German advance and were much diverted by Pussy, who was taking everything in his stride.

That night Winifred and Eugène slept in their flat in Rue Dulong for the first time in six months. At the Belgian embassy next morning Eugène was told to be ready to leave the following day with his group of reservists for training in Narbonne in south-east France. Winifred was resigned to waiting for him in the Paris flat. Her female friends were in the same position, left behind while their men went off to the front. They had just a day before Eugène left to see friends, settle some of their more urgent affairs, withdraw funds from the bank. Winifred went to see Eugène off the next day and was stupefied when his commanding officer took her aside and warned her not to stay in Paris: the Germans would be there in days, he said. Eugène was due to leave in a few minutes. They had just time to agree that she would join him in Narbonne.

The mood in Paris, where many were blaming the Belgians for their policy of neutrality and for failing to stop the German advance, and were losing confidence in the military commanders, was such that Winifred was now glad to leave the city. The next morning she and Pussy boarded a train for Narbonne.

Now began a second trial of endurance on the railways. That evening everyone was told to get off the train at Limoges, a town not on the usual route to Narbonne, where there was the usual scene, with the station teeming with people. Winifred was told that there was no guarantee she would get a train to Narbonne, but that there might be one to Montpellier in the morning. The problem of where to spend the night – not made any easier by the fact that Pussy had of course to be included in any arrangements – was solved by an offer of accommodation from a polite young Boy Scout who was helping out at the station. He took her to his aunt's house, where he and his mother, introduced as the 'Comtesse de Solmes', had themselves taken refuge. The house was full of Louis XVI furniture, and the old-fashioned courtesy of the two ladies was in keeping with the decor. Winifred spent the night in some style on a velvet-upholstered divan in the drawing-room and Pussy seemed quite at home in these surroundings.

Miraculously, there was a train bound for Narbonne the following morning – and, miraculously again, it did eventually reach its destination. But there was no Eugène. A Belgian officer told her that his group of reservists had not arrived there and suggested various other towns she could try. She was distraught until she had a sudden brainwave and hurried to the post office. Sure enough there was a telegram for her from Eugène, telling her to join him in Alès, a town near Nîmes in southern France.

The train she boarded for Alès took two days to get there, for the entire duration of which she sat on her suitcase in the corridor with Pussy's basket on her knees, surrounded by troops, mainly Moroccan. She arrived on the morning of 28 May to find the usual crowds of refugees, with Red Cross workers distributing coffee. The question of accommodation was solved when one of these white-clad workers turned out to be a Paris friend from Alès, who told Winifred she had been in touch with Eugène since his arrival at the town. It was at the house of this friend's family that Winifred first heard the news that Belgium had surrendered that morning. To her indignation, as she walked into the house she heard the French Prime Minister, Paul Reynaud, on the wireless lambasting Leopold III for betraying France. Britain took a similar line, but Winifred was one of the many who defended the King's decision. In her view he had no choice but to surrender in order to stop the carnage. Those fleeing blocked the roads and prevented the artillery from advancing, and army and refugees alike were trapped by the German attack both on the ground and from the air.

The reunion with Eugène was overshadowed by concern about their changed status as Belgians in France (under the law of the time Winifred was a Belgian national through marriage), now that Belgium had capitulated and its citizens were being reviled in the streets as traitors. Eugène's regiment, led by him and an army sergeant, was assembled outside the town, near a village called Saint-Hilaire-de-Brethmas. Winifred joined him at the farm where he and the sergeant were billeted, a fortress-like building standing in the midst of vineyards. Here they spent several weeks waiting to know the fate of his group of reservists. The farmer and his family showed them a hospitality as genuine as that of the young woman who gave up her bed to them at Armentières, and in both cases Winifred was struck by her hosts' stoicism and kindness. After France's capitulation she remembered this family and others like it as embodying for her the values of

Portrait of Winifred by Nell, 1960s (courtesy of Brontë Parsonage Museum)

Above: Plombières-les-Bains, the spa town in eastern France where the Bournes frequently spent the summers in the 1920s (railway poster by F. Hugo d'Alesi, *c.* 1900)

Right: Plombières-les-Bains (photo reproduced by courtesy of Roland Conilleau)

Below: Winifred's father, Frederick Charles Bourne (undated photograph)

Facing page: The interior of Winifred's 'Richard III' cottage in Stanford

Painting by Nell of St Denys Church, Stanford. According to an unsubstantiated legend, Richard III, then Duke of Gloucester, married Anne Neville here

Top: Winifred's mother, Katharine Hill (undated photograph)

Left: Undated photograph of Winifred as a teenager

Opposite top: View from Whitehorse Lane, at the junction where it turns into South Norwood Hill. The Bournes' house stood a little further up the hill, off the left of the photo (courtesy of the Museum of Croydon)

Below: 'Bill' and Dorothy Moore with their eldest son Nicky in April 1919 (courtesy of the Moore family)

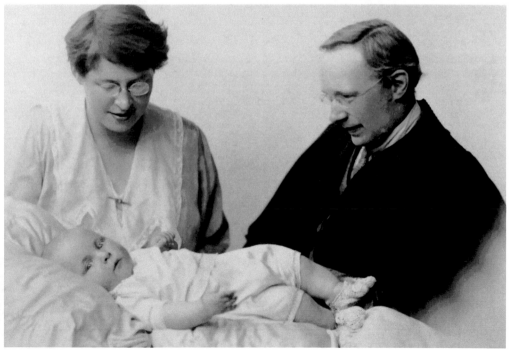

The young Eugène with his cello

Top left: *The violoncelliste poète*. Cartoon published in *Le Nouveau Dijon*, 19 September 1925

Top right: Eugène Gérin. A photo probably taken in the early 1930s

Below: Winifred and Eugène on the Riviera around the time of their marriage (1932)

Top: Photo of Winifred and Eugène dating from the same period (1932)

Far left:The newly-weds. Winifred and Eugène are on the right; Eugène's brother Maurice and his wife Marthe on the left. Both couples married in 1932

Left: Winifred and 'Pussy', the Gérins' white Persian cat, in the Paris apartment. He accompanied them on many of their wartime adventures

Top left: In the Gérin family home in Anderlecht, Brussels, in 1934. From left to right: Eugénie (Eugène's mother), Maurice, Eugène, Marthe. Paul is sitting on his mother's knee

Top right: Alfred Rode and his Orchestra of Tziganes (gypsies). Eugène, pictured on the far right, toured with this orchestra in the early 1930s (cartoon dated 1931)

Below: Eugène in gypsy costume

Above: Marthe and Paul in 1942

Opposite top left: Winifred, Eugène and Eugénie with Paul
Opposite top lright: No 60 West Cromwell Road in Earls Court, the house shared by Winifred and Nell after Eugène's death

Opposite below: Nell and Gilbert with Rowley and Minette

Top: Winifred in the house in West Cromwell Road, 1950s. Eugène's portrait hangs on the wall

Above left: A scene from Winifred's first play, Juniper Hall, performed at the Leatherhead Theatre Club in May 1952. From left to right, Rosemary Webster as Fanny Burney, Michael Allinson as General Alexandre D'Arblay and Wilfrid Walter as Talleyrand (© W.R. Ayling, courtesy of Surrey History Centre)

Above right: Winifred after receiving her M.A. in 1949

Left: Winifred and John in the garden of his mother's house in Purley around the time of their marriage (1955)

Below right: Winifred and John in West Cromwell Road

Below left: The cast of Winifred's play *My Dear Master*, performed by the Leeds Art Theatre in October 1955 (cartoon reproduced by courtesy of the *Yorkshire Evening Post*)

"MY DEAR MASTER"

CHARLOTTE BRONTË
(Cecily Bradbury)

MONSIEUR HEGER
(Peter Beasley)

THE BARONESS DE SWARTZ
(Bertha Keighley)

FATHER LETELLIER
(Philip Wright)

MADAME HEGER
(Marian Walker)

Reprinted from *The Yorkshire Evening Post*

Top: Nell at work in her studio

Left: A sketch by a friend of Nell painting, dated 1968

Below: Winifred and John on the moors near Haworth. In the background is Lower Laithe Reservoir near Stanbury

Top left: Winifred and John by the Church of St Michael and All Angels in Haworth

Above: Winifred with Anne-Marie and the three eldest Gérin children (Marthe, Hubert and Eugène) on the Thames in 1970

Left: Winifred and her godson, Eugène, in August 1967

Below: Postcard of Church Green, Stanford in the Vale. Winifred's cottage, No 3, is the second from the right

Top: Winifred in her last decade. Photo taken in the garden at her cousin Agatha Pearce's house in Goosey, near Stanford, in August 1971

Above left: Winifred and Paul on a visit to Blenheim *c*. 1970

Above right: Winifred with Jamie

the true France, the country she loved. The accommodation and food offered was basic but dignified in its timeless simplicity. She and Eugène and the sergeant slept on sheets in horse boxes full of straw and shared the family's fare of goat's cheese, bread and fruit, dining on the vine-trellised terrace and talking late under the stars.

While they were there the news came that the Germans were in Paris, that the Prime Minister, Reynaud, had resigned and that France's new premier, the eighty-four-year-old Marshal Pétain, was suing for peace. News of France's capitulation soon followed. One of the terms was the repatriation of all Belgian military personnel on French soil. But as a civilian volunteer Eugène was not obliged to return with the others. He had no wish to return to occupied Belgium; he wanted to serve in England.

Under the armistice with Germany, France was divided into a northern zone occupied by the Germans and only nominally adminis-tered by France, and a southern, unoccupied area – the so-called 'free zone' governed by Pétain, with its capital at Vichy.

Meantime, a Belgian government in exile, committed to continuing the fight, was being formed in London by Marcel-Henri Jaspar and Camille Huysmans, who led the exodus of anti-Hitlerite Belgian politi-cians to England. In October of that year, the Prime Minister, Hubert Perliot, and the Foreign Minister Paul-Henri Spaak would succeed in joining them, having escaped through Franco's Spain hidden in a truck. At the end of the year this government of four was formally recognised by London as the legal representative of Belgium.

The Gérins knew that many members of the Belgian cabinet had gone to Nice in the 'free zone', from where some were hoping to make their way to England. There was now a veritable colony of Belgian 'dissidents' in the town. It seemed a good place to head to for the moment, particularly as Winifred's cousin Louie was living there. Now widowed and in her seventies, she was a member of another colony – that of elderly British ladies drawn by the benign Riviera climate. She encouraged them in the scheme. When, in the early autumn of 1940, the other reservists boarded the train that was to take them back to Belgium – in the event, many soon escaped to England – Eugène did not join them. He and Winifred made their way to Nice.

8

Nice
The Pit of Darkness

Winifred and Eugène arrived in Nice on a mellow autumn day. Behind them were hours and days spent crammed in crowded trains, with the fear of being bombed from above and the uncertainty of reaching their destination; the continual hunt for lodgings; nights and weeks billeted in strangers' houses. And now they found themselves on the Côte d'Azur where they had both spent some of their happiest times. In his youth Eugène had left the grey skies of Brussels to join the Monte Carlo orchestra; Winifred, fleeing the London fogs with her family, had been enchanted by the Mediterranean even before it became the scene of her first encounter with Eugène. After their marriage, his concert engagements had brought them back here to places they both loved, such as Menton on the border with Italy.

Nice, with the perfect curve of its beach set in the Bay of Angels, looked, as always, like paradise. A local legend that provides an origin for the name 'Bay of Angels' suggests that the town is indeed an earthly paradise, claiming that after Adam and Eve were barred from the Garden of Eden and were wondering where to go next, they were guided by a host of angels to the French Riviera and took up their residence in the town. It has to be said, though, that Menton also makes a claim to be the destination of the banished pair.

At first glance, life in Nice in that autumn of 1940 appeared to be going on as normal, as far as life in a luxury seaside resort for the wealthy can ever be said to be normal. The War seemed far away. The town was full of visitors and there were bathers on the beach. The hotels were doing business. The Palais de la Jetée on the pier was still in place at that time. The dome and towers of this extravagant Moorish-type palace in doubtful taste were partly inspired by the Crystal Palace of Winifred's childhood.

Sea-bathing or strolls on the pier, however, were not what the Gérins had in mind on this visit to the Riviera, and this time it failed to have their usual effect on their mood. They were set on a single purpose, reaching Britain and joining the war effort there. Nice was intended to be simply a stepping-stone on the way to achieving that objective. Not for the first time since the start of the War, things did not go according to plan.

First on their list of things to do was a visit to Cousin Louie's for tea. The term was rapidly to become a euphemism, as tea was soon a commodity available only on the black market. After that, their goal was to find lodgings and make contact with the Belgian community in the city, people who, like themselves, had fled occupied Belgium and were intent on joining those of their countrymen who had managed to get to England. The lodgings – with a balcony overlooking the street where Pussy could pass his days – were found in the sunny Rue St Siagre off the Avenue Masséna, the city's central avenue leading to Place Masséna, and they were soon in touch with many Belgians in the town. Some, like them, were hoping to reach London. But the Gérins soon learned from them that this was not going to be as straightforward as they had hoped. They had assumed that once in the 'free zone' they would be able to obtain visas fairly easily for North Africa or Spain, but it turned out that no 'exit visas' were being issued for foreigners in any direction. For the moment, along with many other fellow Belgians, they were trapped in Nice.

The practical problems confronting them were many, the most pressing being lack of funds. Their money was in their bank in Paris, and they had been unable to access it since the division of the country into two zones. The English banks in Nice had been closed, as had the British Consulate. Some British residents in similar straits managed to obtain small loans from the American consulate, but as Belgian citizens the Gérins were not eligible for such arrangements.

They got by with money from English lessons given by Winifred. Among her first pupils were two exiled Belgian government ministers, Paul-Émile Janson and Eugène Soudan. Janson, who had been Prime Minister for a time, was the uncle of Paul-Henri Spaak, now the foreign minister of the Belgian government in exile in London. He was a cultured and humane man who made a deep impression on her and became a friend. Through the two ministers and their families she soon acquired other pupils.

Many of her these were members of the town's Jewish community, which was growing by the day. The Gérins soon realised that many of the visitors on the Promenade des Anglais and in the hotels and restaurants were not ordinary tourists come to Nice to enjoy themselves – despite the guidebooks some clutched to give this impression – but Jewish refugees, both French and foreign, who had fled to the south coast of France as a temporary safe haven. Some of them had diamonds sewn into their coat linings, having taken with them all the valuables they could smuggle out. These visitors had swelled Nice's permanent Jewish population of a thousand or so to five times that many at the start of the War. Thousands more were to flock there in the following years.

Under the authoritarian Vichy regime of Marshal Pétain, foreigners were forbidden to seek employment and tolerated only as tourists with independent means. As a man of military age, Eugène was particularly suspect and had to report each month to the *Préfecture de Police* to renew his tourist permit. To do this you had to produce a specified sum of money (10,000 francs) to prove that you had sufficient means of support. Renewal of permits entailed queueing for hours at the police headquarters, and money would be passed surreptitiously from hand to hand by groups of friends to ensure that each applicant had the requisite sum when his turn came.

During their time in Nice they had many dealings with the Vichy police. They were questioned by them when reported for listening to the BBC, which they and all their friends did at every possible opportunity, with the windows closed however stifling the heat. They were questioned when Winifred was reported to be earning money giving English classes. The police officers were collaborators, rewarded for their services with extra rations and other privileges. Other pro-German organisations were the unsavoury collaborationist militia *Service d'ordre légionnaire* and a youth organisation modelled on that of Hitler, whose adherents marched about chanting their anthem in praise of Pétain – 'Maréchale, nous voilà!' – at the tops of their voices. Members of both these uniformed, flag-waving groups constantly paraded the streets, where Marshal Pétain's portrait was in every shop window, and were zealous in denouncing all 'dissidents' critical of the regime. In the early days there was still general support for the government and anger with Britain for 'prolonging the War' and the people's sufferings. Pétain was seen as the country's protector against the rigours of the occupation. As time went on and he was perceived to be betraying that trust, public opinion turned gradually against Vichy, but in Nice open protest was rare.

Winifred and Eugène spent much of their time in the streets of the city. When they were not queueing for documents they were queueing for food in the markets. Those who had the means used the black market, which benefited many profiteers, but the Gérins could not afford to do so and were limited to their meagre rations. Meat, eggs and milk were scarce or non-existent; there was no tea or coffee apart from the 'ersatz' substitutes, no sugar, very little bread. The only luxury still available at this stage of the War was the wine ration; this went a little way towards making life tolerable until it was cancelled at the end of 1941, when the wine was requisitioned for Italy. Fortunately there was an abundance of local fruit and vegetables. On a good day there would be tomatoes, on a bad nothing but turnips and such root vegetables. It comes as no surprise to learn that the Gérins' scant meat (or rather offal) ration, their one egg a week, and the occasional fish (most went on the black market) were allocated to Pussy, who, sunning on his balcony, thus escaped the worst of his owners' privations. They were always hungry and, in common with everyone else on rations, lost weight dramatically. As the War went on and the rationing became stricter, real malnutrition was suffered by many.

An elderly American resident of Nice, Elizabeth Foster, kept a diary in which she recorded life in the town under Italian and German occupation a little later in the War. Its pages are a testimony of just how obsessive thoughts – and dreams – of food can become when your diet is so restricted that an extra lump of sugar with your ersatz coffee counts as a treat, and friends are reduced to *borrowing* a few lumps from you, to be repaid when they get their next ration. What she found almost harder to bear than the hunger was the 'reign of corruption', the dishonest means by which the Niçois endeavoured to supplement their rations, and the general moral disintegration that was the consequence of indifference and lack of resistance in the face of defeat. She felt sure that elsewhere in France things might be very different, but 'If one lives on the Riviera it is very hard to believe in the Resurrection of France . . . I try not to forget that the Riviera is, as someone said of Palm Beach, an atmosphere which "melts the moral marrow."'[64]

Apart from food, Winifred's and Eugène's constant, gnawing concern was their apprehension about their respective families. Communication with Belgium and the Gérins in Brussels was impossible, and the Vichy government propaganda kept up a barrage of news about air raids on London and the Home Counties. Letters to and from London took months and were censored, but Winifred exchanged occasional telegrams with her mother and Nell and thus had regular assurances that they were safe and well. For Eugène there was no such reassurance about his own family.

His and Winifred's own situation improved thanks to a new acquaintance, the son of an elderly resident of Nice called Mme

---

[64] Diary of Elizabeth Foster 1942–4. MS Am 1612, Houghton Library, Harvard University.

Bigwood, Belgian despite the English name. In the winter of 1941–2 André Bigwood, an army officer, escaped from Belgium and passed through the city on his way to England. Having already endured a hazardous journey across the Belgian border and through France, he now faced the further dangers of crossing the Pyrenees on foot in the hope of reaching England via Francoist Spain and neutral Portugal. Many had attempted the journey before him. Some succeeded in joining the growing community of Belgian exiles in London; the less lucky were returned to the German occupying forces in Belgium or detained in the Spanish concentration camp of Miranda del Ebro with other refugees.

The Gérins gave Major Bigwood messages for the family in Surrey. He was one of the lucky ones who managed to reach England, and he was able to visit Katharine and Nell in Virginia Water. With his help they arranged to send Winifred and Eugène modest but regular dispatches of money through a Quaker organisation in Marseille. Thanks to these funds and the proceeds of some jewellery that Winifred sold, she and Eugène at last had enough money to follow in André Bigwood's steps and hazard the journey to England. Very importantly, they also had a guarantor in England, an essential prerequisite for the journey, since Bigwood had made contact on their behalf with their former boss Cecil De Sausmarez, now at the Foreign Office in London.

To get out of France they needed an exit visa, but these were not granted either for European destinations or for French North Africa, where De Gaulle was assembling an army, since from there applicants might head for England. They were advised to apply for a visa to an independent African territory and to provide reasons for their journey. A contact of Major Bigwood's who dealt with their application suggested they apply for Angola on the somewhat absurd pretext that Eugène had been engaged for a series of concerts there. One of the many papers required for their application (the one document *not* requested was proof of the supposed concert tour!) was a medical certificate attesting that he was unfit for military service.

This was supplied by a sympathetic doctor recommended by Bigwood. Clearly it was not the first such service he had performed, and he asked no awkward questions about their plans. Nor did he ask for payment. His examination did not find Eugène to be suffering from any health problem, which was a difficulty, but he soon came up with a solution. The X-ray showed a slight shadow on Eugène's left lung; the doctor did not suppose it denoted anything serious and Eugène himself thought it might be caused by enlargement of a muscle on his left side as a result of his cello-playing. The doctor promptly entered it on the certificate as a scar caused by tuberculosis. It was almost closing time at the Préfecture and he advised them to get the certificate stamped there that evening, as the officers would be in a hurry and would not examine the papers too closely. After a heart-stopping half-hour wait at the police station, the certificate was returned to them duly stamped and the application posted to Vichy. Friends warned them that the visas might take months to be processed and they must be ready to leave the moment it arrived in case the police decided to carry out a last-minute check.

The wait did indeed prove to be a long one, and the monotony of the months of waiting might have been intolerable, particularly once the summer heat was upon them, had they not soon found themselves caught up in increasingly dramatic events. The first change was that after Major Bigwood's arrival in London they began to receive unannounced visitors from Belgium. Their flat was being used as a halfway house for refugees who, using fake papers, had negotiated the perilous journey across the Franco-Belgian border and the demarcation line between the occupied and free zones. All they wanted before continuing on their way was a wash and a rest and something to eat (the last of these posed a puzzle). They would take refuge in the Gérins' flat during the day, while the police were around, and leave at nightfall. They were always cheerful and always grateful for any help. From time to time Winifred and Eugène would hear a coded message on the BBC which would tell them that one of their visitors had made it safely to England. Throughout the long, hot days and nights of the spring and summer of 1942 they dreamed of their own escape from the Riviera resort that was proving to be little like the paradise of the legend. By the time they finally did get away they would have had a glimpse into what Winifred called 'the pit of darkness'. Once seen, she said later, it changed you for ever. It could never be forgotten or forgiven.

It was one of Winifred's Jewish pupils, a Viennese girl, who first told them, in July 1942, of the reports of arrests of Jews on the French south coast. She had heard that the police were carrying out raids in Marseilles and working their way along the coast, and, through a contact, she was going to procure forged visas for herself, her mother and brother which would enable them to escape to Switzerland. Her family was wealthy and could pay the thousands of francs needed to obtain the papers. She calculated that they had only two or three weeks before arrests started in Nice, and could not risk the long wait for official exit visas from the Vichy government.

The Gérins were at first incredulous, since they had always believed that under Pétain's agreement with the Germans when the country was divided, the safety of refugees in the 'free zone' was guaranteed, but over the next few weeks events were swiftly to prove how right Winifred's pupil had been. An anti-Semitic propaganda campaign was soon being waged by the Vichy government in which the Jews were portrayed as 'enemies of the state' and blamed for many of the ills caused by the War. They were accused of hoarding wealth and of responsibility for the black market – which, of course, was used by all who had the wherewithal to do so. There was no shortage of people more than ready to believe the accusations, which became increasingly virulent. In early August police raids started in Nice.

The Gérins got wind of them the day before they started from a hint dropped by the wife of a police constable who worked for friends of theirs. Among their best Jewish friends was a family called Kurtz. Winifred was giving English lessons to their eighteen-year-old daughter Renée. At their house she first had a glimpse of Jewish family traditions at first hand; Renée's father, an engineer, was a rabbi. He was partly paralysed after a stroke brought on by the sufferings they had undergone on the journey from Austria. There was also another daughter, Hannah, aged twelve.

The Gérins resolved to try and procure a medical certificate for Mr Kurtz as they had for Eugène, since seriously ill people could escape arrest. The night before the raids began, Eugène went to see the doctor who had attended Mr Kurtz after his stroke. Unfortunately he turned out to be very different from the one who had made out the certificate for Eugène. As his arm-band proclaimed, he was a staunch supporter of the Vichy government. Eugène must have had strong powers of persuasion; by reminding the doctor of his Hippocratic oath and duty to the sick, and in particular to this patient whose life he had saved, he was able to wheedle or bully him into writing out a certificate, which he presented to the grateful Kurtz family late that night. To make matters more convincing the patient was put to bed, his wife even donning a nurse's uniform to care for him.

The following day the first raids were carried out in Nice. Initially only foreign Jews were targeted; French Jews, because of their influence, wealth and sheer numbers, were left alone for the time being. Anyone harbouring non-French Jews or aware of their presence had to report the fact and it was an offence to hide them. These first raids took place only at night. Many people had already gone underground, but hundreds were caught and bundled into the tourist coaches requisitioned by the police for the purpose. They started by searching the biggest hotels, working down to smaller lodging houses.

The Kurtz parents could hope to gain a reprieve thanks to their strategem, but the risk remained that their daughters, Renée and Hannah, might be taken away in one of the raids. Here again Eugène and Winifred came to the rescue, and a change in their accommodation arrangements made it easier for them to do so. Their lodgings had recently changed hands and their new landlady was a collaborator; they had therefore decided to move to some rooms within the flat of a family called Revelli in the same building. The new accommodation was more likely to escape attention since, being part of a private dwelling, it was not on the police list of registered lodging-houses. Moreover, M. Revelli was no admirer of the Vichy government. His wife was more easily swayed by government propaganda, but she was at present on holiday in the hills with her daughters. The Gérins were renting two bedrooms, and they offered to take in the two Kurtz girls each night. During the daytime the girls felt safe enough to go home to see their parents.

The night came when it was the turn of their street to be raided. They watched from a window of the darkened flat. Watched – and listened, hearing the screech of brakes as three coaches came to a halt in their street and the police jumped out, followed by the pummelling on doors and, a little later, the cries and screams of the women as they were led from neighbouring buildings and bundled in. Most of the men, Winifred noticed, went in silence. When it was the turn of their building they stood in the dark listening to the banging on the street door, the footsteps on the stairs, and the voice of their former landlady, eager to collaborate with the police and tell them about her Polish Jewish tenant, who was now renting the Gérins' old flat; for the time being he had gone into hiding elsewhere. The two Kurtz girls were silent in the next room. For that night they were safe; the police left without hammering on the door of the Revellis' flat.

Soon the raids were also taking place in daylight in the heat of those August days, and residents became increasingly accustomed to the sight. Those arrested were either herded straight to the railway station or detained in the *Pavillon des Fêtes*, a pavilion used for the annual carnival festivities, until they were put on a train. Many were sent to the internment camp at Drancy on the outskirts of Paris to await deportation to Germany. The Polish tenant in the Gérins' former flat was handed over to the police by the virago of a landlady when he risked a quick dash back to the flat to collect his belongings. Winifred, on her way upstairs to their new lodgings, overheard the woman yelling on the phone to the police, telling them to hurry; she had locked him into the flat. Winifred heard him being taken away. He was a sensitive-looking young man whose features reminded her of Chopin's.

From the time of the first raids she and Eugène became more and more involved in helping not just the Kurtzes but many other Jewish friends and acquaintances. Through the Kurtzes they knew any number of foreign Jews in Nice and became familiar with the network of individuals and organisations working to get them to places of safety, for example the pharmacist who provided forged papers, cash and addresses for refugees from his chemist's shop in Place Masséna, and the chief rabbi of Nice. The Christian clergy were also involved. Some of the safe centres were operated by nuns who ran cover organisations in the hills near the town, such as holiday camps for Girl Guides.

It was the chemist in Place Masséna who arranged for the Kurtz sisters to be received at one of these camps when it became unsafe to keep them any longer in the Revellis' flat. Mme Revelli was due to return from holiday, and Winifred and Eugène had been notified that their exit visas were being considered and might arrive any time; once they did they would leave Nice at once. Renée and Hannah were kitted out in Girl Guide uniforms collected in a suitcase from the chemist's shop by Eugène, at some risk, since anyone carrying a case was liable to be stopped and searched. He and Winifred set out with the two girls to put them on a train. They were heading for a small station some way from the centre, as the main one was guarded by police, but had to turn back when they were warned that the smaller station had now been cordoned off as well.

The plan to get the two girls out of Nice had to be abandoned, and much of the next few weeks was spent searching for alternative lodgings for them as well as for other Jewish friends, a task that was becoming more difficult by the day. Few people were willing to harbour Jews for more than a night or two.

On the daily quest for lodgings for their friends on those sultry August and September days Winifred had many glimpses on the pavements of Nice into the 'pit of darkness'. One incident in particular stuck in her memory. Passing by a doorway, she saw an elderly woman being dragged out of the building by the police while an old man, evidently her husband, tried to cling on to her. Both were distraught. They were pleading with the police, who did not understand, as the couple spoke only German. Winifred stopped to translate. It transpired that only the woman was being taken away, as she was under seventy, the maximum age for arrest; her husband, being older, was exempted for the moment. What they were trying to explain was that she was being treated for cancer of the head with a radium plaque, and her husband had to help her daily with her treatment. He was begging to be taken with her. The police's reply was that the couple would in any case be separated, since once in the camps the sexes were segregated. The woman was dragged away. For the next few days, until the wife was put on a train, Winifred accompanied the husband each day to the entrance of the *Pavillon des Fêtes* where she was being kept. Each time, he was denied entrance and told that it would be impossible to find her in the tightly-packed crowd awaiting deportation. The Gérins tried to obtain a medical certificate for her, but the doctor who had helped out in the case of Mr Kurtz was no longer open to persuasion. It was too dangerous, he told them.

With the arrival of their visas now imminent, they had to hand over responsibility for the safety of Renée and Hannah Kurtz to the chief rabbi and take leave of the few friends who knew they were planning to get to London. Their Belgian minister friends gave them oral messages – it was considered too dangerous to give them letters to carry – for Janson's nephew, Paul-Henri Spaak, and other members of the Belgian government in exile in London.

At the beginning of October 1942, hours after receiving their visas, Winifred and Eugène boarded a train to the Spanish border, torn between elation at getting away at last and fears for those left behind.

Many of those they left in Nice were less lucky and were trapped there until it was too late. For the next year or so, however, things improved for their Jewish friends. The following month, November 1942, after the Allied landings in North Africa, the Germans occupied most of the southern zone of France, but Nice was in a south-eastern pocket that was for the moment governed by the Italians. Under their watch, the Jews were left in peace despite German instructions to the contrary, and this encouraged them to flock to the south-east coast in even greater numbers. By the end of the period of Italian rule the numbers congregating on that part of the coast reached 30,000, of whom about 20,000 were in Nice. But in September 1943, after the Allied invasion of Sicily and southern Italy, the Italians capitulated. They left Nice and the Germans overran the area. Raids on Jews were immediately renewed, overseen by SS Hauptsturmfuhrer Alois Brunner from his headquarters in the Excelsior, the hotel where the victims were kept until they were marched to the station. Arrests were now made everywhere, anywhere, in broad daylight, the police often carrying out 'medical checks' on men to weed out those who were circumcised. Thousands were taken to Drancy.

Winifred's erstwhile pupils, the Belgian ex-ministers Paul-Émile Janson and Eugène Soudan, were arrested as political prisoners and taken to Buchenwald. Janson, who was in his seventies, died of exhaustion there in March 1944. Soudan survived to be freed by the US Army.

Towards the end of the War, as the resources of the occupiers became ever more squeezed, they stripped the Palais de la Jetée, the fantastical domed palace on the pier, of its copper and other metals and of anything else that could replenish their resources. Reduced to an iron skeleton, the building that had once provided amusement for Nice's tourists was left to rot into the sea.

9
Aspley Guise
Political Intelligence

When they left France, the Gérins travelled without Pussy, who had developed a cancerous ulcer some time before and had to be put to sleep. The loss of the pet who had been the companion of their Paris years as well as their recent tribulations had cost them many tears, but it obviated the problem of having to find him a new home in Nice, since taking him with them on this trip would not have been feasible.

Their ludicrous visas for Angola were not challenged and they had just enough money to take them to the Spanish border. Their safe passage through Franco's pro-Nazi Spain was guaranteed and financed thanks to Mme Bigwood, or rather her niece's husband, a Belgian businessman with offices in Madrid and Lisbon. As his contribution to the war effort he had already helped many volunteers fleeing occupied Europe via Spain to join the armed forces in Britain, and had assisted André Bigwood on his journey.

The Gérins' adventures in Spain on this occasion were very different from the light-hearted ones of their concert tour in the Republican country of the early 1930s, when everything had charmed and amused them. Most of the memories Winifred bore away from their few hours in Franco's Spain as it was in the years of the Second World War were of a 'sinister' atmosphere. Even the kind man who met them at Figueras, bought their ticket for them (so that their foreign accents would not be detected by the booking clerk) and put them on the night train to Madrid looked at first 'sinister' to her eyes. They journeyed in a malodorous compartment full of country women, their produce, and even some of their hens. At Madrid they were met by another initially 'sinister-looking' or at any rate seedy-looking individual who took them to the Belgian and British embassies. They were advised to leave the city as soon as possible and to keep away from restaurants and shops, where the police were on the watch. They had always wanted to visit the Prado, and their guide encouraged them to spend the day there while they waited to catch the night train to Lisbon. The paintings that most haunted Winifred on her one visit to this museum – haunted her for evermore, her last memory of a country for which she always retained affection despite the fearful impressions of this brief visit – were Goya's portraits of the Spanish royal family. These, too, she found 'sinister'. The expression on the faces of Goya's royal sitters, so vividly painted that they seemed to be alive, she perceived as mocking and malignant, as if they were about to give some deadly command.

Their Madrid contact, having taken them for a meal in a secluded café, put them on the train for Lisbon. They shared a carriage with a couple of German women who had tired of the nightly Allied bombings raids on their cities and were joining their husbands, diplomats in Lisbon. They spoke openly of their weariness of the War and their doubt that Germany could win it, not suspecting that Winifred, who was listening in silence, understood what they were saying and was drinking in every word.

Their arrival in Lisbon in neutral Portugal on 7 October – it was Winifred's birthday; the telegram she at once sent her mother reached Katharine on her own birthday the following day – marked the end of the two-year nightmare that had begun on the day the Germans invaded Belgium. The recollections Winifred took away from Lisbon were of a beautiful city where they could at last breathe relatively freely despite the presence of numerous German spies posing as 'businessmen'. The weather was benign and everyone they encountered kind and welcoming. All that remained was to wait their turn to board the plane that would take them to England and enable them at last to join the war effort being waged from London.

As in Madrid, they had first to visit both the Belgian and British embassies. From the Foreign Office, Cecil De Sausmarez had already contacted the British embassy to act as a guarantor and confirm that once they reached England they would be in his employ. Guarantors were essential given the numbers of enemy agents who were infiltrating themselves among the volunteers. Eugène had to sign papers volunteering for the Belgian armed forces in England, although in view of his age (46) he would in fact be on loan to the Foreign Office. This was confirmed by a telegram from Paul-Henri Spaak.

It was judged too dangerous for them to stay for any length of time in Lisbon itself. Instead they were lodged in a *pension* in the seaside resort of Cascais, where for the next six weeks they lived in considerable comfort at the expense of the Belgian government. The weather remained splendid and there was good food in the kind of abundance they had dreamed about incessantly in the long months in Nice. In the renewed good spirits induced by these comforts they did not forget those they had left behind, and made visits to Lisbon to exert themselves on behalf of Mr Kurtz, contacting a Lisbon engineering firm willing to employ him, as well as other Jewish friends.

It was while they were in Cascais that news arrived of the Allied landings in French North Africa in response to which the Axis powers occupied Vichy France. They learned later that Mr Kurtz did not succeed in getting out of Nice and was arrested when it was later occupied by the Germans. His wife and daughters managed to reach one of the so-called 'holiday camps' run by nuns and survived.

At Cascais they were in the company of other refugees also waiting for a flight to England, many of whom had just been released from the camp in Miranda. To pass the time profitably Winifred and Eugène organised English lessons for their companions. In the hall where training drills were held for the volunteers, the Gérins also drilled them in simple conversational English, getting them to act out scenes in restaurants and shops.

When their turn at last came to be flown out, Winifred was the only woman on board a BOAC plane, a Short S.26 G-class 'flying boat' called 'The Golden Hind', carrying around 50 Belgian and Dutch volunteers.[65] They boarded at night under cover of darkness at a small airport some miles inland from the capital; it was dangerous to fly from the coast because of the Germans who had taken villas there and could alert German planes, patrolling just outside the neutral area, to British planes leaving the country. A civilian plane carrying the actor Leslie Howard on a flight from Portugal to England was shot down by German fighters in June 1943.

It was not a comfortable flight, but they were far too happy to care. It was extremely cold, the wooden panelling having been removed to increase the space available; the seats were primitive and the pilot had to take a devious route out over the Atlantic to avert the danger of German interceptors. The flight to Poole, with a stopover at Shannon where they were given a delicious breakfast, took 12 hours instead of the usual four. Their reception on arrival in Poole was not quite what they had expected; they were met by plain clothes security men, who explained politely that because of the danger of foreign agents all volunteers had to be arrested until their identity could be established. These officers escorted the party on the train to London. Eugène was detained for some days at Wandsworth with the other Belgian and Dutch nationals but Winifred was

---

[65] Built for transatlantic flights, these planes were used by the RAF at the beginning of the war and converted to passenger use at the end of 1941.

released at once and was at last able to visit her mother, Nell and Gilbert at the house in Virginia Water.

Katharine, now 83, had almost given up hope of seeing her youngest daughter again. Winifred was shocked to find how much her much-loved mother had aged since their last meeting in August 1939.

Once Eugène was at liberty they lost no time in visiting Cecil De Sausmarez at his offices in Bush House, where he introduced them to his boss, Terence Harman. They were told that De Sausmarez and Harman were working for the Foreign Office's Political Intelligence Department (PID). Harman was the Regional Director for the Low Countries Section, De Sausmarez his deputy. Before the War, Harman had lived for a time in Brussels, where he used the HMV record shop as a cover for intelligence activities, but it was De Sausmarez who had the greater knowledge of Belgian affairs. He was involved in the BBC European Service's radio station for occupied Belgium, Radio Belgique.

Both Winifred and Eugène were to be employed by the PID, where their foreign language skills and knowledge of Belgium would be useful. They were told that the work would be secret and required to sign the Official Secrets Act, which they did on the spot. Eugène's job was the one De Sausmarez and Harman were most interested in; it was to involve broadcasting, and he was at once borne off to a studio to do a test recording, which was found to be satisfactory. For the time being he was told nothing more about the secret work he was to do.

After the years of exile and frustration they had achieved their long-standing goal of joining what Winifred called 'the army of workers for Victory'. Before they took up their duties in the New Year of 1943, though, there were practical matters to attend to such as visits to the bank and the replenishing of their much-depleted wardrobes, for which they were given generous clothing coupons. After that, there was Christmas to celebrate in Virginia Water with Katharine and Nell.

Terry Harman had told them that they would be working not in London but at the PID's Headquarters in the country, somewhere in the Home Counties, where he was based for much of the time. When, in January, instructions came to take a train to Bletchley in Buckinghamshire, where they would be met at the station and taken to their lodgings, the name meant nothing to Winifred. She could have no inkling then how often it would recur after the War in conversations with other former members of the 'army for Victory'. There seemed to be few war workers who had not spent some time being trained at Bletchley Park near Milton Keynes, or had not, at the very least, passed through it at some stage.

The village where she and Eugène were driven, by a member of the department called Tony Parker, was in fact Aspley Guise about five miles away. Again, on arrival at this charming place full of Georgian and Victorian buildings, they could initially have had no idea that it too had become a hub of secret war work, and that many of these gracious houses lodged those involved in the 'black propaganda' campaign – disseminating information purporting to originate from dissident groups within the occupied countries. A secluded residence in Church Street called The Rookery, near the splendid Aspley House, lodged the man leading this campaign, Dennis Sefton Delmer.

The Georgian building where the Gérins were to live with 'house-master' Terry Harman and his wife and about six other colleagues was called Netherhill House. Writing her memoir in old age, Winifred remembered the name as Netherfield, surely by unconscious association with the house mentioned in the third sentence of *Pride and Prejudice* as being taken by Mr Bingley, the 'single man in possession of a good fortune' whom Mrs Bennett hopefully supposes to be 'in want of a wife'.

Under normal circumstances, Jane Austen and her heroines might have felt quite at home in the streets of Aspley Guise. The 'hush-hush village', as it was sometimes called in later years for its role in the War, had been popular over the centuries for its dry and invigorating climate, attracting the wealthy merchants whose handsome villas nestled among the pine-trees. In the war years, however, the area hosted not just over a hundred evacuees from Walthamstow in East London but the numerous secret propaganda workers of various European nationalities, whose presence was explained to the residents on the grounds that they were engaged in 'research'.

Eugène, who was now one of these so-called 'research workers', was to have his office in Netherhill House. Winifred, however, was to work a few miles away in the more splendid setting of Woburn Abbey, the home of the Duke of Bedford, which had been requisitioned as the country headquarters of the PID. After lunch she was driven there with Harman. She was to be P.A. to Joseph Saxe, one of the bosses in the Belgian and Dutch section, a very tall and somewhat fierce-looking man with pebble glasses – Jewish Hungarian by birth, Belgian by adoption – who despite his alarming appearance turned out from their very first acquaintance to be all cordiality and endearing spontaneity. With this affable boss and a cheerful nineteen-year-old typist called Jill Barrington-Ward – Winifred could at that time only type with one finger – she was to spend the next 18 months. Her new colleagues told her that in the weeks since her arrival had been announced, while she and Eugène were waiting in Portugal for their flight to England, she had always been referred to as 'the lady from Lisbon'. Once she was installed in the Abbey, Jill dubbed her 'Madame'.

Joseph Saxe had been one of the leading journalists on the Belgian socialist newspaper *Le Peuple*, attacking the policy of neutrality under his pseudonym of 'Jexas'. He was a friend of De Sausmarez, who helped to get him out of Belgium after the invasion and found him a job when he arrived in London. 'Jexas' was one of a group of anti-Hitler, mainly Socialist Belgian journalists whom De Sausmarez had gathered around him in Brussels and subsequently encouraged to follow him to London. They were close to the Belgian government in exile and kept him informed of Belgian affairs. Of all these journalists it was 'Jexas' whom De Sausmarez admired the most for his journalistic skills and knowledge of European affairs.

Winifred's task was to write up the reports flown in from agents in Belgium, which were used to provide information for broadcasts to Belgium and instructions to the Resistance, for example for sabotaging infrastructure targets. Saxe also used them to compile weekly reports for Churchill's cabinet. One of Winifred's tasks was supposed to be to correct her boss's written English, though in fact Saxe, who was married to an Englishwoman, had a perfect command of the language.

As Winifred soon found out, the 'Political Intelligence Department' was a cover name for the Political Warfare Executive (PWE), a clandestine propaganda organisation, reporting to the Foreign Office, created by Churchill in 1941. It was born out of the propaganda arm of the sabotage and subversion department known as the Special Operations Executive (SOE) and incorporated staff from the Ministry of Information and the BBC. It was based at Woburn Abbey and had its London offices in Bush House. The Abbey, near the government's code-breaking centre at Bletchley Park, had been used as a centre for propaganda activities since the start of the War, when the staff of the propaganda organisation set up during the Munich crisis, 'Department Electra House' (later absorbed into the SOE) were evacuated to Woburn. Fifty miles from London, the Bletchley Park area was far enough from the capital to escape bombing but close enough for easy access, and well connected by road and rail.

Under an agreement with Herbrand, the 11th Duke of Bedford, PWE staff at Woburn were initially housed in Abbey outhouses such as the stables. The old Duke would not allow them to occupy the main house itself on the grounds that it was already occupied. In fact the Duke, who was widowed, was the sole member of his family left in the huge building; many of its 100 rooms were standing empty, although, admittedly, accommodation had to be found for the 50 indoor and 200 outdoor servants employed to tend him and his estate.[66] The Duke was lukewarm about the activities of the new occupants of his stables, seemingly viewing the invaders from London as the real enemy rather than Hitler. He died in August 1940 and his son the 12th Duke, even more of a Nazi sympathiser, was considered a security risk and advised to keep away from the Abbey. He followed the advice by staying on his Scottish shooting estate, and the PWE took over the whole of the Abbey, moving its officials and typists and telephone operators into the gilded rooms, where they could admire the Savonnerie carpets under their desks and the Canalettos on the walls as well as the views of rolling parkland through the windows.

The office workers slept not just in the servants' bedrooms but in the Duke and Duchess's personal suite. They used lavatories of Wedgewood porcelain with rosewood seats in Regency-style bathrooms and bathed in the Duchess's vast porcelain bath – a freezing experience in winter, as reported by Jeanne Fawtier, a young intelligence research assistant who worked there in 1941.

By the time Winifred took up her post, however, the number of staff occupying the main house had greatly diminished, since the PWE now considered it safe enough to move its main headquarters to Bush House and relocate most of the essential staff in London. In 1944 the Abbey was used to quarter Wrens from the code-breaking centre at Bletchley Park.

At its height, the PWE occupation of Woburn was a hive of activity producing 'white' (overt) and 'black' (covert) propaganda. The equipment for the printed propaganda was accommodated at one stage in the hangar that had housed the aircraft of the 'Flying Duchess', Mary Russell, wife of Herbrand. She had learned to fly in her sixties and travelled as far as India, making many solo flights. In 1937 the DH.60 Moth she was piloting crashed into the North Sea and her body was never recovered. Some years into the PWE's occupation of the Abbey, the staff at this supposedly hush-hush country headquarters were asked by the RAF if they were aware that the word WOBURN was written in large letters on the roof, placed there to guide the Flying Duchess home on foggy evenings.

Winifred's days passed pleasantly enough at Woburn, though she would have liked to have more time to spend with Eugène; her working day was eleven hours long. After lunch in the Abbey Mews she and Saxe would sometimes walk in the grounds; in spring the surrounding woods were full of bluebells. She enjoyed listening to Saxe, and in turn told him about her time in Nice. As a Jew, he foresaw

---

[66] Details of Woburn and its owners and its occupation by the PWE are taken from Seebohm, *The Country House: A Wartime History, 1939–45.*

the Holocaust at a time when most British people were still incredulous about the reports emerging from the extermination camps. After what she had witnessed at first hand in Nice Winifred had no difficulty in sharing his premonitions. The staff in the Belgian and Dutch unit headed by Saxe included a Jewish girl from Amsterdam who had lost her entire family. It was not until after the War that Winifred had news of the friends they had left behind in Nice, and learned the fate of the Belgian former ministers Janson and Soudan.

Saxe lodged with the Gérins and Harmans at Netherhill House. Winifred and Eugène were privileged in being billeted with their bosses rather than in the chilly expanses of Woburn. Terry Harman, a quiet, sympathetic man, was a genial 'housemaster'; his wife did the catering and she and their young children provided a family atmosphere. They would all gather each evening in the 'drawing room' to listen to the 9 o'clock news, after which Winifred and Eugène would slip away as soon as possible to their comfortable bedroom to talk over the day.

Sometimes Cecil De Sausmarez stayed overnight on one of his visits to oversee the country operations. He was close to Harman despite their different views on PWE activities; he did not share Harman's enthusiasm for black propaganda, considering that much of the black broadcasting was a waste of time. The garrulous Cecil would stay up talking until late. He had many anecdotes to tell them. There was the story, for example, of how, in his endeavour to repair Belgium's reputation in Britain after its capitulation to Germany, he had persuaded the director of the Windmill theatre to change the words of a cabaret number from 'When we were left by Belgium and France' to 'When we were left by poor old France'. He also claimed to be one of the originators of the 'V for Victory' propaganda campaign launched by the BBC in July 1941. The chief instigator was the announcer on the BBC's Radio Belgique, the Belgian former cabinet minister Victor de Laveleye, who urged Belgians to take as their 'rallying emblem' the letter V, as the first letter of 'victoire' in French and 'vrijheid' (freedom) in Dutch as well as of 'victory' in English. The first four notes of Beethoven's 5th Symphony became the Victory signal on broadcasts to occupied Europe, echoing the Morse code for the letter V.

Fond as she was of De Sausmarez, Winifred, who wanted to make the most of her precious time with Eugène, wished he would not keep them all up so late.

Meanwhile, Eugène was finding his broadcasting tasks congenial, if tiring, for he had not been in very good health since their privations in Nice. As a broadcaster for the Resistance in occupied Belgium he was one of numerous speakers and scriptwriters lodged in various houses in and around Aspley Guise under the supervision of British 'housemasters': houses such as Dawn Edge, where the housemaster was the socialist politician Richard Crossman, who worked with Sefton Delmer. The teams of 'research workers', as the foreign broadcasters were denominated, were called 'Research Units', R.U.s. They were supposed to be kept separate from each other and never meet or discuss their work. To this end they were banned from the local pubs; needless to say the ban proved difficult to enforce and it was not completely unknown for conversations in foreign tongues to be heard at the Anchor in Aspley Guise!

Scriptwriters and broadcasters would write and rehearse their scripts in the houses where they were accommodated. The broadcasters were then taken to the recording studios by chauffeurs in secret service cars, black Hillman Minxes, accompanied by a 'censor' (a role often undertaken by the housemaster, who also edited the scripts), who had to ensure that the programme that went out adhered to the agreed script. The need for censoring was one reason why programmes were pre-recorded rather than going out live, though care was taken to give the impression of live broadcasts, made in the country concerned. A complex shuttle system was operated to ensure that each car journey was made in isolation and that teams from different R.U.s did not encounter one another. In the studios, the broadcasts were recorded on discs that were then taken by the drivers to the transmitters. Fifteen minutes was the maximum recording time allowed by the capacity of the discs.

Eugène never knew the exact location of the place where he was taken to make his broadcasts. This was the recording studio housed in Wavendon Towers, a country house near Woburn code-named 'Simpson's' after a nearby village.[67] Security was tight, and passes were examined both by the police guard at the gate and the well-spoken young female receptionists in the entrance hall who supervised the arrivals and departures of 'The Funnies', the unofficial name for the secret broadcasters.[68]

There were occasional failures of the strict rules designed to keep teams apart, particularly teams of the same nationality but different political persuasions. There was the occasion, for instance, when the French Socialist R.U. made an unscheduled return to Simpson's to re-record their programme in order to incorporate some breaking news. Listening to the playback in the billiard room, they heard the French De Gaullist R.U. in full flow in the studio next door. Apparently the

---

[67] Eugène's name was added to the Simpson's pass list on 6 February 1943. Memo in Foreign Office file FO 898-51, CEGESOMA.
[68] Taylor, *Bletchley Park's Secret Sisters*, p. 25.

Socialist team resigned in a body on the spot.[69] One reason for trying to keep each R.U. in isolation, unaware of the existence of the others, was to give each the impression that it was unique in being accorded facilities by the British government for conveying its views to its countrymen.

The clandestine station or 'freedom station' for which Eugène was broadcasting was called *Sambre et Meuse*, the name of a historical Belgian region roughly corresponding to the modern province of Namur in Wallonia (the French-speaking, southern part of Belgium), the Sambre and the Meuse being the two main rivers in the area. The station, which had been operating since May 1942, was Socialist in sympathies. Aimed at workers in Wallonia, where much of the country's industry was concentrated, it encouraged industrial non-collaboration with the Germans (a similar station broadcasting in Dutch targeted a working-class audience in Flanders). Eugène was required to speak with a Walloon accent, which probably came easily enough to him since he had lived as a child in a village in the province of Namur.[70]

Such underground stations were independent of the official BBC programmes for the occupied countries but were intended to complement the work done by them. Less inhibited by considerations of diplomacy and good taste, the freedom stations could allow themselves to depart to some degree in tone and policy from the official line. They could also comment on the BBC programmes and recommend them to their listeners.[71]

Despite being in theory part of a concerted effort with the BBC, the content of these stations was not always approved of in official quarters. The foreign governments in exile were not supposed to know about the black broadcasting activities at all, but Spaak, the Belgian government in exile's Foreign Minister, did become aware of *Sambre et Meuse* and complained on at least one occasion to De Sausmarez and Harman about not being consulted or informed about the material broadcast.[72]

Eugène's rousing broadcasts were transmitted twice daily, at noon and in the evening, six days a week. He was a born *raconteur* and

---

[69] 'Report on the Operation of R.U.s', 11 October 1943, FO 898-51, CEGE-SOMA.

[70] *Ibid*. This report does not refer to Eugène by name, but his name is recorded in the Simpson's log book as a broadcaster for *Sambre et Meuse* (Political Warfare Executive Papers 1941–5, catalogue No 12843, Imperial War Museum).

[71] Report on R.U.s in Low Countries, FO 898-57, CEGESOMA.

[72] Belgium Files (General Correspondence), FO 898/238, National Archives.

entertainer, had warmth and dramatic talents and brought a personal touch to his programmes by inserting background music carefully selected to move his listeners, thanks to a collection of records placed at his disposal by a member of the studio team. Thus, a warning of the probable fate of collaborators would be accompanied by the March to the Scaffold from Berlioz's *Symphonie Fantastique*!

Eugène, the 'violoncelliste poète' with his romantic soul and classical music excerpts, was an anomaly among the Belgian exiles involved in *Sambre et Meuse*. The others were trade unionists from the industrial area of Charleroi, who carried out their black broadcasting activities under cover of their London offices. A trade union leader called Arthur Gailly wrote many of the scripts, assisted by a former metalworker, Georges Keuwet. It was important that broadcasters' voices should not be recognised, and Gailly was too well-known in Wallonia to be used as a speaker himself.[73]

It is not clear whether Eugène was involved in preparing scripts as well as providing the 'voice' of *Sambre et Meuse* 'in the country'. Where possible, broadcasters doubled up as scriptwriters, but clearly Eugène would have lacked knowledge of the industrial milieu. Nor is it clear whether anyone else at Netherhill House was involved in writing the material or whether this was all done by Gailly and Keuwet in London. Winifred herself was involved in administrative aspects of Eugène's work; she liaised with the studio staff, who informed her of problems such as breakdowns of 'Pansy' or 'Poppy' (the radio transmitters), and on occasion acted as 'censor' when nobody else was available.[74]

By his own account, Gailly's scripts consisted of unsophisticated rants, crude invective aimed at whipping up anti-German sentiment among Walloon workers and lashing them on to greater resistance. They were urged to annoy and obstruct *les boches* by every means at their disposal – through strikes, go-slows and sabotage – and to resist deportation to Germany for forced labour. '*Les boches* are defeated, victory is nigh! *Courage, courage, courage!*'[75] There was also commentary on the day-to-day events reported by the secret agents. Thus, the assassination of a collaborationist politician by a member of the Resistance would be related as if the speaker had witnessed it with his own eyes, perhaps even fired the gun with his own hand: 'I saw him fall on the steps of the Town Hall . . . '

---

[73] Interview with Arthur Gailly, AA 2268/296, CEGESOMA.
[74] Simpson's log book, Imperial War Museum.
[75] 'Take heart', 'Keep your spirits up'.

How effective was the black radio propaganda? Results seem to have varied greatly from station to station. How many Walloon workers actually listened to *Sambre et Meuse*? The PWE had to judge this from reports of agents and of Belgians arriving in London, but their feedback was inconclusive. When De Sausmarez and others first spoke of the station in interviews thirty years after the War, few Belgians seemed to have heard of it.[76]

Life in that period in Aspley Guise, when its salubrious air was thick with the intrigue of psychological warfare, must have been rather like being in a spy novel. In the Rookery, the tree-screened Victorian villa opposite the church, Dennis Sefton Delmer, best-known of all the 'black' broadcasters, reigned over his secret empire. Born in Germany of Australian parents but registered as a British citizen, he had been the first British journalist to interview Hitler. After fleeing to England at the start of the War he was employed by the British intelligence services and since 1941 had been running GS1 ('Gustav Siegfried Eins', based on the German army's phonetic alphabet), the first of his highly effective black broadcast stations purporting to be made in Germany. His team recorded in a purpose-built studio at Milton Bryan using 'Aspidistra', a powerful radio transmitter sited near Crowborough.

Long after the Gérins were sleeping soundly at Netherhill House, the portly Delmer – who lived at The Rookery in some style, enjoying a well-stocked wine cellar and game from the Duke's estate – would be working into the small hours writing scripts for GS1 based on an invented character called 'Der Chef'. By pretending that this character was a Nazi supporter who had become disenchanted with the regime, the station aimed to undermine Hitler and demoralise German listeners by convincing them of growing disaffection in Germany against the regime. A German journalist also quartered in The Rookery played 'Der Chef'. GS1 was highly popular. Delmer was not fastidious about the material and language used to get his listeners' attention and his propaganda methods were much 'blacker' than those of *Sambre et Meuse*. They were not endorsed by Richard Crossman, who ran the German department with Delmer and wanted to use propaganda to appeal to the 'good' Germans he saw as making up the majority, or by Sir Stafford Cripps in the War Cabinet, who described the station as 'beastly' and 'pornographic':

---

[76] Confusingly, there may have been at least one clandestine station of the same or a smiliar name operating in Belgium itself. According to one report, which may not be authentic, a station called *Entre Sambre et Meuse* operated for years under the noses of the occupiers in a garden near Charleroi (*Historique du poste émetteur clandestin wallon Entre Sambre et Meuse.* AA 1056/91, CEGESOMA).

'If this is the sort of thing that is needed to win the War, I'd rather lose it.'

Typical of the spy novel atmosphere were the code names for people and places. Wavendon Towers was of course 'Simpson's', Woburn Abbey was 'CHQ' (Country Headquarters), Peter Seckelmann, the journalist who impersonated 'Der Chef', was known in the village as 'Paul Senders'.[77] De Sausmarez's visits to 'PWE Country' were made under the name of 'Mr Salter' and everyone 'in the country' was supposed to address him by that pseudonym, even those who knew him well. De Sausmarez found these precautions rather ridiculous except where used for secret agents. He was forbidden to disclose the location of the country headquarters even to his wife, and had to swear her to secrecy when she inquired about a train ticket she found in his coat pocket. It seems fitting that Ian Fleming, creator of the most famous spy of all, was a frequent visitor to The Rookery on Naval Intelligence business.

As 1943 wore on there was plenty of reason for optimism about the Allied cause, but at the close of the year a personal loss made that winter a sombre one for Winifred. Just before Christmas, Katharine died at the age of 84. Winifred could not have imagined that the Christmas of 1942 soon after her joyous reunion with her mother and sister would be the last one she would celebrate with her mother. She had been shocked to find Katharine an old, crippled woman, but had soon found that the war years had not succeeded in quenching Katharine's vivacity. Her loss was a hard blow for both sisters. For Nell it was the loss of a companion from whom she had never been separated.

Years later, Nell wrote about Katharine's death in the little piece entitled *The Threshold* cited in Chapter One of this book. As has been seen, the piece began with a description of how each Christmas Eve Katharine would open the nursery door and admit the children to a 'foretaste of Heaven' – the magical Christmas world she had created – until the year the Christmas lights went out for ever after Phil's death.

---

77 Taylor, *Bletchley Park's Secret Sisters*, p. 43.

That little composition closed with Katharine's own death.

> When my mother went, many years later as a very old woman, she chose a dreary December night, in the second World War, for her going.
>
> Stunned by grief and want of sleep, it was not until I was driving along the Surrey roads behind her hearse, in the solitary car with my sister and the faithful old servant who had never deserted us, that I remembered the date – December 24th – the Christmas Eve of my childhood . . .
>
> Suddenly, as we turned in at the gates under the dripping pines of Brookwood, which looked for all the world like Christmas trees exiled from Paradise, the Vision returned . . . I saw my mother once again opening the nursery door – and this time, not from within but from without – not to admit others but to enter herself – not to give joy, but to receive . . . and beneath those unlit trees, in the icy still-ness of that city of the dead, my heart was glad . . . [78]

After the Normandy landings in June 1944, Eugène's station was closed and most of Winifred's section disbanded. What remained of it was transferred to London and she and Eugène were told to report to Cecil in London for instructions. He told them with his usual insouciance that their utility in the department was effectively over. However, he found employment for them; Eugène was incorporated into the Belgian services and assigned an administrative job at the HQ of the Belgian government in exile in Eaton Square, while Winifred was given a post in the department's remaining section, which was operating from Ingersoll House in Kingsway.

One of her new colleagues, who became a friend, was called Betty Maclean. She was the widow of Gordon Maclean, a Foreign Office diplomat who was on the DC-3 on flight BOAC 777 from Portugal, carrying the actor Leslie Howard, shot down by the Germans over the Bay of Biscay a few months after the Gérins' own flight to England. There has been endless speculation about why the plane was brought down in a supposedly neutral zone. One theory is that the Luftwaffe mistook the civilian airliner for an enemy aircraft, another that German spies thought that Churchill was on board, having mistaken Howard and his portly cigar-smoking manager for Churchill and his

---

[78] BPM papers.

bodyguard. Yet another is that Leslie Howard was the target; of Hungarian Jewish origin, like Winifred's boss Josef Saxe, he had made anti-Nazi propaganda films.

By this time Winifred was no longer working with Saxe. Before she was transferred to London he had died suddenly after a supposedly minor surgical operation. She took some comfort from the fact that he was spared the full disclosures about the Nazi extermination camps.

Her new tasks involved drawing up records of resistance fighters and collaborators. She liked the work, as she did working with Betty Maclean, but in other ways the move to London was less pleasant. Hard on the heels of the invasion of Normandy, as the tide turned overwhelmingly in favour of the Allies, the Germans were retaliating with their last hope: dropping flying bombs, V1s, over London and the Home Counties. Winifred and Eugène were now living with Nell in the bungalow in Virginia Water. All three of them took the train each day in to London where Nell, too, had a war job, at the Air Ministry. Their lives, day and night, came to be dominated by the buzzing of the approaching 'doodlebugs', the sudden silence as the engine cut off before impact, the guilty sense of relief once they knew they were safe. The family home in Norwood was destroyed in a raid in June 1944. The Crystal Palace had burned down in 1936, and after the War, new developments completed the transformation of the Norwood of Winifred's childhood.

From October the V1s were replaced with the V2s, which gave no warning before impact. The bombing took its toll on Eugène in particular. He did not enjoy his administrator job in Eaton Square. More seriously, he was still in poor health. The tiredness and headaches that had plagued him throughout his broadcasting months continued and seemed something more than the exhaustion everyone was feeling after the years of war. His family had been a constant worry throughout those years. With the liberation of Belgium in September 1944, communication with the Gérins was renewed, but their account of how things had gone for them in the war years did little to lift Eugène's spirits. Their privations had been severe, Maurice's recovery from his stroke had been slow and Eugénie had had an operation for breast cancer. Eugène ensured that his name was among the first on a list of administrators from his department to be allowed to travel on a mission to Belgium, but by the start of 1945 had still not been called. He and Winifred had, for some time, been preparing provisions of food and clothing to take to the family, and the call for Eugène to go to Brussels seemed at last to be imminent, when he was taken ill. The family doctor diagnosed thrombosis and ordered complete rest, and Winifred was given leave from her job to nurse him.

After some weeks of this enforced rest Eugène seemed to be improving under her care and the doctor's supervision. In those few weeks they had extended time together for the first time since their arrival in Britain, and with the end of the conflict now in sight they talked over their plans for after the War. Their thoughts turned to the apartment in Rue Dulong, which they had of course not seen since the day in May 1940 when Winifred had shut it up and set off for southern France. Shortly after the occupation of Paris it had been requisitioned by the police. Eugène longed to have the energy to play his cello again. He dreamed of renewing his musical career and of embarking on new projects and engagements.

Meanwhile, the Gérins in Brussels had been getting through the years of occupation as best they could. They were cold, dark, hungry years. The winters of 1941–2 and 1942–3 were severe and under blackout regulations the streets were only dimly lit; indoors, behind the regulatory blackout blinds, the electric light was weak and the coal rations inadequate. Gas for cooking was restricted. Not that there was much food to cook; with Maurice unemployed for much of the War, there was no money for expensive extras on the black market. Like Winifred and Eugène in Nice, the Gérins in Brussels dreamed constantly of meat and eggs and cheese, of having white bread to eat instead of the brown, gluey stuff that stuck to the knife. It was always a red-letter day when Maurice brought home a bag of macaroni, a present from a musician colleague who worked in a pasta factory, or Marthe some herrings from the fishmonger who supplied her school. The Gérins did not have a garden in which to grow a few extra vegetables, and in any case Maurice was not fit enough for gardening.

Charities such as the *Secours d'Hiver*[79] organised food supplements for primary school children considered to be in particular need. The lucky beneficiaries were designated by the doctor who examined the children each month. When the first of these examinations failed to obtain the desired result, Paul had a tactic ready for the next time. He made sure that as the doctor examined him he breathed in hard, holding in his stomach as far as it would go. The stratagem worked, and from then on he was among the recipients not just of cod-liver oil capsules but of a daily bowl of soup or mug of cocoa.

These counted as treats in those years. Chocolate was almost unobtainable, and the Côte d'Or factory by the Gare du Midi produced an

---

[79] 'Winter aid'.

ersatz version under the name of 'Congo Bar'. Tobacco was rationed and Maurice never had enough cigarettes. There were no butt ends on the pavements during the War; they were recycled into cigarettes the ends of which could be wetted with a liquid sold in little tubes to give the approximate aroma of your favourite brand. Every three months or so in the latter part of the War a small parcel would arrive from Portugal. It contained two tins of sardines. Eugène had placed an order with a grocer in Lisbon for this regular consignment for his family back in Belgium. This was all they knew of him during the years of occupation.

Like everyone else, the Gérins sold off possessions to put food on the table. Among the most treasured of those disposed of was a little collection of gramophone records on which there were recordings of Maurice's and Eugène's playing; selling them was one of the hardest things Eugénie had to do during the War.

Worse than the cold, the dark and the hunger, of course, was the fear. It was not the ordinary German soldiers they were afraid of but the Gestapo, the SS, and the militias organised by the collaborationist parties. You lived in fear of your own neighbours, who might report you, for example, for listening to the BBC. You would hear the police cars going their rounds to catch any covert listeners, or Gestapo boots thudding by in pursuit of the Resistance workers who distributed the clandestine press. You never knew who these workers were until they disappeared. If caught, as often as not they were deported to work in Germany or the occupied countries of Eastern Europe.

One of the worst days of the War for Paul was that of the funeral of a well-known collaborator, a Flemish party leader who had been killed by the Resistance. It was a day of reprisals by the militia. Some of their members boarded the tram on which Paul and Marthe were returning home from school. They shouted and made everyone get out off, and forced the men to do the Nazi salute, beating up those who resisted. Paul was still shivering with fear when he went to bed some hours later.

Before the War was over, certain events left an even deeper mark. His primary school, like the family home, was in a predominantly Jewish area, near a synagogue. One day in 1942 the headmaster came to speak to his class. This was unprecedented, and Paul never forgot what he said. 'From now on your Jewish classmates will have to wear a yellow star. The occupiers have introduced this measure as a way of mocking Jews. I forbid you absolutely to make fun of any classmates wearing the star. On the contrary, you should behave even better towards them than before, and go out of your way to treat them kindly.'

Until then, his Jewish classmates and their many Jewish neighbours in Anderlecht had had no occasion for shame or concealment. Soon after their appearance wearing the mandatory stars, however, one by one the classmates started to disappear. In the Gérins' neighbourhood, the fear in the streets became palpable as raids on houses began that August. On the night of 3 September the German forces cordoned off an area a few hundred metres from Rue Georges Moreau. Each house was searched, every Jew found put into one of the waiting trucks.

The Jewish tenants who had been renting the ground floor of the Gérins' house were not among those who lay awake in fear that night. Some time before the German occupation, alarmed by Hitler's expansionist plans, they had taken the decision to emigrate to America.

One scene Paul witnessed was branded in his memory deeper than any other. He and his mother were walking home from the tram stop when they found their way blocked; in a street near their house a large group of German soldiers were standing around a line of Jewish men who were performing limbering-up exercises of the kind done in gym classes. The soldiers had lined up all the men they could find wearing the yellow star and hit on this way of entertaining themselves. As the soldiers watched and laughed, they kept a close eye on passers-by. Paul had just time to observe that many of those being forced to perform were old men with long white beards before he and his mother made a quick getaway. Like Winifred in the streets of Nice, nine-year-old Paul was learning new lessons about human nature in the streets of his native city.

The most important of all the lessons of those war years was one that was constantly instilled by his parents, by word and example. It had, moreover, been demonstrated daily since his earliest childhood in the most vivid and visual way possible, by a familiar household ornament. On the sideboard in the dining-room sat three china monkeys. The first was covering his eyes with his hands, the second his ears, the third his mouth. His grandmother had often reminded him of the significance of these three wise monkeys of oriental tradition: 'See everything, hear everything, but say nothing'. The Gérin family were firm believers in 'keeping themselves to themselves'.

One thing best kept to themselves was the English sister-in-law, who, they suspected, might be doing some kind of war work for Britain. Years later, Paul wondered whether there were other things too, things his family had kept concealed even from him. It was not until later in life that he learned about the integration and assimilation of Jews in France, and it was a long time before he first wondered, in this connection, about the genealogy of his own French grandmother, Eugénie Nicodème. Be that as it may, the lesson of the three wise monkeys was one that was quickly learned by a boy growing up in a Jewish quarter of Brussels in the years of occupation.

Anderlecht did not escape the Allied bombardments of Brussels which began early in 1944. Marthe's father, on his way to visit them, came close to death when a bomb fell on the tram on which he was travelling.

Paul never forgot 3 September 1944. The little boy of six whom Eugène and Winifred had last seen just before the German invasion was now eleven and about to start at the Athénée de Bruxelles high school. He was old enough to know the meaning of the British tanks rolling into Place du Conseil at the end of his street, where he and his parents were among the jubilant crowds who had turned out to watch. They meant that the Allies had liberated Belgium from the occupiers. The last of the Germans had fled and flags had been hung at all the windows and balconies – French, British, American, Russian. There was a pall of smoke above the Palais du Justice, the law court building, which had been set on fire by the retreating Germans. People had rallied round to put out the fire but the heat melted the great copper dome that was a landmark in the city.

Liberation did not bring an immediate end of the War, and well into 1945 Belgium, in its turn, received the visitations of the V1s and V2s. Liberation did, however, bring the renewal of correspondence with Paul's aunt and uncle – chiefly with his aunt, Eugène's contributions being brief addenda to Winifred's letters in his miniscule handwriting. Winifred congratulated Paul on his exam results and promised him presents from England as a reward. Parcels were planned for the whole family; she had been laying by much-needed items of clothing for them and would send them via the Red Cross as soon as it became possible.

One new development in Paul's life provided relief from the privations of wartime life and the sombre atmosphere at home. Since liberation he had become a Boy Scout. He was very proud of his uniform, but preoccupied by the difficulty of acquiring all its components; the price of clothes in Belgium was still exorbitant and many items unobtainable. Winifred expressed approval of this venture and promised to look out for a neckerchief in the requisite colours for Baden-Powell's new recruit.

In the last months of the War Paul looked forward to seeing his uncle and aunt again. He knew that Eugène was hoping to come to Brussels soon, although Winny had told them about his illness. Paul had missed the visits that used to transform the house in Rue Georges Moreau into a place of laughter and fun, with Eugène the life and soul of every family gathering, the entertainer who made everyone feel happy.

Apart from Liberation Day, the day Paul never forgot was the one in February 1945 when he returned home from school to hear a sound he had never heard before coming from Eugénie's apartment on the second floor. His grandmother, the strong matriarch of the household, was lying on the floor of her bedroom sobbing, with a letter in her hand. It was from Winifred and brought the news that Eugène had died of a pulmonary embolism on 16 February, a few days before his 49th birthday.

10
West Cromwell Road
The Long Road Back

Eugène was buried with full military honours in the Belgian section of Brookwood Military Cemetery. The funeral was attended by André Bigwood, at that time the Belgian Military Attaché at the War Office, who had been so instrumental in helping Eugène and Winifred to escape from Nice.

In the first months after Eugène's death Winifred went every week to Brookwood. The military cemetery, mostly occupied by Commonwealth war graves, was a tranquil place of green turf and tall masses of evergreens, a short walk from the little train station along a path skirting the railway line. Giant sequoias guarded the modest Belgian plot of fifty or so graves, adjoining the Polish and Czech sections. An unassuming memorial was raised there next to those displaying the Polish eagle and the Czech lion, and in time the wooden crosses were replaced by white headstones. The inscription chosen by Winifred for Eugène's stone, under the lion rampant of the Belgian coat of arms, read: 'Soldat. E.J. Gérin. 24-2-1896 – 16-2-1945. Mort pour la Belgique. La mort n'atteint pas ceux qu'elle glorifie'. The text was taken from a poem by Eugène himself.

> La Mort n'atteint pas ceux qu'elle glorifie,
> Ceux qui sont le suprême orgueil de la Patrie,
>   Ses immortels Sauveurs;
> Ne sont-ils pas déjà la lumière perdue?
> Leurs noms ont les accents des cloches disparues,
>   Qui sonnent dans nos cœurs.[80]

'The Long Road Back', subtitle to this chapter, is the phrase used by Winifred in her memoir to refer to the years following Eugène's death.

[80] Death cannot harm those it glorifies, those who are the supreme pride of the Fatherland, its immortal saviours; are they not already the lost light? Their names ring in our hearts like vanished bells.

The lights had gone out for Winifred. With the passing of the years life would gradually become less dark for her than in those first months of 1945, but the particular light that had illuminated the years with Eugène, the Côte d'Azur of their courtship, the parks of Paris where they had walked and planned their lives before the War, would not shine on her again. Years later she would experience a different kind of happiness in the light of the sky over the moors at Haworth and a different kind of fulfilment in the literary vocation she finally discovered there. With Eugène at her side, just being alive had been fulfilment enough. From now on she would have to seek a measure of consolation and compensation, as well as an outlet for her energies, in some kind of purposeful activity.

In early April Paul received a letter from his godmother. It had been written on Good Friday.

> MON CHÉRI,
> *Te voilà face à face, peut-être pour la première fois dans ta petite vie, avec le deuil, le chagrin, la désolation.* Perhaps for the first time in your short life, you find yourself face to face with mourning, with sorrow, with desolation. You see Grandma crying, *Papa* and *Maman* crying, and your heart aches. I'm writing to you to comfort you and to show you how you, *petit Paul*, can do something big and beautiful that will at the same time be a comfort to you yourself.
>
> Will you carry out a mission for me? I know that you can do it and that nobody can do it better than you. Isn't it a wonderful thing to be able to say to oneself 'I am necessary, I am needed by others for something'? We all need you – I myself as much as those who live with you. What I want to ask of you is to make it your aim in life just now to comfort Grandma and your parents. I know that your life is very full. But what I am asking of you isn't a matter of time. It is simply to show your family as much affection as you can. Don't let yourself be influenced by other boys who tell you that people nowadays don't show their feelings in that way, as if it were something to be ashamed of. Follow your heart, which is loving, and be ten times more affectionate than in the past.
>
> Your grandmother has had the most terrible sorrow anyone can have – to lose one of her children. Imagine your mother's despair if she lost you. But she would still have your father to comfort her. Just think: your grandmother no longer has her husband and has to bear this terrible sorrow alone.

Will you make it an aim in life to replace *Parrain*[81] in your grand-mother's life? Would you like to be like him? When I come to visit you, would you like to be able to say 'Godmother, I've fulfilled my mission as well as I could'? You are already necessary to your family just by being yourself, but you would be doubly so if you made it your ideal to console them for what they've lost. You know that Grandma and your parents live only for your happiness and their happiness or grief depend on you.

Now that you're a big boy and a member of the noble Boy Scouts movement, you can understand what an ideal is. It is something infi-nitely bigger and more beautiful than ourselves. It's something we devote ourselves to with all our heart, something we would give our lives for if necessary. That's what your godfather did. All his life he served an ideal of truth and beauty. He was a born artist and spent his whole youth perfecting the gifts he received. It wasn't easy and it wasn't always fun, but he stood fast; he wanted to achieve perfec-tion, and he succeeded. I've been with *Parrain* in European capitals where he played before rooms full of people and I've seen musical connoisseurs stand up in their enthusiasm and run towards him to take his hands and say: 'Monsieur, you are an artist!' He achieved the ideal of his youth.

But life is a staircase. We can either go up and up – or go down. If I talk to you about *Parrain* it's because I witnessed his ascent.

When the War came, *Parrain* had only one idea in his head; to devote himself to freeing the world from the worst threat humanity has ever faced. It wasn't easy to do what he did – to leave a country occupied by the enemy and reach England, the only place where the immeasurable effort that was to bring about liberation could be organised. Yet he did it.

Before the War, he loved peace, the contemplative life, order and beauty. He sacrificed all that. After the War he never had another peaceful day. He worked twelve and fourteen hours a day in a state of constant alert. And yet he was happy. He could have taken days of leave, but he never did. He always said, 'We'll have time to rest after the War.' He refused all relaxation. The ideal that filled his life demanded perfection and he couldn't be content with less. He had great satisfactions, the greatest: the knowledge that what he was doing was of supreme importance, the respect his bosses had for him, their praise of him. But it was too much for his strength. He didn't live to see the day he had been working for and denying himself for – the day of victory. But on that day, think of him. Think

---

[81] 'Godfather'.

of the fact that if he and millions of other idealists had not given their all, there would never have been a victory day and Europe would have been a huge slave camp working for the most brutal of tyrannies.

You can see from my handwriting that I have been very poorly since *Parrain* died. And yet I have a lot of things to comfort me. His life is such a wonderful example I am full of happiness and pride at having had the honour of sharing it. I don't see death as an end but as a continuation. Nothing will ever be able to separate me from *Parrain's* love. That's why I wanted to talk to you about ideals. On the one hand there are the transient things in life, on the other the eternal things – love, generosity, greatness. If you aim for these three, you will never feel bereft.

If her eleven-year-old godson had been more like the boys she warned him not to heed, the emotional tone of this long letter might have been a cause of discomfort rather than consolation and added to the oppressiveness of life as an only child surrounded by grieving elders. But Paul was fond of his English aunt and he was also thoughtful and considerate for his age. Just as she thought of his grief as well as her own, so he, as her next letter shows, thought of hers.

In that letter she told him how much she had been touched by his reply and his promise to write to her regularly. As a child, she too had loved writing so much that she was often designated by her family to correspond with relatives. 'Thank you for understanding me so well, and thinking of me and *Parrain*. I'm sure this will make you happy, for one of the most beautiful things in life is to communicate in thought with those we love. When we do that, distances can no longer separate us even when death has taken those we loved out of our life. We can always be beside them in the innermost depths of our soul.' On a lighter note, she promised to search for shoulder loops for his Scout shirt and to send him some chocolate. Eugène and she had been saving their chocolate rations for Brussels.

Her thoughtfulness showed itself to each individual member of the family in such practical ways. Very soon after Eugène's death Winifred's thoughts had turned to his family, who had been awaiting his visit to Brussels announced since the previous autumn. Despite her own grief she entered not just into their sorrow but also into their material needs. 'The only pleasure left to me in life now,' she wrote to Marthe, 'is that of serving others.'

The parcels she and Eugène had been preparing for his visit to Brussels, containing the things they knew his family most needed, were still waiting to be posted. Everyone in the family was short of clothes, and Winifred had all Eugène's cleaned for Maurice. But it was not until May, just before V Day, marking Germany's surrender and the official end of the War, that she was able to send the first batch of clothing via the Red Cross. Parcels were still limited to one a month, and took a long time to arrive. In a second parcel she sent Maurice some of Eugène's shoes and asked whether he would rather she sent Eugène's suit or raincoat in the next one; because of the weight restrictions it had to be one or the other. Over the next months she also sent parcels via Belgian friends travelling to Brussels. For Marthe there were clothes of her own, hardly worn at the time she went into mourning.

Besides such practical considerations, she was deeply concerned about Eugénie. Prostrated by the loss of her adored youngest son, she lost all will to live and her health, never good since her cancer diagnosis and operation, deteriorated steadily. Winifred wrote bracing letters to her mother-in-law and exhortations to Marthe. Had *Maman* seen a specialist? Was she taking something for her high blood pressure? Should she take a *calmant* for her nerves?

'For Eugène's sake,' she implored Eugénie, 'don't give way to grief. He would want you – does want you – to be happy and to laugh. Eugène is happy; don't mar his happiness.' 'Encourage *Maman* to look after herself and tell her that it makes my own grief worse to know that she is so overcome,' she told Marthe. 'I can fully enter into her feelings – neither she nor I have much to keep us on earth now, but it seems to me we have an important reason to go on living: the love for Eugène that we have in common. There are so many things I want to tell *Maman* about the last few years and there are so many things she can still tell me about his childhood and youth. Most importantly of all, I know that Eugène would have wanted his mother to take care of herself. After what you've all been through in the last five years you must help one another and try to make life easier for each other. *Maman* must take comfort in the thought that we all need her.'

Delays in authorisation to visit Belgium, compounded by her own prostration and reluctance to revisit scenes of former happiness with Eugène until she felt more able to undergo the ordeal, postponed the visit to the Gérins that she knew she must undertake. Meantime, on Paul's twelfth birthday she wrote to him again about Eugène. '*Parrain* can't be visibly at your party but he is happy when you're happy. He loved so much to laugh . . . He accompanies us on our way and supports us with the strength of his love.'

Winifred took seriously her duty, as Paul's godmother, to ensure that he was set on the right course in life. He was now old enough to choose the path he would take, she told him, and once more she held up to him the example of his godfather. But perhaps her need for Paul was even greater than his for her. She needed to talk to him about Eugène, almost as if her dead war hero had been Paul's father, and Paul the son she and Eugène never had.

However bracing her letters to the Gérins, after nights of sleepless hours thinking of Eugène, or dreams haunted by him, Winifred often wondered how she herself would find the strength to go on. In between the visits to Brookwood she was trying to come to terms with her loss by writing. She had not produced much little verse since the poetry of her twenties and the years of courtship. Then she had written exuberantly in the intoxication of youth and love. But the poems she wrote in the eighteen months after February 1945 were born in pain and record her struggle to assimilate what she called the 'calamity' of the loss of Eugène. They were the working through of an inner dialogue about his death and about what death signified. It was a dialogue that in those first months of bereavement she was holding ceaselessly with herself – and with him.

As soon as she felt able, which was not until the end of 1945, she went not only to Brussels to see the Gérins but to Paris. She went ostensibly to sub-let the apartment there and do necessary paperwork, such as taking out probate, but even more important for her was to revisit the places most associated with her years with Eugène. Nature, even in wintertime, could comfort by speaking of the continuity of emotional experience and of the past in the present.

Paris just after the War was no longer a happy place. In every queue for food or coal the hatred and resentment between those who had resisted and those who had not, those who had had access to the black market and those who had not, was palpable. It was no longer the city Winifred had loved. Whenever she could she got out of it, to the royal parks of St-Cloud and Marly-le-Roi, the *Petit Trianon* at Versailles, Bougival, seeking the essence of what she and Eugène had experienced there. Associations with places were all-important in her memories of him and the names of the places that formed the landscape of their love and that she visited without him on this wintry trip to Paris recur again and again in the poems recording the inner journey she was taking at the same time.

These poems, which often take the form of questions, express the paradox of the death of someone who has been one's whole life. Eugène was lost to her, yet since he was a part of her and could not, therefore, cease to be so, he was still with her.

In a poem called *Full Circle* she recalls how once, during her time

with him, she had a foretaste of what it would be like to lose him. He
was climbing ahead of her up a winding mountain track and whenever he turned a bend in the path she temporarily lost sight of him.
Now and then he looked back and smiled at her, and his smile seemed
to her like an adieu. Each time he disappeared from view,

> As though in premonition of the end
> I first had intimation of the time
> That was to come, as though the tranquil air
> Had cried out with my loss, and with you there
> I'd seen the same path empty I must climb.[82]

Their life together, she wrote, unbroken by any separation longer
'than the short sleep between June dusk and dawn', had been so perfect
it was as if they had been born straight into Heaven without having
to die first. It had been timeless and therefore a kind of eternity. In a
poem called *The Green Paradise: The Journey Back*, in which she
revisits the willows of Bougival nine miles from Paris on the banks of
the Seine, a favourite haunt of Manet and Renoir as well as of hers
and Eugène's, she evokes this lost paradise.

> Life was a summer's day, by nothing bounded
> But a great ring of light;
> An unbroken circle that was rounded
> Without a rift of darkness or of blight
> . . .
> And all our awakenings seemed compounded
> Of a celestial delight . . .

Addressing Bougival, she imagines other couples visiting it,

> Fond twilight lovers who haunt you as of yore
> On summer evenings when the full moon shone;
> Where, oh Elysian fields, is your far shore?
> Oh! my green Paradise! where are you gone?

Was the paradise gone for ever or was it possible, she asked, that the
lost happiness could somehow be regained?

> Somewhere, the paths that we have cherished,
> The chosen sites,

---

[82] All the unpublished poems by Winifred cited are in the Greenwood papers.

The settings, the very witnesses as it were
Of our delights,
Await our coming, for these have not perished
– The elect places – they keep their happy state
Preserved from harm, perennially fair
At the last journey's end; but where, oh! where?

Since they had already experienced Heaven on earth, how could there be a better state awaiting them after death? And if souls did survive death, how could Eugène be happy on the other shore without her? If only they could have been wafted *together* to that further shore during the years when it felt as if they were floating outside time. Her desolation in a world without Eugène is a little reminiscent of Emily Brontë's Heathcliff. Knowing himself to be on the point of the death that he is confident will reunite him with Cathy, who has been dead for the past twenty years, Heathcliff describes himself as being 'within arm's length of the shore. I must reach it first, and then I'll rest.'

Life without Eugène was Hell, a prison, and, like Emily Brontë, she sometimes longed to be released from it. She explored in verse the possibility of reunion with him after death. A poem called *The Passage* was published in *Poetry Review* in August–September 1949:

Outside this wall, across this frontier line
That is myself, spreads everlasting life;
. . . One step and I am through;
So fragile is the barrier and so fine
The shade between security and strife,
Prison and liberation, Hell and you.

On that side freedom beckons; and who knows
To what fresh dedication of our powers
    Death is the gate?
Like any refugee I stand and wait
My chance to cross. They seem to me long hours . . .
No habitations glimmer, no light glows . . .

It will be possible to see the place,
Perhaps even to recognise the way we went
    If in the forward rush,
In the confusion and the shifting crush
Of that arrival, I can find your face,
As formerly at every journey's end.

In a poem called *Appeasement* there are some echoes of Emily Brontë again, in this case of Emily's *The Prisoner*. Emily's captive is visited each night by a 'messenger of hope' whose visions of the Invisible and Unseen allow her to forget that her soul is still the prisoner of her body. Winifred appeals to Eugène to claim her as his own and spirit her away at the 'enchanting hour' of night when the bonds of earthly existence are loosened and her soul seems to float disembodied. Doubtless in those months Winifred did sometimes long, like Keats, to 'cease upon the midnight with no pain'.

> Oh! Cast me even with the present surge
> Of this high passion on your further shore
> Not to come back but perish in your arms,
>   Where all our past alarms
> And the tempest of my grieving shall be stilled,
>   And each in each
>   Be finally fulfilled,
> Conmingled in the appeasement of that love
> From which there's no returning any more.

Through verse Winifred gradually worked her way to a calmer shore than the one where she had been left stranded by Eugène's death. She said later that that had been the most terrible but at the same time the most revealing experience of her life. The revelation she took from it was that death was not an extinction but a continuation. Eugène had died in mid-sentence in the entrance hall of the Virginia Water bungalow, passing a comb through his hair in front of the mirror just as they were about to go out. Winifred had been by his side. When he died it was almost as if he had simply walked into an adjacent room.

She came to feel that the lost paradise was not really lost, because nothing that has been is lost. We are the sum of all our experiences, and what has been becomes a part of us, just as the branches and leaves of a tree grow out of all the summers that have passed through it.

Happiness, she felt, is even more important in forming us than grief. Writing in her memoir of her time in Paris with Eugène, she said that happiness, by which she meant the happiness of love, leaves you a different being from what you were before. 'Like a new language learnt, a great landscape seen, it alters you within and transforms life without.' And in her play about Jane Austen written in the 1950s, Cassandra Austen, referring to Jane's romance with the one and only man she ever loved, observes that: 'I think that when one has experienced great happiness *once*, it colours the whole of one's life. More than grief. I believe *happiness makes us what we are*. It has greater power.'[83]

Winifred wrote in her poem *Happiness* that although Eugène could no longer be there to see the spring with her, nothing could take away the experience of spring that they had had together.

> How can I fear to lose what once has been
> Since what I see still shows me what I've seen?
> Happiness is a colour of the mind
> That does not fade though it be summers old;
> It cannot be confined
> To any place or moment; and this spring's new green
> - Although it find you cold –
> You shared with me for good at Fontainebleau,
> At Bougival and Marly, years ago.

Whether as wish fulfilment or a genuine expression of belief, thoughts of eternity, survival of the soul and reunion with Eugène on the other shore recur constantly. She reproaches herself for wanting him to miss her as she misses him and reminds herself that wherever he is he must surely be happy since he has attained a higher state of being. In life, he always strode ahead of her showing her the way. Now, too, he is ahead of her and she must learn to know his new self 'that with it I may grow/ And with his striding spirit keep apace'. She will not see his face again as it was, but she will have to learn to recognise 'the quintessential he', wherever it is, in this new phase of his being. Sometimes she is afraid of failing to recognise him on that other shore.

Meanwhile, there were the short-lived reunions brought by dreams. She often dreamed of him. She couldn't always remember what he had looked like or what, if anything, he had said, but she would awaken knowing that she had been with him.

> I looked for you and saw you where you came
> Precipitate towards me on the way,
>   With all the old
> Passionate urgency of haste, the same
> Springing and airy tread as though you flew,
> As when we had been parted for a day
> In happy times. So now as we came near,

---

[83] Winifred Gérin, *Jane, or Fallacious Inferences* (unpublished play, 1953).

By every trick and gesture, Love, I knew
By that impetuous straining to enfold
   In quivering arms
   The form that was most dear
That now as eagerly you would repay
With multiple endearments, myriad charms,
The pain we had in parting, and once more
Turn all our grief to rapture as of yore.

Too charged to speak, too wondering to enquire
   How we came there,
We only looked; and every dear desire
That formerly had made your love so fair,
Now found it consummation in the sight
– Restored awhile – of what each loved the best.
To see was all our rapture. Deep delight
Darkened your eyes to a nocturnal blue
Where every tender passion was expressed.
They seemed to search my being through and through
And on my eyes, articulate, to bend:
– 'Never believe the looks of love could lie
That promised once to love you without end'
(Their language clearly said) 'or bliss deny
Because you cannot always see your joy:
Not even Death the vision can destroy
To retrieve which we only have to die.'

(Brief Vision)

On 9 March 1946 there was a memorial service for Eugène at the church of Notre-Dame aux Riches Claires in Brussels. It was attended by many of his and Winifred's friends, including fellow-exiles from their time in Nice, and musician colleagues performed works particularly associated with him.

In the same year, the Paris apartment was sub-let to friends and Winifred's and Eugène's furniture moved to England. By then, there had been a change in Winifred's living arrangements. After Eugène's death she stayed on at the bungalow with Nell, but with Katharine no longer there and the War over there was no reason to remain in Virginia Water except for being close to Roger, and both sisters wanted to participate in the cultural life of the capital. Apart from their shared devotion to the theatre, Nell planned to return to her long-abandoned art studies at last and take up painting seriously, while Winifred, who sought an escape from grief in music, was keen to attend as many concerts as possible. The old home in Norwood was gone now. In October 1945 Nell, who had inherited the Virginia Water cottage, sold it and bought a house in Earls Court in Kensington. She invited Winifred to share it with her, offering her an apartment in the house.

The two sisters settled into life in their new home in a Victorian terrace at 60 West Cromwell Road, SW5, within walking distance of Kensington Gardens and Hyde Park and the Knightsbridge museums. The house was very large, with spacious rooms and high ceilings. Winifred occupied most of the first floor and Nell ('Gui-Gui') the whole of the second, where she had a large studio.

On the ground floor was a dining room, rarely used, and a huge kitchen which was Gilbert's domain. For of course Gilbert went with the sisters to Kensington. She was now 66 and had been with the family for 27 years. She presided over a household much reduced in numbers since the days when she had directed a little army of servants in Norwood. Even so, there were two servants apart from Gilbert: a cleaning lady who came in most days, and a maid who served at mealtimes, opened the door to callers and did whatever else was not done by Gilbert and the cleaner (one wonders what, exactly!). Frederick had left the family very comfortably off, but even so it is rather mysterious how Nell and Winifred could afford to be so well-attended in such a huge house. Until Winifred became a published writer much later, neither she nor Nell appears to have been earning any income.

One source of revenue was the self-contained flat in the basement, which was often let, frequently to friends who had been bombed out of their own homes. Compensation for 'war damage' was ridiculously inadequate; Nell and Winifred received only £600 for the loss of the 16-room house in Norwood. In bomb-scarred London where so many homes and lives had been destroyed and so many women left widowed, homeless, or both, Winifred found some comfort in her bereavement in helping friends who were similarly bereft, and in the sense of solidarity that bound everyone together. As the city was rebuilt around them, she and countless others were also having to rebuild their lives. Betty Maclean, her colleague from PWE days in London, whose husband had died on the plane carrying Leslie Howard, was an early tenant of the basement flat.

The two sisters had good friends. Both had the gift of friendship and of maintaining it for life. Winifred was an indefatigable correspondent and never lost touch with the French and Belgian contacts she and Eugène had made in Paris and Nice. Of her English friends, the Moores in Cambridge were still among the closest. By this time she was following with interest the careers of their two sons; in the years after the War Nicholas, whom she had known as a toddler in Cambridge, was making a name for himself as a poet, his younger brother Timothy starting to be known as a composer. Mina Breed, too, now working at the Monopolies Commission, was still a close friend. Winifred also kept in touch with her Newnham fellow student Jean Stewart, now lecturing at Cambridge, who had married a scientist called James Pace and had two daughters. With Olga Walters, however, one of her closest friends at college, Winifred had lost contact. Olga and Kingsley Martin had divorced in 1940 and Olga gradually became a complete recluse. Many years later Winifred heard that, on venturing out of her flat for the first time in years, she had been run over by a car and killed, leaving a houseful of cats.

Winifred had occasion to remember Olga and her other college friends when she went back to Cambridge in 1949 to receive her M.A., women graduates having finally been granted the right to attend degree ceremonies two years earlier. In a photograph taken to mark the occasion, Winifred looks wistful rather than jubilant at finally donning the graduate's cap and gown. Eugène's photograph stands on the table beside her, but Eugène could not be there to share in her pleasure. But the M.A. after her name was a welcome boost to her confidence when she later launched herself as a literary biographer.

For Nell, the end of the War marked the start of a new life at the age of 47, a life that had not been possible while she had devoted herself to her ailing parents. She did not begrudge them those years. She had always been self-effacing and slow to make demands for herself. But now she quietly set up her easel in her big sunlit studio on the second floor of the Kensington house. And for the first time since the far-off days with Winifred at the Crystal Palace, she enrolled for art classes, this time at the London Polytechnic School of Art, where she spent much of each day for the next few years. She also started to go on annual painting holidays in Greece, and the light and colours of the country flooded into her paintings. She painted in a bold impressionistic style and in vivid colours. Her landscapes, still lives and occasional portraits, which included one of Winifred, were soon being exhibited at art shows.

In the first few months after Eugène's death Winifred had sometimes spoken to the Gérins of her wish to be posted to Belgium. But her work at the ministry came to an end along with the War and either there were no posts of the kind she had in mind, or this idea was simply abandoned.

She did not seek another office job. Return to anything like normality post-Eugène was a process that was to take years. The slow process of healing was helped by the poetry she was writing; another activity that contributed greatly to that process was music.

Londoners had been starved of classical music during the War, and the years following demobilisation were good ones for concerts. The old Queen's Hall had been destroyed in the Blitz and until the Royal Festival Hall opened on the South Bank, the Royal Albert Hall was the main concert venue. It was within easy walking distance of West Cromwell Road, and Winifred became an assiduous concert-goer. It was not long before she found an even more effective antidote to grief than listening to music: participating in music, *making* music. Her piano had been brought over from the Paris apartment with the furniture, but with Eugène's Cremona cello now silent and Eugène no longer there for her to accompany, playing the piano had lost much of its appeal. Instead, she joined choirs: first the Goldsmiths Choral Union, then in 1947 the newly-formed London Philharmonic Choir. She found herself spending more and more time in Westminster Cathedral Hall, where both choirs rehearsed. She took part in performances recorded for the Third Programme with the BBC Symphony Orchestra. Enrico's singing lessons in the 1920s now stood her in good stead.

In the post-war years there was Handel galore to lift up the spirits, along with the rest of the usual repertory – Bach's B Minor Mass and St Matthew Passion, Beethoven's Missa Solemnis, more modern works such as Elgar's Dream of Gerontius, Britten's Spring Symphony, Carl Orff's Carmina Burana. She worked under the great British conductors of the time such as Beecham, Boult and Sargeant and performed with the singers Peter Pears and Kathleen Ferrier.

When the Royal Festival Hall opened on 3 May 1951, Winifred was one of a contingent of singers invited to sing a programme of British music as part of the Festival of Britain celebrating the country's recovery after the War. Six years on from Eugène's death, she was somewhat more reconciled to life without him, and music had played an important part in her own recovery. But a year later she wrote to Marthe: 'It is seven years since I lost Eugène and not a day goes by but I feel the *physical blow* of his death.' And in another letter to Marthe at the end of the same year she wrote, 'It's almost eight years since I lost Eugène but I still live as if he were by my side. I often dream about him. I dreamed about him last night. Everything I do is as if he were still guiding me'.

Singing had, however, proved to be an ideal therapy. Making music demanded and absorbed every faculty. It liberated you from the confines of self and individual preoccupations. She told Marthe and Paul that it was a way of communicating with Eugène. 'Music is the most divine thing we have on earth.' It transported her and took her to Eugène's side. When she sang a Beethoven mass she sang it for Eugène and for '*tous nos chers morts*'.[84]

Winifred continued to correspond regularly with the Gérins. She always regarded them as her family as well as Eugène's: they were in need of her comfort and she needed theirs, not just to share in the loss of Eugène but to fill the gap left by the loss of so many members of her own family. She was solicitous about Marthe, who had to care for a fractious husband on top of her other duties, and Eugénie who never recovered her spirits or health after Eugène's death. Winifred continued to send her mother-in-law translations of nineteenth-century novels and exhort her to live for the members of the family left to her.

To Paul, throughout his teenage years, she continued to write in what she saw as her role of moral advisor and educator as well as affectionate aunt. Good exam results were rewarded with congratulatory telegrams. 'I'm particularly pleased that you got a good result in civics. Serving others is more important than knowledge.' 'The important things are effort, discipline, using your talents. Only that leads to happiness.' Eugène is made to participate in her pleasure at Paul's academic successes: 'Your godfather would have been happy. He was conscientious, hard-working.' She claimed that the death that struck Eugène down – an embolism caused by thrombosis – was frequently the fate of those who worked too hard; she made the same claim for George VI, who died of thrombosis in 1952.

She often held up what she saw as peculiarly *British* values as examples for Paul to follow, and in these too the half-French, half-Belgian Eugène was made to participate. Modesty and consideration for others, for instance. 'The English are very modest. They're brought up to think of others before themselves . . . Everyone loved your godfather because, despite his talent, he was modest and generous.'

She was ambitious for Paul. 'One day, when you're a university professor . . . ' she would say only half-jokingly. Or 'When you're a member of the Royal Academy of Belgium . . . '. Meanwhile, she was as anxious for him to acquire a knowledge of Britain's history and culture as she was for him to imbibe its virtues. Postcards arrived from

---

[84] 'All our dear dead ones.'

Stratford, from the Lakes, from the London art galleries – from the Tate came Henry Wallis's painting of the dead Chatterton.

On her visits to Brussels she was able to impart this moral and cultural training in person. She went regularly, twice a year, during Paul's school holidays, to the house in Rue Georges Moreau. Her visits, without Eugène now and without Pussy, were not as gay as in the old days when his uncle was alive, but they were nourishing to Paul. It was only now that he and his English aunt really came to know each other. Part of her time in Brussels was spent looking up her Belgian friends; the rest was devoted to the Gérins and to Paul in particular. He was intellectually mature for his years but socially gauche. As well as inculcating in him a love of history and literature she took it upon herself to instruct him in social etiquette.

She would take him on outings, perhaps to see a film chosen by her for its literary or historical interest, or for a walk in the countryside around Brussels, ending with 'le five o'clock', for wherever they were, Marraine Winny would find a café where they could round off their excursion with a cup of tea and a cake. Her conversation was always interesting but she could be over-zealous in her insistence on good manners and he did not relish the lectures and scoldings administered to him, sometimes in public. But although he smarted under them at the time, in after years he acknowledged his debt to her for helping him to acquire social ease. Among much else for which he was grateful to her, his English aunt taught him *savoir-vivre*.

In the summer of 1951, when Paul was seventeen, he stayed for the first time with Aunts Winny and Gui-Gui in Kensington. That visit, the first of many to London, was an unforgettable one for a young man who had hitherto seen very little of the world.

The boy from Anderlecht, the future historian who noticed everything, was fascinated by every detail and ritual of life in West Cromwell Road. The Victorian terraced house with its big bay windows seemed like a vast mansion to him. He noticed the features that made it different from Brussels town houses like his own, in particular the steps up to the front door, the 'ground' floor being actually some feet above ground level, and those down to the basement, with the sunken 'area' in front of it. The basement flat, unlet at the time, was his for the duration of his stay. One of the rooms had been made into a shrine to his uncle. His photo hung on the walls, which were papered in Regency style stripes; his cello, placed by the fireplace, seemed to be awaiting its owner's return.

The house had a magnificent staircase painted black, as were the banisters and skirting boards, and regally carpeted in red; the doors on the landings were painted black on the stairwell side and white on the inside. The high ceilings were moulded and there were marble fireplaces. When Paul saw the interior of the Banks family home in the film *Mary Poppins* years later he was transported back in time to the 'Upstairs Downstairs' setting of his aunt's house as he knew it in the 1950s.

Communication with Gilbert, the presiding spirit of the household, was constrained by Paul's limited spoken English. The one aspect of an English education in which Winny had failed her godson was in teaching him her language. His conversations with Winifred were invariably in French – 'Gui-Gui' also spoke good French – and on his few attempts to speak English she criticised his accent so severely that he abandoned the effort. Despite the limitations of conversation with Gilbert, however, Paul felt instinctively that she had his measure. Nothing escaped her. She could be caustic. Had his comprehension of English been better he would have discovered that she could also be very amusing. She always had a cigarette in her mouth and her fingers were stained with nicotine, and in the evening she liked her tipple of whisky or brandy.

Although Winny and frequently Nell dedicated much of the day to entertaining their visitor they did not breakfast with him. His breakfast was served each morning in his basement apartment by the housemaid, who wore a white apron and cap.

After breakfast he would talk to his aunt. Winny loved to talk. They would discuss English and French history. She spoke about the little princes in the tower (the two sons of Edward IV supposedly murdered by their uncle Richard III), and the mystery concerning the fate of another imprisoned prince – the 'Lost Dauphin', Louis XVII, the son of the monarchs guillotined by the revolutionaries. Did the little Dauphin really die in prison, and if so was he murdered? Or was he removed from the Temple prison and taken to safety, and another child substituted in his place? As a child of ten, Winifred had wept on holidays on the Isle of Wight at the tomb of Elizabeth Stuart, imprisoned from the age of six until her death at fourteen. As a woman of fifty, in conversation with her nephew, she still shed tears when she spoke of the fate of child captives who had languished and perished in grim fortresses down the centuries.

Despite the attractions of his aunts' house and of two magnificent angora cats called Minette and Rowley, much of Paul's time in London was spent being piloted around the city by Winny and Gui-Gui. Paul became very fond of his other English aunt. She was quiet and retiring, dominated by her more assertive younger sister. She was tender-hearted towards the needy. Like her mother on their childhood motor tours, dispensing largesse to tramps on dusty highways in the form of bundles of coppers, Nell would keep little piles of coins on a table in the entrance hall, and before leaving the house everyone was instructed to pocket some of them to distribute to poor people begging in the streets. When the doorbell sounded it often turned out to be some protégé of Nell's seeking assistance.

Each day, carefully planned by Winifred, brought a banquet of culture. Paul was taken to the National Gallery, the British Museum and the Victoria and Albert Museum. He saw a Shakespeare performance in Regent's Park and went to the opera at Covent Garden and a promenade concert at the Albert Hall. He would remember his times in London as an initiation in history and the arts, an education in themselves.

Well before the time of Paul's first visit to London Winifred was already absorbed in a new literary venture, and while Gui-Gui painted in her studio on the floor above, Winny was spending much of her time writing in her study on the first floor.

This new creative departure, which would ultimately steer her life into the course that gave it real direction and brought recognition for her writing, had been triggered by chance while reading Alfred Duff Cooper's 1932 biography of Talleyrand, the crafty diplomat whose life encompassed her favourite historical period. In 1792, at the start of the September massacres, Talleyrand and some other French émigrés were given sanctuary at Juniper Hall, a country house near Mickleham in Surrey. What sparked Winifred's interest was that these French exiles became friendly with a sister of Fanny Burney's who lived in Mickleham, and that one of them was General Alexandre D'Arblay, the man who became Fanny's husband. D'Arblay was an enlightened aristocrat who, though loyal to the King, had supported constitutional reform; his views represented a middle way between the Royalists' and Republicans'. It was at Juniper Hall that Fanny and the penniless D'Arblay met, fell in love and began their courtship in the face of her father's disapproval.

Winifred had always liked Fanny Burney's works. Re-reading her diaries, she was struck by an aspect of Fanny's life that her own marriage to Eugène now made more interesting for her: Fanny's marriage to a 'foreigner' in the face of opposition from her family. General D'Arblay's prospects, as Eugène's had been, were somewhat precarious. His only profession was that of a soldier, and as an exile and a supporter of the executed king his chances of serving under the Republican regime in France were doubtful. Despite the difficulties of their respective courtships, however, both Fanny and Winifred found in their partners a strong affinity of tastes and outlook. D'Arblay played the mandolin and was a connoisseur of poetry. Fanny described him as a man of integrity and sensitivity, with spontaneous, open manners.

Parallels between Fanny's and Winifred's destinies continue after marriage. Their paths even cross geographically. Happy as they were with their partners they found that in one respect, circumstances bore out their families' apprehensions about marriage with a foreigner: in wartime it caused considerable inconvenience and led to some hair-raising adventures. Like Winifred, Fanny enjoyed a honeymoon idyll before war turned her life upside down. She and her General married in 1793 and the first years of their marriage, undisturbed by the war with France, were passed in a cottage not far from Juniper Hall, where Fanny wrote novels and her husband kept himself busy gardening.

In 1802 D'Arblay – at nearly fifty already rather old for active service – accepted an offer to serve under Napoleon, and Fanny, with their son, joined him in France to face an uncertain future. They settled first in Rue de Mirosmenil near the Parc Monceau, close to the Gérins' Rue Dulong. When hostilities between their two countries were renewed the following year and communications broken off, Fanny found herself a prisoner in France. Because D'Arblay refused to take up arms against his wife's country he was obliged to accept an administrative post, but took to office life no more kindly than Eugène had in London.

The year 1815 was an unsettled and perilous period for both the D'Arblays, reminiscent of the Gérins' war adventures, with both Fanny and Winifred equally reluctant to stay at home and determined to stay with their men regardless of the risk. In March Napoleon landed in France from Elba. As the deposed emperor approached the French capital, D'Arblay, who was a member of Louis XVIII's bodyguard, rushed off to join the King while Fanny fled to Brussels, making the same trip in reverse as Winifred in 1940. Alone in Brussels while her husband, in Trèves, rounded up deserters from Napoleon's army to fight for the King, Fanny, with her usual knack of being on the scene when history was being made, saw the troops setting out for the fields of Waterloo and the wounded being brought back to the city after the battle, and heard the cry '*Napoléon est pris*' in its streets.

Hearing that her husband had been injured, Fanny set off to Trèves to nurse him. Her lonely journey, beset by frights and misadventures, was reminiscent of Winifred's on her way to rejoin Eugène and his regiment in southern France. Fanny made it to Trèves and D'Arblay eventually recovered, but there was no place for him in post-Napoleonic France and the couple made their way to England where D'Arblay, his health shattered, died three years later. Fanny was so devastated by his loss she hardly left the house during the first year of widowhood. She survived her General by twenty-two years.

It was the first meeting between the two that was the subject of Winifred's play. She visited Juniper Hall, an eighteenth-century house set in a wooded valley in the Surrey Downs. It had just been sold to the National Trust and was looking dilapidated after occupation by the army during the War, but she was able to see the John Adam style room in which Fanny met D'Arblay, wander along the avenue whose cedars were supposedly planted by Talleyrand, and visit Mickleham Church where the couple were married. Her need to see the setting of her drama with her own eyes indicated the importance of places in stimulating her imagination, and it was inevitable that the name she chose for her play should be *Juniper Hall*.

It was of course not the first time she had used drama as a medium – when she was in her twenties, verse plays had flowed from her pen as abundantly as poetry – but period comedies like this one marked a completely new departure.

The comedic elements sprang from the differences in cultural mores and standards of morality between the timid and retiring Fanny, who had spent years closeted as a lady-in-waiting at the staid court of George III, and the sophisticated, uninhibited members of the French 'Juniper Colony'. These included the notoriously unconventional Mme de Staël and her lover the Comte de Narbonne as well as her former lover Talleyrand. Fanny – who at forty was seen by her family as unmarriageable and at the start of the play declares her intention never to marry anyone, let alone a foreigner – is in a continual flutter at the antics of her new acquaintances, too innocent even to pick up on de Staël's relationship with Narbonne and Talleyrand. But as the cynical Talleyrand observes to D'Arblay, a virtue that protests as much as Fanny's is a virtue conscious of its weakness; her prudishness must be a sign of 'combustibles within'. Sure enough, by the time Act 1 has been drawn to a dramatic close with the announcement of the execution of Louis XVI it is clear that Fanny is aflame with passion for D'Arblay.

The feeling is mutual, and by Act 2 they are teaching each other their respective languages, he calling her his 'Professor', and writing essays for each other to correct. Their unfolding feelings are expressed with Austenian elegance. The language of the period came effortlessly to Winifred; she had imbibed the style of *Pride and Prejudice* early in life and even in her own letters was liable at times to fall into eighteenth-century diction. 'Nothing,' D'Arblay tells Fanny, 'could be sweeter to me than your compassion, and nothing could be more dishonest in me than to solicit it; for I think I had never reason to be happier in my life.' In another sense, though, the question of language poses a problem: the script is of course in English, but it is not always clear whether the characters are supposed to be speaking in English or in French.

When D'Arblay declares his love he is repulsed by Fanny, who has taken to heart a warning by Talleyrand that marriage in France is no more than a business arrangement and that when a Frenchman speaks of love it is not marriage he has in mind. Happily she realises her mistake in time. Fearing that she may be throwing away her only chance of happiness, she resolves instead to throw 'the proprieties' to the winds and let D'Arblay know her sentiments.

Fanny Burney was the first of a series of female writers whose lives Winifred was to chronicle both in drama and biography. She was always drawn to her subjects by empathy; in the case of her plays, a particularly crucial episode in her subjects' lives caught her attention and gave her an insight into their character.

She doggedly sought a stage for her play, employing her friends and contacts to assist her. Perhaps her years with Eugène, who had been constantly on the lookout for openings in the musical world, had helped her develop the skills she now needed to market her writing. She asked Moore if he could show the play to his friend Desmond McCarthy, whom Winifred admired as a literary critic, but his opinion, if sought, is not recorded. In 1950 Winifred sent the play to Duff Cooper, whose book on Talleyrand had planted the germ of the drama in her mind. In a kindly reply he wrote that he was no judge of its suitability for the stage, and that he had always longed to write drama himself but had never made the attempt. He told her he had enjoyed reading the play: 'You have, it seems to me, admirably caught the spirit of that age and written a charming comedy.' He had some criticisms, however: there were too many people and not enough plot, and he suggested dropping some of the secondary characters and developing the main characters and plot lines.[85]

After trying in vain for the West End, Winifred found a company willing to produce the play in the vicinity of Juniper Hall. This was

---

[85] Letter of 24 December 1950 (Greenwood papers).

the Under Thirty Theatre Group, soon to be renamed the Leatherhead Theatre Club. Set up after the end of the War to give young actors professional experience, the group had recently found a permanent home at the Victoria Hall in Leatherhead, where it enjoyed considerable success in the 1950s and 60s.

Winifred found having her play staged hugely enjoyable. She adored the rehearsals. The new venture brought back the thrill of Old Vic productions and being on Parisian film sets with Eugène. But then she had simply been an onlooker; this time she was backstage watching her own creation being brought to life. She approved of the cast, finding Rosemary Webster perfect as Fanny because she had an 'eighteenth-century face' as well as the necessary 'charm, inner tranquillity and old-world dignity' for the part.[86] Michael Allinson, later to make a career for himself on Broadway, she found a worthy D'Arblay.

Juniper Hall premiered on 5 May 1952, close to the bicentenary of Fanny's birth (13 June 1752), to enthusiastic audiences, Winifred told the Moores. The reviews mostly praised the play, *The Times* calling Mme de Staël's part 'a gift to the stage'.[87] The actress Yvonne Arnaud even offered Winifred a West End production, which Winifred turned down as Arnaud wanted to make Mme de Staël's the star part at the expense of Fanny's.[88]

Reporting to the Moores on the play's success, Winifred apologised for blowing her own trumpet but could not help sounding exultant. She began to think that she had found her literary calling, and immediately started on her next play.

'Our only recourse is in work', she wrote in a letter to Marthe, written following Maurice's death from a heart attack in April of that year. Widowhood created a fresh bond between Marthe and Winifred, who remembered to write to her on the first anniversary of her marriage after Maurice's death. It was an *annus horribilis* for the family in Rue Georges Moreau: Eugénie died of cancer in the summer of that year after a long illness.

'The void around us would be ten times more horrible if we couldn't use all our energies to do the work each of us is suited to', Winifred wrote to the Gérins in one of her letters of this period. She had discovered the same antidote for grief as Charlotte Brontë, who wrote after the death of her sisters, 'Labour must be the cure, not sympathy –

---

[86] Letter of 11 May 1952. Letters from Winifred and Nell in G.E. Moore papers, MS Add.8330 8 B/17 and G/5, Cambridge University Library [hereafter Moore papers].

[87] *The Times*, 6 May 1952.

[88] According to Winifred's unpublished memoir.

Labour is the only radical cure for rooted Sorrow'.[89] In Winifred's case as in Charlotte's, the labour referred to was, of course, writing.

Apart from the need to lose herself in work, Winifred had enjoyed her taste of making a name for herself through her writing and having a public, and she was soon craving a repetition of the excitement of rehearsals and performances. Over the next two or three years she wrote more plays. She continued to take her favourite women writers as subjects; *Jane, or Fallacious Inferences*, described by her as a 'comedy of manners, a pastiche of the Austen vein',[90] followed *Juniper Hall* in 1953.

Winifred never attempted a biography of Jane Austen, but her play about her is redolent of Austen's books and period. Winifred is comfortably at home in Georgian England. As in *Juniper Hall*, she captures effortlessly every turn of the elegantly balanced Johnsonian speech of the time, as when Jane says of unwelcome callers who have ventured out on a rainy day, 'Their wet stockings . . . should arouse our compassion, even if their folly provokes our contempt.'

The comedy makes Jane the heroine of a real-life romance of her own; writing it must have been a perfect antidote to the flatness of life post-war, post-Eugène in the England of the 1950s. Winifred based it on a sketchy anecdote told by Jane's sister Cassandra in old age about a man Jane met at a Devon resort when she was in her twenties. The man, a shadowy figure in the story handed down, seemed interested in Jane and she looked forward to meeting him at the same resort the following summer – but she then heard that he had died. Winifred developed this merest hint of a romance into the love of Jane's life and set it in Sidmouth in 1801, an unsettled period for the novelist; her rector father had just retired from the beloved childhood home at Steventon and taken up residence in Bath, a town Jane disliked.

In fact more is known about another aborted romance of Jane Austen's – her friendship with Tom Lefroy, an Irish law student with whom she enjoyed a brief flirtation in 1795. In old age he confessed to having had a 'boyish' love for her, but neither had any money to marry on and nothing came of it; Lefroy became a barrister, married an heiress and had seven children. Winifred preferred to build her

---

[89] Letter to W.S. Williams, 25 June 1849. Smith, *Letters of Charlotte Brontë*, Vol. II, p. 224.
[90] Letter of 11 January 1955 to the West of England Theatre Company (BPM papers).

romance for Jane around the mysterious man at the Devon resort. Since nothing whatsoever is known about him, she was free to shape him into a hero worthy of Jane Austen.

For Austenites one of the pleasures of the play is that of spotting characters and situations inspired by the novels. The sprightly Jane herself has much in common with Elizabeth Bennett. She is also something of an Emma Woodhouse, believing herself to be clear-sighted even while being led by 'fallacious inferences' to misinterpret situations and characters. Mr Austen is a Mr Bennett in his ironical enjoyment of others' folly. Ample food for his sarcasm is provided by their Sidmouth acquaintance Mrs Portal, a tyrannical matron reminiscent of Lady Catherine de Burgh. She orders everyone around and bullies a fretful daughter with a nervous cough like Kitty Bennett's who exclaims 'Oh Lord, I'm famished!' in the manner of Kitty's flighty sister Lydia. Mrs Portal provides much of the comedy as she lectures and patronises everyone, accusing Mrs Austen of sacrificing her daughters' pleasures to her own wishes while ordering her own browbeaten daughter to the library to take out *Mrs Pembleton's Advice to the Downtrodden Women of England*, the strong-minded Mrs Portal being a self-proclaimed upholder of women's rights.

Mrs Portal wishes to marry off a rich niece, the spoiled and sulky Lady Honoria Blyh. The suitor on whom she has set her sights is Captain Fitzalan Herbert, a naval officer just arrived in Sidmouth with his fellow officer Lieutenant Bolton. Unlike Bolton, who has only his good looks to recommend him, Herbert is viewed by her as having great expectations, being the heir to a wealthy elder brother who is 'in a decline'. Herbert, however, is himself in poor health, having sustained a wound in a naval battle.

When the Captain shows signs of being more interested in the rector's younger daughter than in Lady Honoria – who, in turn, seems to have a perverse inclination to chat to Lieutenant Bolton – Mrs Portal's aim becomes that of keeping Jane and Herbert apart. Meanwhile, Jane herself risks alienating Herbert, a man she finds 'sensible, agreeable, modest and heroic', by rejecting his overtures and treating him as a sparring partner rather than potential partner for life, suspecting him to be a fortune-hunter intent on marrying Lady Honoria's £15,000 and of showing interest in herself only to make Honoria jealous.

When Jane realises – too late, as she believes – that her suspicions were false, she fears she may have 'forfeited a life of felicity'. Winifred fashions a delightful hero in Captain Herbert. Lacking Lieutenant Bolton's obvious good looks but possessing 'something more subtle', he combines the virtues of the man of action and the man of feeling, the glamour of Austen's naval hero Captain Wentworth with the modesty of a Darcy, and has a sparkle to match Jane's own.

The love drama unfolds against a backdrop of comedy, with a final dénouement on the cliffs where Mrs Portal has organised a pleasure party. Lady Honoria and the two naval gentlemen fail to appear and, to Jane's anguish, Honoria is believed to have eloped with Captain Herbert with Bolton's aid. A letter from Honoria, boasting of her elopement in Lydia Bennett style, reveals Bolton not Herbert to be the groom, but Jane's misery is not yet over since she fears that her behaviour has driven Herbert away for good. A gentleman is descried ascending the cliff path but at that moment a sea mist breaks up the party. Jane, the last to linger, bumps into Captain Herbert in the mist as he reaches the top. By the time it has dispersed, so have their doubts about each other, and Jane now regrets her tendency to see plots and intrigue everywhere she looks. Like Emma Woodhouse when the scales fall from her eyes, she wishes in future for a life free of deception, and like Anne Elliot when united at last with Captain Wentworth, she is happy in the prospect of being a sailor's wife despite the inconveniences.

The play ends with an epilogue that jumps forward 14 years. Jane's novels are enjoying increasing popularity and her brother Henry has invited her publisher and fans to a surprise party for her in London. Jane's sister-in-law Mary wonders why Jane never married and Henry reveals that she gave her heart away once and for all many years before.

'And the man jilted her?' Mary surmises.

'No,' Henry tells her. 'The man died'.

The play ends with an apprehensive Jane, like Fanny Burney when she was revealed to be the author of *Evelina*, or Charlotte Brontë when the London literary world discovered her to be the creator of *Jane Eyre*, preparing with trepidation to meet her fans in the flesh and be lionized.

Once again, Winifred had written about a favourite writer falling in love. *Jane* was unusual in that the romance in question was an imagined one, something that might have happened rather than something that did happen. In this it strikes a modern note and looks forward to the later fashion for fictional biographies, fertile in building on any suggestion of romance in the lives of certain nineteenth-century female writers or fabricating imaginary love stories for them.

She did not find a company to produce the play. As with her first one, the size of the cast and the expense of the necessary period costumes was a deterrent. However, on 7 October 1953 *Juniper Hall* was broadcast on radio by the Canadian Broadcasting Corporation under the name *The Reputation of Miss Fanny Burney*, with Aileen Seaton and Budd Knapp as Fanny and D'Arblay.[91]

By 1954, Winifred was working on the play that was to prove a turning point in her life and take it in a direction she could never have imagined, the play that set her on the path to Haworth. It was called *My Dear Master: The Love Story of Charlotte Brontë*.

It was natural that, having 'done' Fanny Burney and Jane Austen, Winifred should turn next to Charlotte Brontë, a favourite author since the days of listening to her mother reading *Jane Eyre* on the balcony at Norwood. Since Winifred's marriage she had been espe-cially intrigued by Charlotte's time in Brussels – a time of emotional ferment in her life. In Charlotte's love for Heger and her relationship with both him and his wife during her two years as a pupil-teacher at the Hegers' boarding school, Winifred found a theme as suited to her as Fanny's encounter with D'Arblay and the other French émigrés. Her experience of French and Belgian life gave the subject of cultural differ-ences a personal appeal. In *My Dear Master* the struggle between Charlotte and Zoë Heger, the directress of the Pensionnat whose husband Charlotte has come to love, is a clash of cultures as well as a battle between rivals in love and between two temperaments antago-nistic to each other.

Winifred said of this new play, 'What has interested me particularly in this incident of her life is the contrast it affords between the racial, religious and moral codes of two opposed natures like Mme Heger and Charlotte. My object has been to show how strong was Charlotte's moral fibre in the greatest crisis of her life, and how heroic, when all is said and done.'[92]

The precise nature of Charlotte Brontë's feeling for the tutor to whom she wrote desperate letters after her return to Haworth, pleading for some sign of affection and concern, has always intrigued students of her life, and these letters can be read in various ways. Was her infatuation an acute case of a schoolgirl 'crush' on a teacher? Did she simply yearn for his friendship, for fellowship? Or did the letters reveal real passion, and if so – most intriguing of all – was Charlotte fully aware of her real feelings? Equally uncertain is precisely how Heger and his wife interpreted her appeals; what is known is that as her tone became more intense, Heger instructed her to write less often

---

[91] *CBC Times*, 4–10 October 1953.
[92] In the *Yorkshire Post*, 11 May 1955.

and finally stopped replying. In *Villette*, written ten years later, Charlotte develops a love story between her volatile hero, the teacher M. Paul – into whom she put much of the personality of Heger – and her apparently mousy but inwardly fiery narrator Lucy Snowe, who shares many traits with Charlotte herself. The spying Mme Beck, the directress of the Pensionnat in the novel, who jealously tries to come between Lucy and M. Paul, is generally supposed to be based on Mme Heger, though clearly caution is required when matching the characters and relationships Charlotte explores in fiction with the real-life ones that provided the germ for them.

In Winifred's interpretation of the Charlotte–Heger–Mme Heger triangle her sympathies are with Charlotte and against Madame. When Charlotte's letters to Heger were published in 1913, some saw them as an expression of a guilty passion while others asserted the innocence of Charlotte's feelings. Winifred ranged herself with the latter, seeing Charlotte's love for Heger as essentially innocent because Charlotte herself was unaware of anything wrong in it, or at any rate refused to view it through the eyes of convention and small-mindedness. In Winifred's play, Charlotte experiences her encounters with Heger as a meeting of minds in a place removed from mere sensuality, a place she describes as her 'Eden'. Mme Heger's inability to appreciate this and jealous suspicions make her the serpent who introduces guilt and shame into the 'Eden' by forcing Charlotte to view her feeling for Heger in a light in which it can be seen as romantic passion.

Inevitably, the romantic and fiercely unconventional Charlotte gets more eloquent lines than Mme Heger, who is the defender not just of her marriage but of prudence and *les convenances* (the proprieties, keeping up appearances). Charlotte, claiming to be more able to understand Heger's real nature than his wife, is given lines such as:

'He moves in a world that will always be closed to you! A world of the spirit, where only the pure in heart can come . . . That he has been good to me, generous of his time and knowledge, kindling by his imagination, comforting by the warmth of his compassion, healing by his laughter: all this I acknowledge, and for all this I love him and *shall* love him for as long as I live. If it is evil to love what is good, then I have done evil. But, for your suspicions of him, they are as false as they are unfounded. Your husband has *never* . . . sought to express a sentiment that he should *not* express for me. His conduct has been as exalted as *yours* has been beneath contempt.'

Madame's defence of herself is, by its nature, inevitably less fiery and stirring. When accused by Charlotte of cruelty in trying to prevent her from having a final meeting with Heger before she leaves Brussels, Madame retorts, 'I am a practical woman. I see things as they are. Not distempered by the fever that men call "poetry". One day . . . when this frenzy is over . . . you will thank me that I spared you the worst remorse a woman can know.' But Madame does have an eloquence of her own when defining her own culture, which has come into collision with Protestant and English values as well as with Charlotte Brontë's particularly free and individualistic spirit:

> 'I value decorum, it is true; and you do not. You are an Englishwoman, very free in your opinions and your language . . . And though you have chosen to reside abroad, you have not chosen to conform to the pattern of behaviour that obtains abroad. Oh, I am quite aware that you despise the rules of conduct generally accepted among women of our milieu. But the regrettable result is that you lay yourself open to misapprehension. I follow a rule of life which is as good as any other I have met with – and better than some. It is to *avoid* the appearance, even, of opprobrious conduct. This you have, to my infinite regret, neglected to do . . . '

The threat to the reputation of Mme Heger's Pensionnat caused by gossip about Charlotte and Heger is one reason why Madame has to get rid of her.

As for Heger, the cause of the hostilities, Winifred of course paints him as delightful, as everything his wife is not: childlike and spontaneous, impulsive and unsuspicious. Fond of his wife, kind to everyone, he feels no guilt in having a genuine interest in and affection for Charlotte. But in Winifred's portrayal he does have something beyond that: there is in him a romanticism, alien to his wife's nature, which responds to Charlotte's own. Like M. Paul reading Lucy's character in her face, Heger is able to see into Charlotte's soul. 'There is below this forehead, behind those flashing eyes, a world struggling to be born.' He wishes to help her genius to find expression: 'It is Chaos yet, but who can tell how soon there may be light? I cannot *make* that light, I am not God; but I can perhaps bring it nearer.'

Winifred manipulates the triangle for dramatic effect, and in the play's dénouement things are said and done that are more likely to have taken place in Charlotte's fantasies than in the decorous setting of the Pensionnat. Mme Heger confronts Charlotte openly, and Heger accuses his wife of cruelty and unworthy suspicions; as Charlotte is about to set off on her homeward journey Heger embraces her and pleads with her to stay, with echoes of Rochester trying to dissuade

Jane from flight. He pleads with Charlotte for his own sake as well as hers. He needs her; she is the 'child of his spirit'.

Another, surely more credible reading of the situation is that the bourgeois and deeply religious Heger, despite his love of Romantic poetry, his eccentricities and temperamental outbursts, was as concerned with the proprieties as his wife; that he was in no way attracted by Charlotte in a romantic way, and that her obsession with him was something both the Hegers found excessive and dealt with together, as a couple. His lack of response to her letters was probably the result of a joint decision by both husband and wife that it was best to be cruel to be kind. As for Winifred's portrayal of Madame Heger, although Charlotte was antagonised by the ceaseless surveillance she exercised, other ex-pupils remembered her as a wise and fair superintendent rather a cold-blooded Mme Beck.

By the time Winifred wrote her biography of Charlotte Brontë in 1967, her view of Madame Heger had evolved into a much more nuanced one with greater sympathy for her predicament:

> By all accounts – from family, friends, pupils – she was an upright and charitable woman accustomed to dealing with a large school with no harsher measures than a grave reproof. Miss Brontë, however, was no child to be reproved . . . She was a woman of 27, with exceptionally complex feelings and sensibilities, vulnerable to pain as few adults are vulnerable, secretive and proud. Even if Madame Heger had felt so inclined she could not have spoken to Charlotte without outraging her pride and bringing upon herself the odium of harbouring thoughts unworthy of a lady. The very frankness Charlotte accused Madame Heger of *not* possessing was made impossible by the very nature of the case: for, of the three principals involved, only *one* was fully awake to what was going on. Madame Heger cannot be blamed for having greater insight than Charlotte or her husband; her nature was simply different from theirs. Nor can she be blamed for hesitating to rouse them to a consciousness of the danger lying ahead. She was obliged therefore to use methods that very likely appeared underhand to Charlotte, in order to isolate Charlotte both from her master and her fellow teachers. She was prepared to watch over her privacy, and Charlotte did not hesitate to call this spying.[93]

Throughout 1954 the play went the rounds of London actors and producers but Winifred did not find a stage for it in the West End.

---

[93] Gérin, *Charlotte Brontë: The Evolution of Genius*, Chapter 14.

Common criticisms, levelled also at her previous plays, were that there was too little action, the speeches were over-long and the language too literary. As in *Juniper Hall*, the language issue was felt to be confusing; on the one hand the dialogue is peppered with French expressions while, on the other, Heger sometimes misuses English idioms even at times when he can be supposed to be speaking in French.

As with *Juniper Hall*, Winifred had to seek outside London for a home for the play. She found one at the Playhouse Theatre in Amersham, Buckinghamshire. Since opening in 1936, this repertory theatre had attracted young actors of the calibre of Dirk Bogarde, Denholm Elliott and Rosemary Leach at the start of their careers. By the time Winifred's play was produced, however, the theatre was on its last legs, with dwindling audiences; it closed the following year. *My Dear Master* opened on 16 May 1955 under the direction of Terence O'Regan, whose performance as Heger was felt by critics to be overly bombastic; the greatest praise was reserved for Megan Latimer as his wife. While reviewers praised some aspects of the script, it was on the whole received with less enthusiasm than *Juniper Hall*. Winifred herself, despite the pleasure of being once again admitted backstage and involved in decisions on sets and costumes, felt that the actors were miscast and was disappointed with the production.

Her disappointment is likely to have been tempered by a new buoyancy in her emotional life, which for the past few months had been undergoing a metamorphosis. She was already contemplating a change – personal, professional, geographical – that was to take her far away from her life in West Cromwell Road and give her a creative focus that would drive her for the rest of her life. This sea change had come about as a result of an encounter in the summer of 1954 which proved to be the most momentous since she heard Eugène Gérin playing Ravel's *Pavane* in Cannes over twenty years earlier.

11

Haworth
Brontë Atmosphere

In June 1954 Winifred and Nell went to Yorkshire for a two-week break. For Nell it was a sketching holiday, for Winifred an opportunity to visit Haworth, for despite her lifelong interest in the Brontë family she had never been there. Charlotte's rapturous description of the moors in *My Dear Master* had sprung from Winifred's imagination before she saw them with her own eyes:

> When the full moon rode out on the moors, and the winds unleashed their coursers in the sky, and we stumbled and ran and plunged in the surging heather as in a sea – ! Oh, yes! *Then* we were gay! Delirious, drunken, with the hum and howl of the earth and sky in commotion – Spring dusks, when the rain was driving and the curlews hounded us on, and the lash of the wind fell on the back of the tall thin blades of the grasses – and the roar and turbulence of a rocking world were in our ears like an incantation to escape and to speed with all things – like spirits – to an appointed spot! though no one could tell and we never found, *where* that was! Since no path showed on the moors – only a dazzle of lights in the distance that might have been stars – or the front of a house illumined, to beckon us home!

After seeing Haworth, however, Winifred was to claim that in order to understand the Brontës you had to experience the moors for yourself; that in order to write about the Brontës you had to experience the moors in all seasons and weathers; and that the way to do this was to live in Haworth yourself.

Winifred was in need of a holiday that summer. She had been working too hard at both her music and her writing, and since 1953 had had periods of feeling unwell. Angina was diagnosed and for a time she became a virtual invalid, cutting down on her singing and other activities. The angina in fact proved to be mild and their doctor was not unduly worried, but both she and Nell had been under strain since Gilbert had finally decided it was time to retire and taken herself off to live with cousins in Kent. Predictably, she proved to be irreplaceable. A Mrs Gullich who succeeded her seemed to get through far less work, and 'servant problems' had started to figure frequently in both Nell's and Winifred's letters.

They had booked into what was at the time virtually the only bed and breakfast accommodation in Haworth, the Brontë Guest House at the top of Main Street (today the Old White Lion), run by a Mr and Mrs Standish. They were congenial hosts, and friendships would often be struck up among guests.

Arriving in Haworth shortly after completing her play about Charlotte and Heger, her head full of the biographical reading she had done to refresh her knowledge, Winifred experienced an epiphany on her first sight of the Parsonage and the moors. She had hitherto pictured the grey house and the landscape through the eyes of the biographers she had read. In the opening lines of *The Three Brontës*, for example, which Winifred had read in her twenties, May Sinclair had written:

> It is impossible to write of the three Brontës and forget the place they lived in, the black-grey, naked village, bristling like a rampart on the clean edge of the moor; the street, dark and steep as a gully, climbing the hill to the Parsonage at the top; the small oblong house, naked and grey, hemmed in on two sides by the graveyard, its five windows flush with the wall, staring at the graveyard where the tombstones, grey and naked, are set so close that the grass hardly grows between. The church itself is a burying ground; its walls are tombstones, and its floor roofs the forgotten and the unforgotten dead.
>
> A low wall and a few feet of barren garden divide the Parsonage from the graveyard, a few feet between the door of the house and the door in the wall where its dead were carried through. But a path leads beyond the graveyard to 'a little and a lone green lane', Emily Brontë's lane that leads to the open moors.
>
> It is the genius of the Brontës that made their place immortal; but it is the soul of the place that made their genius what it is. You cannot exaggerate its importance. They drank and were saturated with Haworth. When they left it they hungered and thirsted for it; they sickened till the hour of their return. They gave themselves to it with passion, and their works ring with the shock and interchange of two immortalities. Haworth is saturated with them. Their souls are henceforth no more to be disentangled from its soul than their

bodies from its earth. All their poetry, their passion and their joy is there, in this place of their tragedy, visible, palpable, narrow as the grave and boundless.

Despite the impact that Haworth has invariably had on Brontë biographers from Gaskell onwards, and the effectiveness of some of their descriptions, when Winifred saw the place for herself she felt that something essential had been left out of their accounts, namely a real sense of the *beauty* of the natural setting. The legendary grimness of Haworth and the moors were almost always emphasised to the detriment of all else.

Seeing this setting for herself, being able to stand in the tiny playroom where the Brontë children had acted out their stories, remembering her own childhood make-believe games with her three siblings in the house in Norwood, being able to look out of the window and see the view over the churchyard that the little Brontës had seen, was for Winifred quite different from reading about it or imagining it. Her revelation in Haworth was something hard to put into words. It was a sense of a new understanding of and empathy with the Brontës after seeing their environment, a sense that she had previously only dimly comprehended the physical background to their lives. Countless other visitors to Haworth have had similar sensations; the perception of the Brontës' environment as a powerful formative influence is common enough. In Winifred's case her 'epiphany' was in part simply a consequence of the importance that places always had in her own life and her vision of other lives. 'Places, as opposed to people, have always meant a great deal to me', she wrote in her autobiography. 'The atmosphere and setting of a place has as much character, as distinct features, as the expressions of a face, and is often more instant in creating sympathy and seduction.'

It was at the height of June, the weather was splendid, and while Nell sat at her easel Winifred walked around on the moors in a more ecstatic state of mind than she had known since Eugène's death. She has a companion on her walks, for John Lock, a fellow guest at Mr and Mrs Standish's, had offered to be her guide. He was a keen walker and mountaineer and had, he told them, spent holidays in the Alps and climbed the Matterhorn. His other main interest was the Brontës, and in Haworth he was able to indulge both passions. It was the second summer he had stayed there and he was already familiar with the surrounding countryside.

For him, one of the main appeals of the Brontës was the inspiration they drew from the moors, at least in Emily's case, while the most powerful appeal of the moors, of course, was that they were pervaded by the spirit of the Brontës – though he was quick to claim beauty for them in their own right. He was one of those Brontë lovers who arrive at Haworth as at a shrine, in the religious as well as literary sense of the word; not just as admirers but as worshippers. The Brontës seem to attract more of such adoration than any other writers and as with the saints of old, the veneration in which they are held extends to the places associated with them. Ranging the moors, their devotees seek the 'spirit' of Emily Brontë – often the object of their particular worship – which they feel to be at large there, perhaps hoping for 'mystical' experiences such as they believe hers to have been. At a more prosaic level, they take an obsessive interest in every detail of the Brontës' lives, acquiring an encyclopaedic knowledge of the objects by which the family was surrounded, the smallest incidents that marked their lives, every place they ever visited, every local family with which they had the most tenuous connection – an interest that often surpasses even that taken in their work.

Such fanaticism may be found alongside a certain lack of fulfilment in the devotee's own life. At the time he met Winifred, John Lock had resolved to give up his office job and devote himself to literature, and more specifically to some literary project involving the Brontës. For the moment he contemplated writing a guide to Haworth and walks in the countryside around it. There appears to have been a lack of direction in his life up to that summer of 1954. An only child, born in July 1921, he had grown up in Purley, not far from the Surrey suburb of Winifred's own childhood. His father William was a chartered accountant. John spent three years at Ardingly College in Sussex, leaving in 1937 at the age of 16. He did not go on to university, and the War came before he had had time to settle in a career.

William Lock was something of a war hero. Having been a pilot in the First World War he served again in the Second as an officer in the RAF Volunteer Reserve. Young John followed his father into the RAF, though as an air controller, not a pilot. After the War he had various jobs in banks, including an unhappy spell in Canada, but his dreams were of being a writer. William Lock died in 1953. His widow was left comfortably enough provided for but his estate was fairly modest and it is not entirely clear how John intended to fund a life as a man of independent means.

Be that as it may, he was full of hopes for the future and he and Winifred discussed their respective enthusiasms and plans over breakfast and then on their first walks together, when he impressed her with his knowledge of the Brontës and his ability to recite their verse. Her interest in the family, revived while writing *My Dear Master*, was kindled into new ardour by John's enthusiasm. He shared her deep love of nature and her affinity with the nature-worshipping Emily. They found common ground, too, in their interest in nineteenth-century literature, history (they were both devoted to the Stuarts) and music.

They talked about the War. He was riveted by the stories of her adventures in Belgium and France. His own war had been much less exciting – although he had been posted abroad at one stage, to Gibraltar – and some incidents had made an unhappy mark on him. Before joining the RAF he had been in the Home Guard. A perfume factory in Croydon took a direct hit during the Blitz and images of the dead and dying factory girls he helped to evacuate haunted him for life. Many of his Ardingly friends had been killed, many RAF pilot friends shot down.

He listened with interest, too, when Winifred told him about Eugène, whom she always portrayed as a war hero. Her devotion to her husband's memory made a strong impression on him. Many other things about her impressed him too: her knowledge of literature and history, her writing. John was twenty years younger than Winifred. They met when she was almost fifty-three, he just coming up to his thirty-third birthday. She was gratified by his admiration of her, and in turn was attracted by a romanticism in him to which her own nature responded. The combination of his youthful enthusiasm with nature in its June splendour was having an effect on her spirits that she had not imagined would ever be possible again.

The spell worked on her cannot have been lessened by the fact that John was a good-looking man with charming manners. When she left Haworth they agreed to continue the acquaintance. They started to meet regularly in London, where they went to concerts and museums together.

They also met again in Haworth, to which Winifred made further visits, as she was trying to find a Yorkshire theatre company willing to put on *My Dear Master*. She was helped in this by the Yorkshire writer Phyllis Bentley, author of several books on the Brontës and a leading light in the Brontë Society, who took a particular interest in Charlotte's Brussels period; in 1953 she had met the first member of the Heger family to visit Haworth, Simone Beckers née Heger, a grand-daughter of Constantin. Bentley was encouraging about Winifred's play although she was critical of some aspects, feeling that the portrayal of Mme Heger was too harsh and that the real Charlotte came out of the Heger episode less creditably.

In 1955 a Leeds theatre company offered to stage the play. By this time Winifred's head was seething with ideas for further writing projects focusing on the Brontës, and John Lock was increasingly forming a part of them. One of the first projects she contemplated appears to have been a book on Emily. On 4 March 1955 Nell wrote to Dorothy Moore in Cambridge, 'Winny went off yesterday for a few days to Haworth. She is writing a book on Emily Brontë and wanted local colour. She is staying with the people we were with last year, who will look after her well, and travelled up with a young man Brontë enthusiast we picked up in the summer. So all should be well . . . but I shall be glad to see her safely back . . . Our Scottish house-keeper left us today and I am tackling the new one. She seems very nice but I have grown sceptical.'[94] Nell herself was looking forward to fleeing domestic cares during a painting holiday in Greece, though she would enjoy it more, she told the Moores, if Winifred could go too.

One wonders whether poor Nell had any premonition at all during these months of how soon she was to be left to deal alone with the perennial servant problems at West Cromwell Road. While she was looking forward to having Winny 'safely back' in their placid life in Kensington, where the most traumatic events were the arrivals and departures of unsatisfactory housekeepers, Winny herself, walking the moors again with the 'young man Brontë enthusiast', was by now making very different plans.

In July of that year Marthe and Paul Gérin, alone in the house in Anderlecht since the deaths of Eugénie and Maurice, received a letter from Winifred. This was a common enough occurrence – although her letters had been scarcer in recent months – but this one had the effect of a bombshell in Rue Georges Moreau. Winny began by apologising for being a poor correspondent of late. The explanation was not long in coming.

> You will no doubt be very surprised – and I can hardly believe it myself – when I tell you that I am getting married again. My fiancé, John Lock, is a charming man, full of delicacy and goodness; very well-read, a great lover of music, a keen mountaineer and, above all, a great nature lover. Like me, he loves the past. He is not of this century. He went to one of the best English public schools and was in the RAF during the War. We met over a year ago in the village of the Brontë sisters (of whom he is a fervent admirer) and then got to know each other better in London. He was only waiting for me

---

[94] Moore papers.

to accept his offer of marriage in order to establish himself in Yorkshire (he is an accountant) and take a house in the place I love more than any other. We will spend most of the year there but I will often come and keep Nell company. It was on her account that I hesitated most, but she is very fond of my fiancé and knows how I will be spoiled and how well I will be looked after and is happy for me. She will often come and stay with us – the district is ideal for her painting.

We will have a very quiet wedding at the end of October, as soon as our house is ready and my play on Charlotte Brontë has been staged in Yorkshire. My fiancé will be going to Yorkshire from next week and I will often be joining him to oversee the work on the house and attend rehearsals of my play. Nell will join us for a holiday in September.

I don't need to tell you that I thought long and hard before taking such a big step, and one that I so little expected. My fiancé shows great delicacy in everything concerning my feelings for Eugène. He says that it's one of the things that most attracted him to me. He wants all the things commemorating Eugène to have their place in our house as they always have in mine.

I will be able to devote myself to literature more than ever with a husband so passionate about it. He himself, in his leisure hours, writes poetry, and spends all his evenings reading. We suit each other perfectly.

'You can feel sure that my affection for you will remain unchanged. I will always be the same Winny for you, and my remarrying doesn't change my sense of duty to Eugène's family in the least,' she concluded.

Paul did not altogether welcome the news and in her next letter to him and his mother Winifred sought to reassure them: 'One of the things that made John fall in love with me at our first meeting was my loyalty to my *amour disparu* of ten years ago. He wouldn't want me to neglect Eugène's family. Paul will understand one day that life brings many changes; nothing stands still.'

As for Nell, the person most affected by Winny's momentous decision, one can only imagine how she felt about it, but whatever her regrets on her own account and her doubts on Winifred's she probably accepted the change with her usual unselfishness. (Ironically in view of the fact that Winifred's literary career took off after the move to Haworth, Nell thought she would have more chance of success as a writer if she stayed in London.) One good thing came out of the change: to Winifred's huge relief, Gilbert agreed to return to West Cromwell Road, this time in her role as companion to Gui-Gui rather than housekeeper, and to live out the rest of her retirement in Kensington rather than Kent.

'Gimmerton', the home John had found for them in Haworth (it was his idea to baptise it with the name of the village near Wuthering Heights in Emily's novel), was a detached Victorian millstone grit house in West Lane, which leads out of the village towards the moors and the village of Stanbury. The house is just past the Methodist chapel in whose graveyard lies another Brontë biographer who lived in Haworth. This was Esther Alice Chadwick, author of *In the Footsteps of the Brontës*, who lived briefly in West Lane as a newly-wed in the late 1880s; after her death she was brought back there to be laid beside her first child, Elsie, who died in Haworth in infancy. Chadwick's biography was written many years after she left Haworth, but in it she drew on her contacts with villagers who had known the Brontë family.

Once the work on 'Gimmerton' was finished, John and Winifred were delighted with their new home. Nell found it 'grey and grim' without, while acknowledging that they had made it charming within. But her painter's eye must have delighted in the views. From the front of the house there were no houses opposite to impede the sight of the fields leading to Haworth moor. But it was the view from the back that was by far the most spectacular. From the bottom of the Worth valley lying below, the eye was swept up sheer green slopes climbing to the villages of Oakworth and Oldfield towards the north-west. The vistas were most glorious in the evenings, just before the sun dropped behind the hills, when the play of light and shade on the valley-side dotted with sheep, cattle and horses was at its most dramatic.

The months of Winifred's engagement went by in a flurry of visits to Yorkshire to get the house ready and attend rehearsals of *My Dear Master*, which opened on 4 October at the Leeds Civic Theatre, housed in what is now the City Museum. The production, by the Leeds Art Theatre, with which a youthful Peter O'Toole had recently made his debut, received better reviews than the one at Amersham. The *Yorkshire Post* praised the play as 'well-made' and its dialogue as excellent in conveying the period. As at Amersham, though, the actor playing Heger was criticised as over-histrionic.[95]

In the succeeding years Winifred continued to believe in the merit of her plays and seek outlets for them on the stage or on radio and television. On 12 April 1956 *Juniper Hall* was televised by the BBC with several members of the original Leatherhead cast, but more than one critic found it heavy-going and the dialogue stilted. Once firmly

---

[95] *Yorkshire Post*, 5 October 1955.

established in her new career as a biographer, Winifred was thankful that her visit to Haworth and meeting with John had led her to abandon playwriting in favour of her new literary departure.

She and John were married quietly in Kensington on 17 October, accompanied only by Nell and a friend of John's, and by John's mother, Sybil. Nell told the Moores that the newly-weds looked very happy as they set off for a ten-day honeymoon in Dublin. As Patrick Brontë's homeland and the country in which Charlotte Brontë spent her own honeymoon with her Irish curate husband Arthur Nicholls, Ireland was a fitting destination in which to launch their partnership in Brontë studies, and they doubtless started as they meant to go on by taking the opportunity for some research; either on this or a subsequent trip Winifred visited Banagher, the town where Nicholls spent most of his childhood.

By the end of the month they were installed in Gimmerton. The house was furnished with some of Winifred's French furniture from the Rue Dulong days and various antiques; either at this time or later they acquired a Yorkshire dresser dated 1801, the year indicated at the start of *Wuthering Heights*. Thanking Dorothy and Bill for their wedding present of two antique chairs, Winifred wrote that John delighted in them as much as she did, since 'nothing later than 1850 finds much grace in his sight; everything that belongs to the past appears naturally beautiful in his eyes.'[96] The sitting room cum dining room, to the left as you entered the house, became Winifred's study; the smaller room on the right, known as the music room, was John's. Space was found for Winifred's piano and Eugène's cello.

Although West Lane was viewed by the villagers as being outside the village proper, the Parsonage and church could be glimpsed from the first-floor windows of the house, and it was only a five-minute walk to the shops in Main Street. In those days, just before the tourist boom which took off in a big way in the 1960s, it was a very different street from the one of today, when practically every building is a gift shop or eatery. In Winifred's time there were still 'real' shops for the inhabitants rather than the visitors. Admittedly, there was already a Brontë café and a Brontë guest house, but there was also a butcher's, a greengrocer's and a hardware shop.

The new arrivals settled well into life in Haworth. Quiet village life suited John, and Winifred was too busy and happy to miss the plays and concerts and social life of London. She had fallen for Haworth's charms as well as John's. She loved the long, dramatic climb up Main

---

[96] Letter dated September 1955 (Moore papers).

Street – after Clovelly, the steepest village street in England – so tightly lined on either side by former weavers' cottages you had the sense of being in an enclosed, fortified place; and the abruptness with which, once you gained the Parsonage past the church at the top, the vista opened out onto the wide moors. She loved the sandstone houses. She loved the gas lamps that still lit the streets in those days. She had the same Wordsworthian sense of timelessness and the continuity of a way of life as on holidays in Plombières. The sheep on the hills were a continual reminder of the ancient trade that had made the township what it was, from the days when the cloth spun in the village by hand-loom weavers was carried on packhorses across the Pennine uplands to market.

In reality, though, despite Winifred's perceptions of timelessness and continuity in Haworth, below the surface all was not as idyllic as it appeared to her and John when they first arrived. They moved there at a time when many of the old ways of life and local amenities were under threat, as they were in other villages up and down the country. Although these were the years of Macmillan's 'You've never had it so good', the textile industry was in difficulties, the mills closing in the face of foreign competition. There was a decline in the local institutions that had been the pillars of community life, for example the friendly societies, dwindling since the National Insurance Act of 1948; the cooperative society, with local co-ops merging and branches closing – though Central Stores in Main Street was still open in this period; the Haworth Institute, which had provided educational evening classes but now offered only crafts for women – it closed in 1965. The new medium of television was killing off local entertainment; the Locks' years in Haworth saw the closure of the village's two cinemas. Another factor in the waning of local cultural and leisure activities was the steady fall in church-going, leading to a decline in the churches and chapels around which so much local culture and sport had been organised. The chapels' music and drama societies were doing fewer oratorios and Gilbert and Sullivan productions than in the days of large congregations. Even the cricket and football teams were lacklustre in these years. As their names denoted (Haworth Methodists, Haworth Baptists), they too had been organised around church and chapel.

Increased car ownership led to cuts in bus and train services: during the Locks' time in the village (they never owned a car themselves) the Worth Valley railway, the branch line serving villages and mills between Keighley and Oxenhope, closed down, to re-open later only as a weekend tourist attraction. The impact of the car, while it brought more visitors to Haworth, caused the traffic congestion and parking problems that were the subject of constant complaints by villagers – the bypass taking traffic out of Main Street was not built until after Winifred and John left Haworth.

The only industry that seemed to be thriving in Haworth, in fact, was tourism. The post-war years saw a surge in enthusiasm for the outdoors and the creation of national parks and official long-distance footpaths. Part of Haworth Moor was declared a country park; the Pennine Way, which passed close to the village and past Top Withens, was created in 1951. Rambles on the moors were one attraction for visitors; the other, of course, was the Brontë connection, with the Parsonage Museum attracting growing numbers of visitors. The hand-loom weavers who had formerly inhabited the cottages had been replaced by the Brontë industry of which Winifred and John were planning to be a part.[97]

Winifred reported that their new neighbours had made her and John welcome and shown them kindness – in their own Yorkshire way, of course, a way she had to become accustomed to. For she also reported that Yorkshire people lived up to their reputation of being blunt. She was discovering the truth of Elizabeth Gaskell's assessment of their character in the second chapter of her *Life of Charlotte Brontë*:

> Their accost is curt; their accent and tone of speech blunt and harsh. Something of this may, probably, be attributed to the freedom of mountain air and of isolated hill-side life; something be derived from their rough Norse ancestry. They have a quick perception of character, and a keen sense of humour; the dwellers among them must be prepared for certain uncomplimentary, though most likely true, observations, pithily expressed.

Surrey-bred Winifred was at first taken aback by the frequency with which this bluntness manifested itself in what she called 'strong language', until she realised, as she put it, that for her Yorkshire neighbours, swearing was an expression of strong feeling rather than of any wish to be offensive, and came as naturally to them as bleating did to the sheep on the hills around. Like Mrs Gaskell and other visitors over the centuries, she found many of the stereotypes about Yorkshire people to be largely accurate. They were independent and stubborn. They were not given to expressing emotion directly, but their feelings, whether of amity or enmity, went deep and lasted long – a friend was a friend for life, while a grudge could be passed down through generations of a family.

---

[97] Some of this information is taken from Baumber, *A History of Haworth*.

It is more difficult to gauge what the people of Haworth thought of the newcomers. Of course they were 'offcomed'uns', outsiders, but this was not in itself a barrier to acceptance. Among the very few villagers who remember them today, none of whom were close friends, John is recalled as having 'charming' manners, with a hint that they were rather suave by Yorkshire standards; Winifred by some as being talkative and friendly, with recollections of kindnesses received from her, such as wedding presents, sweets for the village children, coal for the poor; by others as 'reserved', giving away little about herself – 'the Locks kept themselves to themselves.'

Winifred herself spoke of the many friendships they made locally. New friends included Canon Dixon, the Rector of Haworth, and their next-door neighbours, Herbert and Edith Petty, a couple in their thirties. Mr Petty was the village postmaster. He also sold books and produced postcards of Haworth, and had a fund of knowledge and local lore about the Brontës.

He was one of many people in the village who could tell John and Winifred stories about the Brontë family. For a biographer, one of the charms of Haworth is the sense of living links with the Brontës in the form of villagers who turn out to be descendants of people who knew them. A casual conversation reveals that your interlocutor is descended from one of their friends or servants. Mrs Chadwick, who lived in Haworth only thirty years or so after Charlotte's death, could of course still talk to people who had known and worked for them – Tabitha Ratcliffe née Brown, for instance, the sister of the Brontës' servant Martha Brown (Martha was the daughter of the sexton John Brown, Branwell Brontë's great friend). A century after Charlotte's death, Winifred and John were able to meet Eleanor Stanton, Tabitha's daughter, who died in 1963. When Eleanor was a child, her Aunt Martha had transmitted to her the love of reading and knowledge that she herself had imbibed from Patrick Brontë.

Young Margaret Hartley, who kept the hardware shop in Main Street, was a descendant of the William Hartley who kept the post office in the years when the Brontës were sending manuscript novels by 'Currer, Ellis and Acton Bell' off to London publishers. Margaret married a village man who was descended from Browns and Ratcliffes. (At the time of writing, Margaret Hamer née Hartley still owns a shop in Main Street.) Winifred felt that such contacts helped her, as she wrote in the preface to her biography of Anne Brontë, to absorb 'something of the spirit of the family and of the place'.

With the pleasant young local woman who worked as their housekeeper, Irene – renowned for her wonderful baking – helping to run the house far more competently than any of Gilbert's successors in

Kensington, Winifred had long hours of freedom for rambles with John. The locals' predictions that the rigours of a first winter in the Pennines would drive the newcomers away were not realised, and as with Eugène in Paris, Winifred spent the first months of her new life in the north buoyed up on a wave of elation. The setting could not have been more different, but the mood, coming after years of loneliness and despondency, was similar. It was helped by the fact that the weather was unusually mild in the early months of that winter. In a letter to the Gérins in December she recounted walking to Top Withens, the ruined farmhouse popularly supposed to have inspired the site of Wuthering Heights, on a windless day of blue skies and brilliant sunshine, while London – so Nell reported in their weekly telephone conversation – was suffocating in fog. The days of dazzling sunshine continued, and when the snow finally arrived in February its glittering whiteness merely added to the enchantment of the scene. Winifred found something Alpine in the bracing air, and felt as rejuvenated in health as in spirits. She had no recurrence of her heart problems.

Friends who saw her on her visits to London noted that she seemed radiantly happy. 'I could never have imagined her as having any other husband than Eugène, and John is so different', Mina Breed, who confessed to feeling 'little enthusiasm for second marriages', told Paul Gérin, 'but he is clearly making her very happy.' Winifred herself told the Gérins how devotedly her husband looked after her while assuring them that Eugène, whose grave she continued to visit whenever she was in London, would always be remembered.

Her walks on the moors with John had a purpose, for he was planning a guide to Haworth to be published by their postmaster friend and neighbour Herbert Petty. The bulk of the guide was John's project, but Winifred was to write the foreword and a brief history of Haworth. The guide was to contain six walks near Haworth that had connections with the Brontës, with relevant quotations from their writings. While John measured distances and made notes about every path and stile, Winifred was becoming acquainted with the changing face of the moors in the seasonal cycle of the year. Her contribution to the guide provided an opportunity for the kind of descriptive writing that was to feature in her biographies. No written description, however, she felt, could fully evoke the moors for those who had not seen them:

'The immensity of moor', she wrote in her foreword, 'after the confinement of the village street, is what impresses most . . . There they are, rolling to the horizon's verge in a succession of breakers, like a billowing sea covered with high clusters of heather, clumps of bilberry and fern and broken in all their cavities by cascades of water, whose tinkle, plash and gurgle fill the earth with voices as the sky is filled by the jubilation of lark and linnet.'[98]

She discovered their subtle changes in colour as the pink flush of the bilberry bushes in spring gave way to the blue harebells of summer, to be succeeded in turn by the purple heather of August and September and the copper of the bracken in autumn. Like Emily and Emily's heroine Cathy, Winifred loved to lie on sunny days gazing up at the sky, studying cloud formations and listening to the larks and lapwings and curlews. At the invitation of a gamekeeper friend, she and John also spent hours lying flat on their stomachs, concealed among the heather, watching the grouse and their chicks in their friend's preserves.

Their *Souvenir Guide to Haworth, home of the Brontës*, published in May 1956, sold well and was reprinted in 1961. It style was far more rhapsodic and emotional than that of previous Haworth guide books. In the foreword Winifred expressed her view that most writers had dwelt on the more forbidding aspects of Haworth and its surroundings and failed to do justice to their beauty.

Did she and John go too far the other way and claim too much beauty for the Haworth moors? It is interesting to note that Charlotte Brontë, in a note in an edition of her sisters' writings published after their deaths, gives rather the opposite view of the landscape Emily loved, stating that it was a case of beauty being in the eye of the beholder.

The scenery of these hills is not grand – it is not romantic: it is scarcely striking. Long low moors, dark with heath, shut in little valleys, where a stream waters, here and there, a fringe of stunted copse. Mills and scattered cottages chase romance from these valleys; it is only higher up, deep in amongst the ridges of the moors, that Imagination can find rest for the sole of her foot: and even if she finds it there, she must be a solitude-loving raven – no gentle dove. If she demand beauty to inspire her, she must bring it inborn: these moors are too stern to yield any product so delicate. The eye of the gazer must *itself* brim with a 'purple light,' intense enough to perpetuate the brief flower-flush of August on the heather, or the rare sunset-smile of June; out of his heart must well the freshness, that in latter spring and early summer brightens the bracken,

---

[98] Lock and Gérin, *Souvenir Guide to Haworth*, p. 5.

nurtures the moss, and cherishes the starry flowers that spangle for a few weeks the pasture of the moor-sheep. Unless that light and freshness are innate and self-sustained, the drear prospect of a Yorkshire moor will be found as barren of poetic as of agricultural interest: where the love of wild nature is strong, the locality will perhaps be clung to with the more passionate constancy, because from the hill-lover's self comes half its charm.

My sister Emily loved the moors. Flowers brighter than the rose bloomed in the blackest of the heath for her; out of a sullen hollow in a livid hill-side her mind could make an Eden. She found in the bleak solitude many and dear delights; and not the least and best-loved was – liberty.[99]

The Locks' guide book, in contrast, refers to the splendours of the moors with the breathless excitement of enthusiasts to whom they were a recent revelation. The Brontës are descried everywhere we turn, effusively evoked with the fervour of votaries: 'But the Brontës live on; their presence felt in every ripple of the long grass; in every shimmering pool; every twig of heather; and their voices are heard mingling with the winds . . . '.[100] Of all the family it is Emily who is most omnipresent. 'What would these moors, that high carpet of grass, these rolling hills, what would they mean to us without the memory of Emily Jane Brontë?' wonders John Lock. 'Would they seem beautiful or grim? Haunt us or be forgotten? Most of us will never know, for it is her life, her writings, that have led us on, will draw us back again, just as surely as if she held our hand.'[101]

It is impossible to answer the question of how Haworth and the moors would appear to us if we were not viewing them through the medium of the Brontë legend, just as we cannot know how the Brontës' talents would have manifested themselves if they had grown up among the hills of Surrey rather than the Pennines. May Sinclair had written about the impossibility of 'disentangling' the Brontës' soul from the soul of Haworth. But did Haworth merely give the Brontë temperament an ideal setting in which to develop, or was it largely responsible for forming that temperament in the first place?

---

[99] Charlotte Brontë, *Prefatory Note to 'Selections of Poems by Ellis Bell'*, 1850. Reprinted in Smith, *Letters of Charlotte Brontë*, Vol. II, pp. 752–3. In her concern to win sympathy for Emily by presenting her as an unsophisticated child of nature living in a remote spot, Charlotte may, of course, have deliberately exaggerated the moors' bleakness in this passage.

[100] Lock and Gérin, *Souvenir Guide to Haworth*, p. 78.

[101] *Ibid.*, p. 84.

In 1961, with the Brontë 'industry' burgeoning and Main Street increasingly clogged by seekers after what was frequently referred to as the 'Brontë atmosphere', a reader of the *Keighley News* signing himself 'a puzzled native' dismissed as 'cant' this term so often on the lips of the enthusiasts who haunted Haworth. 'We can feel with Emily Brontë the influence of the nature of our beloved hills, and we do not need anyone to explain to us the true Brontë atmosphere of their charm.'[102] More than one reader pointed out that it was in the Brontës' writings rather than in Haworth that the 'Brontë atmosphere' was to be found. It was something created in the minds of readers; it was possible to breathe it without even having been to England, to live on the other side of the world and be more immersed in it than many of the natives of Haworth.

John's guide book was published in May, and with this first venture behind them the Locks began at once to capitalise on their familiarity with the 'Brontë atmosphere', however one chose to define it, by each setting to work on a new project.

Their friend Canon Dixon, the rector of Haworth, had suggested that he and John should write a life of Dixon's most famous predecessor, Patrick Brontë. The Locks' research on the history of the village for their guidebook had led them to the church registries, where Mr Dixon made available to them to a wealth of information on the forty years of Patrick's ministry. Just as John wanted his guide to correct the perception of Haworth as grim and bleak, so he and Dixon now set out to counter the image of Patrick as grim and tyrannical, an image first diffused by Mrs Gaskell. Although much toned down by subsequent biographers, it still lingered in the popular conception of the Brontës.

Both the Locks felt they had a mission to refute or revise certain elements of what Lucasta Miller was to call the 'Brontë myth'[103] initiated by Mrs Gaskell (it is doubtful whether, without her biography, the Brontës would ever have become the object of fascination they did). In fact the Locks were not alone in this, since many biographers since Gaskell had set about their task with a similar sense of mission and, as Miller shows, the mythology is in fact in continual evolution, each generation bringing to the interpretation of the Brontës different tastes, perceptions and preoccupations.

To say that Mrs Gaskell created the Brontës of popular mythology is not to say (as the Locks had a tendency to claim) that the image

---

[102] *Keighley News*, 30 September 1961.
[103] Lucasta Miller, *The Brontë Myth*, 2001.

created in her book was untrue. Patrick Brontë himself acknowledged that her account of Charlotte's life was substantially true even though he complained of certain exaggerations and inaccuracies. Some of the most glaring of these are found in her treatment of Patrick himself. John was indignant at her portrait of an eccentric recluse and domestic tyrant who shut himself up in his study leaving his motherless children to their own devices and, in the first edition of Gaskell's *Life*, cut up one of his wife's dresses because he disapproved of the cut and burned the children's boots because they were too brightly-coloured – anecdotes repudiated by Patrick and dropped by Gaskell from subsequent editions. John aimed to present instead a less entertaining but more accurate portrait of an affectionate father and conscientious parish priest toiling tirelessly to improve the lot of his parishioners.

Although the idea for the biography came from Canon Dixon and it was eventually published under both their names, most or all of the actual writing appears to have been done by John. The text included numerous citations from Patrick's letters. Scattered in libraries and private collections, these turned out to be far more in number than John had anticipated, and the book grew steadily in volume as more and more of Patrick's correspondence came to light.

Meanwhile, Winifred had chosen Anne Brontë rather than her more famous sisters as the subject of her first biography. In this she was influenced partly by John, who had a special affection for Anne and made annual pilgrimages to Scarborough to lay heather from Haworth on her grave high on the cliffs. But as a novice biographer, Winifred's main reason for focusing first on the sister who had always been kept in the shade by her own reserve as well as by the greater talents of her sisters – perhaps, too, by Charlotte's tendency to underestimate her – was diffidence about approaching either Charlotte or Emily as yet. Despite the lack of really comprehensive and well-researched Brontë biographies, a gap Winifred was to be one of the first to fill, one way and another a great deal of ink had been expended on both Emily and Charlotte in the century since Gaskell's *Life*. Much earlier biographers than Winifred (May Sinclair, for example, writing in 1912) had already felt daunted at the prospect of venturing onto such well-trodden ground. But there was no full-scale biography of Anne, and Winifred saw her as a means of feeling her way into familiarity with the rest of the family. At this stage of her and John's respective careers she knew much less about the Brontës than he did, and had some reason to feel diffident.

Another attraction of tackling Anne was the desire to do some myth-demolishing of her own. The more Winifred read about the youngest Brontë sibling the more she respected her and felt that she

had been underrated by previous chroniclers. Far from being colourless and weak, Winifred found her well worth knowing and indeed
heroic. 'In many ways she was even more admirable than her sisters,'
she wrote to Paul. She admired Anne's tenacity and sense of duty, and
the way she demanded so much of herself yet was so compassionate
towards others.

Winifred embarked on her first biography with zest. It is no wonder
that she appeared so happy to friends who saw her in her early years
in Haworth. She was in the first flush not just of her new marriage but
the discovery of what she now felt sure was her true vocation. Her
other literary ventures she now saw as false starts. Her plays had been
primarily exercises in character analysis, exploring character through
dialogue, which proved good preparation for becoming a biographer.
Biography, combining as it did character study, drama, history, and
descriptive writing, was for her the most complete and satisfying
literary form, the one towards which she had been groping her way all
her writing life.[104]

She was exhilarated by the detective nature of the research involved.
'One discovery leads to another, all the time,' she wrote to Dorothy
Moore. 'A name, a note, a title, if followed up, is continually throwing
light onto a whole, unsuspected sequence of events. I find it all
absolutely enthralling.'[105]

One of her primary concerns was to fill out, in all its density, the
physical and social background to the Brontës' lives that she felt had
often been no more than sketched in by previous biographers.

'I have followed her everywhere,' she wrote in her preface to her
biography of Anne, 'to see what she saw, to trace her passage and to
pursue every available trail that might give a feature and a shape to
those persons who, at the turnings in her life, accompanied her upon
part of her way and peopled her world – that world which every writer
from Mrs Gaskell down to the present time has represented as a kind
of a void, a social vacuum in which the Brontës moved alone without
human contact or sympathy of any kind. Thus the shadowy forms of
the Thornton godmother whose beautiful home, Kipping House, I was
privileged to visit; the enlightened schoolmistress, Margaret Wooler,
whose traces I was not content to follow to Roe Head and Heald's
House only, but from whose neglected grave in Birstall churchyard I
could not rest till I had removed the tangle of ivy and bramble; the
friend, Ellen Nussey, in her elegant homes at the Rydings and

---

[104] These views are expressed in her memoir.
[105] Letter of 9 January 1960 (Moore papers).

Brookroyd, the pupils, the clergymen who taught and influenced Anne, sprang to life for me. All these I have sought out wherever the traces of them can be found, even to the humblest relic. For sometimes it is from silent witnesses that much may be learned, as all, I think, will agree who have seen Aunt Branwell's lustre teapot with its text: "To me to live is Christ, to die is gain."'

She and John researched together, and their outings on the trail of the Brontës were one of the most enjoyable aspects of their partnership. It is difficult to imagine Winifred's marriage to John ever coming about without their common interest. Not only had it brought them together in the first place, but it was the bedrock of their marriage, forging a bond strong enough to overcome the twenty years' age difference and making them partners in both senses of the word, colleagues. Marriage with Eugène had been like a perpetual holiday, but this second marriage was about work rather than play. John and Winifred had given each other an occupation and a mission.

'This writer's life is ideal', Winifred told Paul, himself hard at work writing assignments for his university course, in July 1956. 'We spend eight hours a day writing, each in our own study looking out on the moors and the last rooftops of the village. We work all day and in the evening, after supper, at 9 or 9.30 we always go for a walk on the moors on these lovely evenings until sunset at 11 pm, and sometimes by moonlight. I feel wonderful and am very happy. Next month Nell is going to stay with us and do some painting.' Apart from regular visits from Nell and John's mother, they do not appear to have received many visitors in their Haworth retreat.

In breaks from writing there was work to be done in their garden with its incomparable view of the hills behind the house. They were as surrounded by animals as Emily Brontë had been, Winifred told the Gérins – horses and sheep, rabbits and birds. Either because of the danger from traffic in West Lane or because John was more enthusiastic about wild animals than domestic ones, they did not keep a pet in Haworth. However, they often borrowed a friend's dog for walks, and Winifred compensated for the lack of pets of her own by feeding all the stray cats in the neighbourhood and joining the committee of the Keighley RSPCA.

For much of the essential background to the Brontës' lives the Locks need seek no further afield than the Parsonage, where they could look at their relics and spend long hours reading their manuscripts. Here, their indefatigable search after knowledge of the former inhabitants of the house sometimes brought them into conflict with its present tenants. In those days there was a live-in custodian, Harold Mitchell. Since the opening of the Brontë Parsonage Museum in 1928 he and his family had lived in a flat in the Victorian wing added in the 1870s by Patrick's successor, John Wade. There was also a curator, Wyndham Vint. With both these men Winifred sometimes clashed over her requests for access to material. Mr Mitchell, in particular, found her demands too insistent and got on better with Daphne du Maurier, who was projecting a biography of Branwell Brontë and made friends with the Mitchells on visits to the Parsonage. On occasion she was known to sit long into the night in their flat discussing such points as the authorship of *Wuthering Heights*.[106]

Winifred could be impatient and imperious at times. Paul Gérin, who had been at the receiving end of her scoldings as an awkward schoolboy, had witnessed her, in London department stores, demanding peremptorily to see the manager when the service did not meet her standards and making sure that matters were arranged to her liking. Many people testified to her good-heartedness, but to some she could appear overbearing on occasion.

Clearly it was in Winifred's interests to be on friendly terms with the Brontë Society and its trustees, who oversaw the running of the museum, and the staff they employed. Apart from her and John's need to access the museum's collection, contact with the scholars the Society counted among its members arguably had its value as well as roaming the moors in search of 'atmosphere', and it might be imagined that the benefits of life as Haworth's resident Brontë biographers would include close relations with the Brontë Society. Unhappily, although they were friendly with individual members such as Phyllis Bentley, relations with the organisation started to turn sour from the very start of their time in Haworth.

In the mid-1950s the Brontë Parsonage Museum was thriving, with visitors averaging around 50,000 a year following a renewed surge of interest after the War, partly fuelled by popular film adaptations such as the 1939 *Wuthering Heights* starring Laurence Olivier. The Society was headed by the solicitor and mill owner Donald Hopewell, who was its President for over 40 years, and Sir Linton Andrews, editor of the *Yorkshire Post*, its Chairman. Both these scholarly men appear to have led the Society ably enough, and in 1957 it was described by a

---

[106] Dinsdale, *At Home with the Brontës*, pp. 71–3.
[107] *Keighley News*, 8 June 1957. The writer was Fred Taylor, the Keighley Borough Librarian. (Footnote call on opposite page.)

Council member as 'a body noted for its unity and decorum'.[107] But at the time the Locks arrived, it had just become embroiled in one of the periodic controversies that tear it apart.

As so often in these disputes, it related to plans for the Museum. The one now mooted involved the biggest change to the structure of the house since the wing added by the Rev. Wade in the 1870s. Even with the addition of this wing there was not enough space to accommodate the growing numbers of visitors and house the collection, some of which had to be exhibited in glass cases in the rooms of the original parsonage. The proposal was to build an extension at the back of the house which would include a new flat for the custodian – thereby freeing up exhibition space in the Wade wing – and to make the original Parsonage rooms look much more lived-in. They would also be re-decorated to make them look less austere, based on Mrs Gaskell's account of the interior in 1853 after Charlotte had refurbished it.

John and Winifred were among the most vocal opponents to an extension which they believed would alter the character and atmosphere of the original building, and felt strongly that the Society was failing in its duty as custodian of the Parsonage. They resigned their membership in protest, and would therefore have missed the talk on Emily's poetry given at the 1957 AGM by Cecil Day-Lewis, later Poet Laureate, a tall, elegant, willowy figure whose lecture Linton Andrews considered one of the best the Society had ever heard. 'We have all wondered again and again what the Brontës were like', he said (did not the Locks, in their respective studies at Gimmerton, pass all their time wondering just this?). 'Mr Day-Lewis has brought us closer than ever to the answers.'

And if John and Winifred had attended the following AGM, in 1958, surely they would have approved of Donald Hopewell's address about the importance of the Brontës' environment in shaping their characters and writings.

> I am myself, I confess, an unrepentant environmentalist, because I believe very strongly that all that is best in the Brontës' lives as in their works . . . is due to their upbringing in this West Riding valley on the edge of these amazing moors . . . They lived among sturdy, independent, noble people, and I for one believe that they drew from these hills and these peoples the best in their lives and their works.[108]

---

[108] *Brontë Society Transactions*, Vol. 13, Issue 3, January 1958, pp. 281–2.

In the same address, Hopewell defined what he saw as the purpose of the Society, saying that he saw its role as that of guardian not just of Brontë relics but of the Brontës' image. The Brontës should be presented to the world in the round, warts and all, free of 'sentimental adulation', and should be defended against 'those who have tried to force them into the straitjacket of their own pet theories and opinions.'[109]

As Lucasta Miller has shown so comprehensively in *The Brontë Myth*, there is of course no consensus on the 'truth' about the Brontës and 'what they were really like'. Enthusiasts and scholars alike reach their own personal conclusions. Both have a tendency to claim unique insights and to appropriate the literary family, sometimes in highly emotional ways, and clearly no literary society can dictate how a writer's life and work is interpreted. What it can do is provide a forum for ideas and scholarship. However, Winifred and John never rejoined the Society and never gave a talk to it themselves.

Reactions to the extension and to the redecoration of the Parsonage were mixed, with the voices of those who deprecated them being raised the loudest. A visitor to the Parsonage lamented the transformation of the Brontës' home as it was when she first knew it, when the rooms were as austerely decorated as in the Brontës' childhood and visitors were free to wander around them without surveillance. She denounced the Brontë Society for wasting money on a 'piece of vandalism':

An extension in the style of a car showroom has been built to front the moors; the original rooms, hacked about and tarted up, papered and carpeted in execrable taste, with paintwork of screaming blue, have been roped off in the manner of the Stately Homes trade while attendants clad in embroidered uniforms, like cheer leaders at a Butlin's camp, watch your step. The whole place, now evocative of the interior decorator's art at its worst – and no longer of the Brontës at all – has become an advertisement for Gracious Living on the Yorkshire Moors.[110]

John and Winifred attacked the Society in similar terms for a refurbishing that in their view had left the house looking more like a brightly-painted 'doll's house' than a clergyman's home.[111] Defending the innovations and the Society's record in managing the Museum, Sir Linton was pained by the furore in the press and by what he saw as

---

[109] *Ibid.*, pp. 280–81.
[110] *Times Literary Supplement*, 18 August 1962.
[111] *Times Literary Supplement*, 21 September 1962.

the Locks' ingratitude towards the Society, which had for years made its research facilities available to them.[112] The arguments rumbled on bad-temperedly well into 1963 while the people of Haworth went about their business as usual, little interested in the latest row at the Parsonage.

---

[112] *Times Literary Supplement*, 29 March 1963.

12

Haworth
Recognition at Last

Squabbles with the Brontë Society, of course, occupied no more than a small part of Winifred's and John's time. Most of it was spent labouring at their biographies and establishing themselves as Brontë authorities, and to judge from their frequent appearances in the press they had what would today be termed good self-promotion skills. There were regular interviews and letters announcing their forthcoming books and expounding their views on all things Brontë.

By the end of 1957 Winifred's Anne Brontë biography was completed and had been accepted by the publishing house of Thomas Nelson. She and John made several visits to the firm's offices in Edinburgh. Their main contact was Leslie Murby, one of the managing directors, who looked after the educational side of the business, a man of great charm and enthusiasm. Although Winifred had initially hoped that Oxford University Press would publish her book, she reported to Dorothy Moore in 1960 (Bill had died in 1958 at the age of 85) that 'Nelson's couldn't be nicer or more encouraging to work for'.[113]

The book came out in May 1959 to favourable reviews. There was general agreement that Winifred had been successful in establishing Anne as an interesting figure in her own right and counteracting the popular perception of her as weak and insipid, and there was praise for Winifred's biographical skills.[114] 'She holds all the threads relating not only to Anne but to the Brontëan community at large. A tireless investigation of original documents and personal relics, a pursuit of minor characters, a topographical and historical approach to towns and houses, a friendly feeling for the Haworth scene, all serve to

---

[113] Letter of 9 January 1960 (Moore papers).
[114] There was also a general consensus that the appearance a few months earlier of Ada Harrison and Derek Stanford's *Anne Brontë: Her Life and Work*, combining biography with a critical study, did not overshadow Winifred's own book.

strengthen and enrich her narrative . . . This absorbing and authoritative biography should remain the standard one,' was the verdict of *The Times*.[115]

The *Times Literary Supplement* review described what its author considered Winifred's main strength as a biographer: 'No other study brings to the reader quite so immediate a sense of intimacy with the Brontë home: the impression of breathing the very air of Haworth and its parsonage . . . The place is made tangible to us as never before. So compelling, at times, is the sense of familiarity with our surroundings that we seem instinctively to stoop where the ceiling is low; to labour for breath in that stuffy little bedroom-cum-nursery, wherein for long hours the little girls stitch resignedly at their calicoes and cambrics under the eye of the inquisitorial Aunt Branwell . . . As through a rift in time we are privileged to overhear the conversation, idle or impassioned, of the children; we witness the entrances and the exits of Aunt Branwell; we appreciate the children's reaction to her conversation, as to her peremptory commands. Across the barrier of a century, we can hear, still, the inflection of their voices. There they are, Charlotte and Emily and Anne, in the big, well scrubbed, shining Yorkshire kitchen – and miraculously, it has been vouchsafed to us to overhear the familiar, everyday speech of Haworth refracted back to us out of another, and mysterious, dimension of time.'[116]

Such reactions endorsed Winifred's own conviction that in biography she had at last found her vocation. Moreover, she must have felt vindicated in her decision to move to Haworth to pursue that vocation by the opinion of the Locks' friend Donald Coggan, Bishop of Bradford, who later wrote the foreword to John's biography of Patrick: 'Miss Gérin has lived on the edge of Anne's moors for four years, felt the fierceness of the winds and snows, smelt the scent of the heather, seen the sunsets; and all this has seeped into the book'.[117]

Winifred's first biography evidences her new-found enjoyment of descriptive writing and the importance of the natural environment in her biographical approach. Apart from the evocations of the moors[118] there is a description of Anne's first sight of the sea in Scarborough, where she accompanied her employers the Robinsons. Anne drank in the sight from the Robinsons' rooms on the cliff overlooking South Bay. Could she have known it, eight years later she was to feast her

---

[115] *The Times*, 21 May 1959.
[116] *Times Literary Supplement*, 29 May 1959
[117] Review for a church publication enclosed in a letter from Donald Coggan to the Locks of 10 June 1959 (BPM papers).
[118] See the passage about Haworth Moor at the end of the prelims.

eyes for a last time on this same view in the Scarborough lodgings where, at her request, she was taken when dying.

> Anne Brontë saw. Never, sufficiently, could she fill her eyes, her ears, her nostrils, all her senses, her heart, her mind, with the scintillating splendour of the scene. She saw the sea for the first time, lying beneath her like a living creature; heaving, shifting, stirring, sighing, in endless motion and with endless murmur . . . The sheer beauty of it was a revelation; but how much more, its mystery and power! . . . She felt her whole being burst open by the onrush of an inexpressible emotion. It swept over her, filled her and flooded her as the incoming tide floods the dual bays of Scarborough.[119]

The scene is viewed through Anne's eyes and charged with her feelings. Winifred's second publisher, OUP, was to take issue with this approach as being too subjective and emotional, but Nelson's allowed her to give imagination and empathy a free rein.

Despite the general acclaim for Winifred's first biography, by readers with knowledge of the facts of the Brontës' lives she was criticised for her interpretation of two aspects key to her account of Anne's life. These were Anne's tendency to religious morbidity, and her feelings for her father's curate William Weightman, whom she is popularly supposed to have loved. Weightman died of cholera at the age of twenty-eight.

Winifred placed the blame for Anne's religious crises squarely on the shoulders of the children's Aunt Branwell, who brought them up after their mother's death. Until Anne worked her way through to a personal conviction of divine mercy for all (even for sinners like her brother Branwell and the dissolute Arthur Huntingdon in *The Tenant of Wildfell Hall*) she was tormented by a sense of sin and doubts about salvation, her own and others'. She was the child closest to her aunt, and Winifred attributed her fears to what she saw as Elizabeth Branwell's oppressive Methodist doctrines. The evidence for this seems somewhat flimsy: the doctrine preached by Patrick, which surely carried more weight with his children, was one of mercy, and it is far from certain that his sister-in-law's was as gloomy as Winifred makes out. But Aunt Branwell, who quit the balmy air of Penzance for the cold stone flags of Haworth Parsonage to care for her sister's six children, and later provided financial support for some of their ventures, comes out of this biography so badly one wonders whether Winifred's childhood dislike of her own 'maiden aunts' could have had

---

[119] Gérin, *Anne Brontë*, Chapter 13.

anything to do with it. Elizabeth Branwell is reproached not just on religious grounds but for insufficient love of animals (apparently she failed to appreciate Emily's menagerie, which included tame geese and a hawk) and for not being known ever to have gone for a walk on the moors. It would be hard to say which of these two failings was the more reprehensible in Winifred's eyes.

For evidence that Anne was in love with the curate Willy Weightman, Winifred looked to her writings: poems mourning a lost love, and the hero of *Agnes Grey*, the curate Mr Weston, whom Agnes loves. There is certainly some justification for seeking literal accounts of Anne's real experiences in her first novel; Anne herself claimed that Agnes's trials as a governess, deemed exaggerated by some readers, were 'carefully copied from life', and the amiable Mr Weston may well have had traits of the amiable Mr Weightman. However, even if Anne was susceptible to Willy Weightman's charms, one cannot be sure that Agnes's love for Mr Weston reflects Anne's for Weightman, or that Anne's poems mourning a lost love refer to a real love any more than Emily's 'Cold in the earth – and the deep snow piled above thee', which is in fact a lament by a character in the imaginary world of Gondal.

Winifred's treatment of the Willy Weightman question shows a tendency, for which she was always taken to task by critical reviewers, to read her subjects' lives in their writings. As in all her biographies, too, the combination of exhaustive research with an empathetic and at times novelistic biographical approach sometimes makes for an uneasy marriage. For the general reader, however, Winifred's narrative skills, warmth and detailed evocation of the Brontës' environment brought the family closer than any other biography since Mrs Gaskell's a century earlier.

It was an impressive achievement for a newcomer to biography who, moreover, was not from an academic background. It was particularly so in view of the dearth of comprehensive, well-researched biographical works on the Brontës at the time. There had been none to rival Mrs Gaskell's *Life* in the hundred years since its publication. The studies produced by such writers as Swinburne, May Sinclair and E.F. Benson, many of whom were novelists by trade with a highly personal approach, provided illuminating insights but were biographical essays rather than exhaustive biographies. Closer to Winifred's own time there had been Phyllis Bentley's *The Brontës* (1947), Ernest Raymond's *In the Steps of the Brontës* in the following year and Margaret Lane's engaging *The Brontë Story: A reconsideration of Mrs Gaskell's Life of Charlotte Brontë* (1953). But although these were competent and readable re-tellings of the Brontë story they offered little new research. Winifred's books, starting with *Anne*, with their mass of detail and their annotations, represented a new trend in biography that was to become common in the 1960s.

Winifred revelled in the recognition brought by her study of shy Anne Brontë. She did not trust Nelson's to do enough publicity for the book and worked tirelessly to promote it herself, helped by John. 'He is mad with happiness about the whole thing and helping me like a Trojan with all the rush of correspondence, phoning, appointments etc.,' she wrote breathlessly to Nell, instructing her to check whether certain London bookshops were stocking the book.

From now on there were fan letters from readers, press interviews, invitations to give talks, visits from American academics and postgraduate students passing through Haworth. As the author of a forthcoming Brontë biography himself, John had a share of her new celebrity status. 'Between you, you and your husband seem to have cornered the Brontë field,' wrote a reader.[120] In fact there were plenty of other scholars doing work on the Brontës at the time, but the perception of the Locks as *the* Brontë experts was one they themselves were not averse to fostering.

By now, Winifred had less time to walk on the moors with John. When *Anne* came out she was already hard at work on her next Brontë book, promised to Nelson's by the spring of 1960. Rather than going on immediately to tackle one of the other sisters, she had taken Branwell as her next subject. No full-length biography had yet been dedicated to him apart from an early memoir by his friend Francis Leyland. Having dealt with the sibling who was in some ways the strongest of the four, Winifred now turned to the Brontë brother, as seemingly promising in childhood as her own brother Roger but destined in adulthood to a life of failure and frustration.

There was much new research to do. Weeks were spent poring over manuscripts of Branwell's voluminous juvenilia. Perhaps more enjoyably, weeks were also spent perusing copies of the young Brontës' beloved *Blackwood's Magazine*. Although Winifred may have overstated the importance of the moors in forming the Brontës' imagination ('Without the moors,' she wrote in the Preface to *Anne Brontë*, 'Anne would never have been a poet'), she did give due consideration to other influences such as their childhood reading.

Particularly enjoyable was the research into Branwell's short-lived career as a clerk on the Manchester–Leeds railway, abruptly terminated when he was dismissed in disgrace after a shortfall of £11 1s 7d was discovered in the accounts due to careless book-keeping. There was a trip with John to the Railway Museum in York to find out about

---

[120] Letter from a correspondent dated 16 April 1960 (BPM papers)..

the early rail companies. There were visits to the little branch stations where Branwell worked, at one of which the booking office appeared to be virtually unchanged since his day.[121] There were records of his employment to be chased up: staff at one of the branch stations referred her for these to the head office in Manchester, which in turn told her that the records were now kept at the central office in London. 'One of the great rewards of long correspondence, fruitless journeys, comes with the day when a letter brings the positive statement that the document you have been pursuing exists, and is being kept for you to see at any time convenient to you! The many entries relating to Branwell's engagement and service with the railways preserved at the British Transport Commissions Office seemed to me, on that first day I read them, to be as enthralling as the opening of *Wuthering Heights*.'[122]

The only dark cloud on the horizon was the knowledge that Daphne du Maurier was also writing a book about Branwell, due out, in all likelihood, before her own. Winifred's opinion of her more famous rival is made clear in a letter to Dorothy Moore. 'You know that Daphne du Maurier is writing a book on Branwell also? Nelson's seem quite happy about it, in spite of her enormous following, because they know that the books can't be alike in any respect. I hope they don't lose over it, because however uninformed hers will be, it will sell like hot cakes!'[123]

Could Winifred have known it, the knowledge that she had a rival was causing Daphne even more apprehension. Despite her commercial success since the publication of *Rebecca* in 1938, Daphne was on the whole the less self-confident of the two women, and felt convinced that after the success of *Anne Brontë*, Winifred's life of Branwell stood a much greater chance than her own of meeting with critical approval. 'My novels are what is known as popular and sell very well, but I am *not* a critic's favourite, indeed I am generally dismissed with a sneer as a bestseller and not reviewed at all, so . . . I would come off second-best, I have no illusions to that!'[124] She wrote Winifred a friendly letter wishing her success and acknowledging that Winifred was the better placed of the two to do a full biography – her own work, she said, would be a less ambitious study or portrait – and received a friendly letter back wishing her well in turn. However, her competitive spirit

---

121 Letter to Dorothy Moore of 9 January 1960 (Moore papers). Winifred was probably referring to Luddenden Foot station, which closed in 1962.
122 Draft for a lecture (BPM papers).
123 Letter to Dorothy Moore of 9 January 1960 cited above.
124 Forster, *Daphne du Maurier*, p. 308.

was roused and she viewed their rivalry as a race to be the first to get their respective books published. This was not altogether surprising, since her own publisher, Victor Gollancz, was less relaxed than Nelson's about the imminent publication of a rival work and told Daphne that if Winifred's came out first it would kill her own book's chance of success.[125]

After embarking on her Branwell project Daphne had visited Haworth in 1955 and, like Winifred, stayed at the Brontë Guest House. Like her, she had stood in the nursery at the Parsonage and felt it to be a happy rather than gloomy place. She had walked the moors, playing at being the Brontë sisters with two women friends who accompanied her. Like Winifred she had been ploughing her way through Branwell's juvenilia. She researched as diligently as she could under difficult personal circumstances; Winifred had every advantage over her in this respect. Not only was Daphne's Cornish retreat, Menabilly, far from Haworth, but she was often tied to it by her husband's ill health and depression. Again and again, in her research enquiries, she found that Winifred had forged ahead of her on the trail. They never met, but Daphne sometimes wondered whether they would 'clash on the doorstep' at some point, and she became somewhat paranoid about the contest.

Daphne's *The Infernal World of Branwell Brontë* was published in October 1960, Winifred's *Branwell Brontë* in July 1961. The earlier appearance of Du Maurier's work appears to have done little harm to sales of Winifred's; the first edition of *Branwell Brontë* had sold out before the publication date, it was well received by the reviewers and was chosen by the Book Society as Book of the Month.

Daphne's book, too, was well received, although she was disappointed that it did not make more of a stir. The two biographers were not dissimilar in their approach and in their verdict on Branwell Brontë, both feeling sympathy for him but finding him lacking in real talent and ultimately responsible himself for his failures.

Winifred's assumption that her rival's book would be 'uninformed' was unjustified. Her own book is more comprehensive than Du Maurier's, but Daphne had done her research. She gave a strong analysis of what she saw as Branwell's dual personality; the Branwell still loyal to the faith and the influences of his childhood versus the sceptical, mocking and irreligious Branwell who sought an escape from reality in his alter ego Alexander Percy, and in the 'infernal world', Charlotte's name for the fictional world of Angria she created with her brother.

---

[125] *Ibid.*, p. 309.

The two writers differed in their treatment of two key episodes in the chronicle of Branwell's failure and decline that have always kept Brontë biographers guessing: his abortive trip to London to study at the Royal Academy, only to return to Haworth a few weeks later penniless, and the exact nature of his relations with his employer Mrs Robinson. Accounts of both escapades have been handed down by possibly unreliable narrators, one of the most unreliable being Branwell himself.

Although the Royal Academy scheme was referred to by members of the family, and a there is a draft of a letter from Branwell to the Academy inquiring about enrolment, no surviving family letters mention his visit to London as having actually taken place. The evidence – oral accounts of Branwell's ignominious return to Haworth with a tale of having been robbed, a railway engineer acquaintance's claim to have seen him squandering some of his money in a tavern in Holborn – is rather unsatisfactory. As in her reconstruction of Anne's life, Winifred turned to Branwell's writings to fill in the gaps. Her theory was that on arrival in London – until then his Mecca – all his self-confidence collapsed. She looked for the evidence in an Angrian story written some months later recounting his hero Charles Wentworth's failure of nerve on a visit to a great metropolis.

Wentworth set forth self-confidently on his 'journey of 300 miles'. However, as he neared 'the mightiest city in the world, where he was to begin real life, and in a while, maybe, take a lead in it', he did not feel as happy as he expected and found that 'happiness consists in anticipation'. On his first morning in the city he lost all sense of purpose. 'He threaded the dense and bustling crowds and walked for hours, never staying to eat or drink . . . with a wildish dejected look of poverty-stricken abstraction. His mind was too restless to stop and fully examine anything.'[126]

Winifred believed that Branwell was, as she put it, 'relating his adventures in the person of Charles Wentworth'.[127] Her account of Branwell aimlessly wandering the streets of London is one of the most vivid passages in the biography, but although the Wentworth tale may throw light on Branwell's character and the reasons for his failures, it is speculative to see in it the key to the mystery of his London trip. As with the possible parallels between Anne's writings and her feelings for Mr Weightman, Winifred was indulging a tendency to equate fiction and real life without allowing for the transformations wrought by the creative imagination. Although, of Branwell's two biographers,

---

[126] Quoted in Gérin, *Branwell Brontë*, Chapter 9.
[127] *Ibid.*

it was Daphne Du Maurier who was the novelist, Daphne in fact kept her imagination in check more than Winifred, concluding that exactly what took place during his stay in London must remain a mystery. Writing many years later, Juliet Barker, author of the most factually authoritative biography of the Brontë family, found no convincing evidence that the projected trip ever took place.

Equally problematic is the question of exactly what happened at Thorp Green to lead Mr Robinson to abruptly fire Branwell – who had apparently given satisfaction during several years' employment as tutor to his son Edmund – for behaviour 'bad beyond expression'. The Robinson episode precipitated Branwell's rapid decline and his death three years later, his constitution wrecked by drink and drugs. His obsession with Mrs Robinson was such that he can almost be said to have died of love. His own version was that the love was mutual, but that his hopes of marrying her when her husband died were shattered when she told him that under a codicil to Mr Robinson's will, she would be disinherited if she married Branwell. The codicil, however, turned out to be an invention, and she soon afterwards married a rich widower.

The remittances Mrs Robinson appears to have sent Branwell from time to time would suggest that she had reasons for wanting to keep him quiet, but was there really any romantic entanglement between the two, and if so which of them bore most responsibility for it? Winifred, like Mrs Gaskell before her, placed much of the blame on Mrs Robinson's shoulders, believing her to have dallied with the susceptible young tutor and then brought about his dismissal once she felt compromised. But the evidence – the fact that Branwell's sisters and father blamed Mrs Robinson, the opinion of a doctor who attended the Robinson family – is hardly conclusive.

Mrs Gaskell was obliged by Mrs Robinson's lawyers to retract her accusations in a subsequent edition of the *Life*, while Winifred was reprimanded by some Brontë scholars, who believed that the affair took place largely in Branwell's head, for condemning Mrs Robinson on insufficient evidence. As in the case of the London trip, the truth is likely to remain shrouded in mystery. Recognising this, Du Maurier, once again, took a more non-committal stance than Winifred. She did, however, advance one highly speculative suggestion, namely that Branwell could have been dismissed for a misdemeanour with Mrs Robinson's son Edmund rather than with the mother!

Branwell was seen as a solid work that built on the success of Winifred's first book and placed her reputation on a still firmer footing. But it is Du Maurier's book that is still on sale today. One reason is doubtless her fame as a novelist, another that her book is more suitable for the general reader. Du Maurier is succinct where Winifred is prolix. Du Maurier focuses on Branwell's inner rather than outer world; Winifred is concerned with the details of both. She explores Branwell's mind through his writings while also providing a wealth of details for those interested in everyday life in the period. We are given two pages on the organisation of the Luddenden circulating library at the Lord Nelson Inn, where Branwell was to be found drinking more often than carrying out his duties in the office at the railway station.

When *Branwell* came out Winifred was already immersed in research for her next biography. The favourable reception of her first two books had by now given her the confidence to tackle the Brontë to whom most pages of biography have been devoted – Charlotte, the eldest of the quartet.

Before setting about this task she had found time, in between writing and proof-reading *Branwell*, to bring out a slim volume on her old favourite Fanny Burney for Nelson's younger readers. *The Young Fanny Burney* aimed to combine education and entertainment for teenagers (how hard it is to imagine teenage girls today reading a book about Fanny Burney). In light, novelistic style, it tells the story of a few months in Fanny's life just after the publication of her first novel *Evelina* at the age of 26. It evokes the cheerful bustle of life with a host of siblings and step-siblings in a house that had previously belonged to Isaac Newton. In Winifred's account, the young people gather in Newton's observatory at the top of the house for clandestine readings of Fanny's first novel, kept secret from her elders, scribbled at odd hours and, rather like Jane Austen's writings, hidden away when guests arrived. It was published without her father's knowledge. When it became the talk of the town the excruciatingly shy Fanny, who was terrified of going into society, preferred to remain anonymous, but once she was identified as the author had to resign herself to being lionised by the likes of Dr Johnson.

The little book seems to have been produced without too much effort between Winifred's weightier Brontëan labours and it is not surprising that the local press spoke of her 'terrific output'.[128] There was growing interest, too, in John's forthcoming biography of Patrick, and in June 1961, 100 years after Patrick's death, a journalist from the *Daily Mail* interviewed both the Locks – inevitably, in the Black Bull of Branwell fame. 'Mr and Mrs John Lock gave up London life

---

[128] *Keighley News*, 6 May 1961.

for the bleak, windswept moors and the undying fascinations of the Brontë story. [Their meeting in Haworth] was love at first sight. Love for each other and for Haworth. So they married and found a stone-built house under the shadow of Wuthering Heights . . . After six years in the village the Locks are determined to stay.'[129]

While Winifred had been producing several books in fairly rapid succession, John had been labouring over his one book, which had yet to appear: *A Man of Sorrow: The Life, Letters and Times of the Rev. Patrick Brontë 1777–1861*. 'Mr Lock's long book on Patrick Brontë' was regularly mentioned in the local press. As the years went by the 'long' became 'very long'. Described as 'likely to appeal to clergymen', its publication was announced at regular intervals as being impending. The ideal year for the book to come out would have been 1961, the centenary of Patrick's death, and in fact, 'Mr Lock is hoping that his very long book on the life and letters of Patrick Brontë will be published this year.'[130] But it was not to be; the date was postponed once again. Presumably the delays were caused by the labour involved in getting such a voluminous book ready for the publishers. When John started out he knew of the existence of 25 letters. By the time he finished his research he had seen around 150. He was reluctant to cut or edit, and the book grew and grew. Nelson's initially balked at the size, but were eventually persuaded to publish it at the length John wanted.

Man of Sorrow, begun as a labour of love, may at times have become something of a sorrow or at any rate burden to Patrick's devoted biographer. Winifred refers in letters to the long hours and gargantuan amounts of work done by both her and John on their respective books. John must have found this more of a strain than the hyper-energetic Winifred. He operated at a more leisurely pace than her, and liked to escape from his study for walks or chats with Haworth acquaintances over a lunchtime drink in the Black Bull or his local, the Old Sun in West Lane. Although he was proud of Winifred's successes, he may not always have found it easy to share life with a partner as driven and forceful as she was, while Winifred, in her turn, must have felt frustrated at the reiterated delays in her husband's project.

In press interviews and in Winifred's letters mention is made of various other literary projects of John's in those years. There were reports that he was working on a novel, writing a book of stories about

---

[129] *Daily Mail*, June 1961. In Brontë scrapbook of cuttings 1955–1970, Keighley library (date not specified).
[130] *Yorkshire Evening Post*, 19 January 1961.

Yorkshire, planning a history of Haworth. None of them was published.

Leslie Murby had great plans for both of them, which he outlined with enthusiasm when they visited Nelson's offices in November 1961. As well as biographies of all four siblings and of Patrick he wanted them to produce a comprehensive work on the whole family – this task was to fall to John – and edit an annotated edition of the complete novels. 'In short, enough work to keep us busy for the next ten years,' Winifred wrote happily to Dorothy Moore.[131]

Winifred was indeed to be kept busy writing for the next ten years and well beyond, but in the event the future she and John had mapped out for themselves in Haworth did not go according to plan any more than Murby's projects for Nelson's.

Periods of concentrated writing and research were interspersed with trips to Kensington to prop up Nell and Gilbert, who was now in her eighties and frail. John and Winifred also escaped for occasional breaks elsewhere, particularly in summer when the streets of Haworth were jammed by tourists' cars. Sometimes they headed for Scotland, John's favourite destination. But one place where Winifred did not go in this period was Brussels. She had not visited the Gérins since around the time of Eugénie's death in 1952. She told them it was painful for her to revisit the house in Rue Georges Moreau. It held too many memories. 'Sorrow is never effaced even when you remake your life. I am deeply happy in my new life and my husband's love and devotion – he does everything to make me happy. But he is the first to understand that there are some affections that are never erased, some memories we should not forget, some sorrows that don't heal.'

In the years when she had been absorbed in her playwriting and then her new life in Haworth, things had not got any easier or happier for the Gérin household. After long years tending her ailing husband and mother-in-law, Marthe fell ill herself. Cancer was diagnosed and treated in 1954, only to reappear again in 1957. Paul's youth was blighted by sickness and sorrow just as his childhood had been. He was studying hard for a post-graduate degree – as Winifred had always predicted, his sights were set on a career as an academic – but some of the care for his dying mother fell to him. Marthe died at the end of 1957 leaving Paul the sole survivor of the family.

---

[131] Letter of 31 Dec 1961 (Moore papers).

Then in the spring of 1958 came more cheerful news. Now twenty-four, Paul announced that he was engaged to Anne-Marie, a fellow post-graduate student. Like Winifred when she moved to Haworth, he was about to restart life on a completely new footing. He and his fiancée were to marry once he took up a post as an assistant lecturer in the history faculty at Liège university. Winifred rejoiced with him and ordered two red armchairs from Maples, the posh furniture store in Tottenham Court Road, a wedding present that was to accompany the couple in all the homes of their married life. From then on, Anne-Marie was included as a matter of course in Winifred's letters to Belgium and in her affection for Paul. She promised to visit them soon in their new home in Liège, which would not hold any poignant memories to distress her. The ghosts haunting the old family house in Anderlecht must by now have been rather too many for Paul himself. After he moved to Liège it was let and eventually sold; he never returned to live in Brussels and in subsequent decades saw the transformation of the Jewish neighbourhood of his childhood as successive waves of new immigrants moved in, first Spanish, then North African.

In September 1962 Winifred at last returned to Belgium, though not of course to Rue Georges Moreau, to see the Gérins and research her book on Charlotte Brontë. She stayed for a week, dividing the time between Brussels and Liège, where she made the acquaintance of Anne-Marie and three-year-old Marthe, the eldest child, and Hubert, born earlier that year. It was the start of two new roles for Winifred: that of stand-in mother-in-law to Anne-Marie (who, happily, took in good part Winifred's benevolent bossiness and tendency to tell everyone what they should do) and surrogate grandmother to the growing family of children. To the whole family she was always 'Marraine Winny'. As with the young Paul, she took this role seriously, taking a detailed interest in the children's progress and playing something of the role of a fairy godmother in their lives.

With the adult Paul, now a university lecturer and often engaged in writing books and articles, Winifred had much in common. He helped her with her Brussels research; he could tell her where to find the information she needed, and save her time by writing to archivists to prepare her visits. The time was too short for all she had to do. She was trying to build up a detailed picture of Brussels in the 1840s, and her reporter's notebook was full of queries. In January 1843, returning to Brussels for a second year without Emily, 'drawn by an irresistible force' by her need to be with Heger, Charlotte made the journey from Ostend by train, rather than by stagecoach as in 1842; Winifred wanted to know the timetables and types of carriages of the early trains. She also needed to look at newspapers to read about concerts in 1842–3 in the Park near the Pensionnat, one of which doubtless inspired the description of the music heard by Lucy Snowe when she joins revellers in the park during a midnight fête.

Winifred's research days were divided between the city archives in the splendid Hôtel de Ville in the old Lower Town, and the Royal Library just off Place Royale in the Upper Town, where she pored over old prints. The Library had recently moved to the 1950s Art Deco building where it is housed today. This was part of a new makeover of the 'Mont des Arts' complex, with its monumental staircase linking the two levels of the town, close to the site where the Pensionnat Heger had stood.

Winifred was already familiar with the topography of Brussels. Now she needed to build up in imagination a picture of the city the Brontës had known, described in her Charlotte Brontë biography as a 'citadel on three levels',[132] the third of these being the intermediate one between the upper and lower towns where the Pensionnat stood before it was razed at the turn of the twentieth century.

The most memorable part of her research was meeting Constantin Heger's granddaughter Simone Beckers-Heger, then in her eighties. Mme Becker was the member of the Heger family who had been hosted by Phyllis Bentley on a visit to Haworth some years earlier; Bentley had spoken of her guest's mental liveliness, charm and innate taste, qualities handed down through the generations of the Heger family.[133] Winifred found her a gracious hostess. The family had always been sensitive to any negative presentation of the Hegers in renderings of the Charlotte-Heger story, but after meeting Brontë scholars in Haworth Mme Beckers had felt reassured that by them at least the subject was handled with justice and discretion. She clearly hoped that Winifred would be similarly even-handed. Winifred planned to deal in detail with Charlotte's time at the Pensionnat, a period she considered so crucial to understanding her development. She spent an afternoon in Mme Beckers' house near the Bois de la Cambre surrounded by memorabilia: the first, pirated version of *Villette* in French that so offended Mme Heger; the keys Madame carried as she padded soundlessly around the school – a habit that suggested the spying habits of Mme Beck; a bust of her to which her granddaughter bore a strong resemblance. Winifred left feeling that she had gained a greater understanding of Zoë Heger than at the time

[132] Gérin, *Charlotte Brontë*, Chapter 13.
[133] Phyllis Bentley, 'M. Heger's Grand-Daughter Visits Haworth', in *Brontë Society Transactions*, Volume 12, Issue 3, January 1953, pp. 211–12.

of her portrayal of her in *My Dear Master* – a portrayal that would certainly not have pleased Mme Beckers. 'Be good to my grandparents', Mme Beckers said as she took leave of her at the garden gate.[134] By the time the biography came out she was dead, but her nephew Paul Pechère read the book and wrote to Winifred to thank her on behalf of the Heger family for presenting the Hegers and Charlotte's relationship with them more justly, he felt, than any English author before her.[135] If this were true, Winifred believed it was attributable not just to that September afternoon's conversation with Mme Beckers but to the knowledge of Belgians and 'foreignness' acquired through her marriage and years abroad.

From her talk with Heger's granddaughter Winifred also brought away little snippets of information about Charlotte's 'master', for example that when dictating letters to his wife or daughters he would walk about with his hands behind his back, and that he hated thunderstorms and would run into the garden in the rain and get his head soaked to ease the oppression they caused him (reminiscent of Lucy Snowe leaning out of the dormitory window in a storm – but Lucy revelled in the violence of the thunder). Winifred returned to England with her notebook well filled.

After a few days with Nell in London she travelled back to Haworth with John, who had been visiting his mother. They arrived at Gimmerton to find that Irene, their housekeeper, had filled the house with flowers in honour of their return and baked one of her celebrated cakes. It was decorated with white roses of York and surrounded by heather from their beloved moors. It was a wonderful welcome, but troubled times lay just ahead.

The mood of the next couple of years, which were unsettled ones for both of them, was set by a fresh storm at the Parsonage. While Haworth endured an exceptionally cold winter, with pipes freezing and some villagers left without running water for weeks, at the Parsonage the atmosphere once again became heated over an issue on which the Locks held strong views. This was the question of who was to be the custodian of the Brontë Museum's treasures. In 1961 Harold Mitchell, the live-in custodian for over three decades, in whose sitting-room Daphne Du Maurier had chatted into the small hours, retired after only a year or two in the new flat in the extension that had caused the previous shindy. An ex-serviceman who lost his right hand in the Great War and taught himself to write with the other, he left a lasting legacy in his design for the wrought-iron sign that hangs outside the

---

[134] Recounted in Winifred's memoir.
[135] Letter of 21 July 1968 (Greenwood papers).

museum to this day, depicting one of the three Brontë sisters writing at her desk.

As a retirement gift, Irene baked Harold Mitchell and his wife a cake so splendid that it was featured in the *Keighley News*: a replica of the Parsonage that included a flowering cherry tree in the garden. Mitchell's send-off was succeeded by a period of instability at the Parsonage. The curator died in the same year; the Society decided to recruit a qualified museum curator as the next custodian and to Winifred's and John's satisfaction chose an experienced candidate called Geoffrey Beard. The Locks viewed his incumbency as the only time in which the museum was run in a professional manner.

After only eighteen months, however, Geoffrey Beard resigned and towards the end of 1962 the Society replaced him with Joanna Hutton, a thirty-year-old mother of three young children without formal qualifications or experience. The appointment proved divisive and prompted the resignation of half the Council members, including Phyllis Bentley. The Locks, though not members of the Society, sided with the resigning members and the local press was soon full of the new row at the Parsonage.

On the face of it Joanna Hutton was an unlikely candidate whose main qualification for the post was her passion for the Brontës – ironically, given Winifred's opposition to her appointment, a passion first kindled by reading Winifred's biography of Anne. She was the daughter of Arthur Brough, the actor who later became famous as 'Mr Grainger' in the TV series *Are You Being Served*, and had herself done some acting before her marriage. This prompted the French press to take up the story and to compare her appointment to putting Brigitte Bardot in charge of the house of Victor Hugo.

The debate in the press soon became as acrimonious as the recent one about the Parsonage wallpaper, and John and Winifred weighed in once again. Winifred accused the Society, having squandered its funds on the costly extension, of running the museum with a view to profit rather than scholarship by failing to provide it with a properly qualified curator. Moreover, in the resigning members of the Council, she said, the Society had lost some of its most eminent people.[136] She and John called on the rest of the Council to resign and claimed support for their views in high quarters: 'What would Emily Brontë and her father make of the present Brontë Society Council?'[137]

Their friend Canon Dixon, who had by now left Haworth, also sided with the protesters. His successor, however, the Rev. Charles

---

[136] *Yorkshire Post*, 28 February 1963.
[137] *Keighley News*, 9 March 1963.

Manchester, appealed to both sides to 'pursue a policy of quietness, peace and love' as recommended in the Prayer Book.[138] A reader of the *Yorkshire Post* considered that 'There is something about the Brontë sisters and their Parsonage which evokes a peculiar acrimony among their devotees.'[139] J.H. Parkins of Bingley, a reader of the *Keighley News*, put it even more strongly in a letter of 9 March 1963.

> Sir. – Does the Brontë Society, or that army of pen pushers who frequently warm themselves in the glow of the Brontë fire, think that it really matters a two-penny damn whether they stick bits of wallpaper on the Parsonage walls, or install an M.A. within?
>
> The Brontë novels and poems remain to be enjoyed by ordinary readers who surely do not require wrangling interpreters – curator or custodian – to sully their pleasures.

After a few months the storm died down, with no further calls for resignations of Council members. Joanna Hutton, who had been keeping her head down while it raged around her and settling quietly into her new duties, proved an efficient administrator in commercial terms at least; under her watch visitor numbers almost doubled.

The local press turned its attention to issues of more concern to Haworthers, such as the threat of electricity pylons on the moor and the need for a bypass to take traffic away from the cobbled Main Street. Charles Manchester, the vicar of Haworth, complained in verse in the pages of the *Keighley News* about the damage done by the stone setts to his old car, 'Delilah'. Parodying Anne's Brontë's expression of faith *The Narrow Way* ('Believe not those who say/The upward path is smooth/Lest thou shoulds't stumble in the way/And faint before the truth'), the Rev. Manchester's version began:

> Believe not those who said
> That Main Street hill was smooth;
> For it has made Delilah dead,
> And that's the honest truth.[140]

It is rather disappointing to discover in the *Keighley News* that Winifred was not among those who were amused by Mr Manchester's parody.[141]

---

[138] *Ibid.*
[139] *Yorkshire Post*, 9 March 1963.
[140] *Keighley News*, 24 December 1962.
[141] *Keighley News*, 5 January 1963.

Admittedly, she had various things on her mind at that period. She and John had had to rush to London more than once to help Nell nurse Gilbert, now 83. The delays over the publication of John's book continued, compounded by printers' strikes. And, just as Winifred's own book on Charlotte was nearing completion, they learned that Nelson's was being taken over by the Thomson Organisation, and that Leslie Murby was leaving to go to Collins in Glasgow. Nelson's, a family firm, had been in decline for some time.

The loss of Murby, their contact at Nelson's who had so recently offered them such ambitious prospects, was a tremendous blow, and it soon became apparent that the Thomson Organisation was not going to fulfil his plans for them. The only one that was given the go-ahead was the publication of *A Man of Sorrow*. Nelson's new owners considered Winifred's biography of Charlotte too scholarly for the firm they envisaged and in 1964 Winifred, with the book completed, found herself without a publisher.

This was followed by another blow: Gilbert's death in May 1964, almost fifty years after she first joined the Bourne household. Throughout their old friend's last illness Winifred's loyalties had been torn between Haworth and Kensington, John's claims and Nell's. She and John hurried to London again and found Nell exhausted after the months nursing Gilbert. Meanwhile, John's mother Sybil had decided to give up her house in Purley and move to a smaller one in Eastbourne. For much of 1964 Winifred, in addition to seeking a new publisher, was in London helping either Nell or Sybil. Despite initial opposition on Sybil's part to John's marriage to Winifred, a cordial relationship seems to have developed between the two women.

By 1965 Winifred had found a publisher for her new biography in Oxford University Press, and the date of publication of John's work was finally set for that year. But things continued unsettled, with Winifred still spending much of her time in London. She was so concerned about Nell that she suggested to John they should move to London permanently, but he was against this idea. In letters she reported concerns about John himself: he was feeling ill and depressed, suffering from overwork and insomnia. At some stage in 1965, ten years into their marriage, what she describes in her memoir as a 'lightning-stroke' coming as unexpectedly as 'a storm on a cloudless summer day' brought to an end her marriage, her literary partnership with John and her Haworth life. The bolt out of the blue was the revelation that John and Irene had fallen in love.

In her memoir Winifred stresses John's honesty to her and writes that his suffering and shock at the turn of events were as great as her own. His own feelings seem to have taken him by surprise. When he married Winifred he was very inexperienced. According to what he told her at the time she was his first love, and his idea of romantic love, as something that was for 'all eternity', was an idealised one that might have been drawn from the pages of *Wuthering Heights*.

Winifred herself, according to the brief account in her memoir, was taken completely by surprise by what had happened because up until then she had been so happy. But their parting appears to have taken place without bitterness. Gimmerton was let to a friend for the time being; Winifred moved back to West Cromwell Road and John made a new life near Bath, a place he had always liked.

Winifred did not want the scandal and publicity of a divorce. There was no announcement of their separation, no mention of it to most of her friends and acquaintances. They were simply told that John was exhausted by getting his book ready for publication and had taken up an office job somewhere 'in the provinces', as Winifred rather oddly termed it, which he found less stressful than literary work. In response to invitations to both of them she would merely say that John was unable to accompany her as he was working outside London. Even to the Gérins she did not refer openly to the separation. John never met them, but on their visits to England in the years after Winifred's return to London he would send them little notes wishing them well and apologising for being unable to see them because of pressure of work. As the months and years went by and Winifred remained in West Cromwell Road with John out of sight in his 'provincial' retreat, people drew the obvious conclusion.

It was doubtless true that John had found the toil and discipline required for the literary life more of a strain than he had anticipated. *A Man of Sorrow* finally saw the light of day in 1965 around the time the marriage was breaking up. The length of the book makes it unsuitable for the general reader and it is marred by its sentimental style, but its wealth of detail still provides scholars with a useful resource on Patrick's incumbency and the Haworth background. It also firmly rehabilitated Patrick's reputation.

While Winifred continued writing at the same frenetic pace after her return to London, producing four more biographies after *Charlotte Brontë*, John lived a life of quiet retirement near Bath and published no more books. But his literary collaboration with Winifred was not entirely at an end; she refers to him proof-reading typescripts for her. Nor did the end of the marriage end a friendship based on common interests and mutual affection. They continued to meet regularly: in London, at his mother's home in Eastbourne, and at the weekend cottage she bought some years after leaving Haworth. After her death he wrote about her in a foreword to her memoir, which he hoped to publish. Referring to the great honour she had done him in making him her literary executor, he ended an emotional tribute to her with the words, 'Above all, she bequeathed to me that most precious and rarest of gifts – forgiveness.'

13

Kensington
The Final Fifteen Years

Looking back on the Haworth years in old age, Winifred remembered them as very happy ones right up to the sudden end of her marriage partnership with John. As for her verdict on their professional partnership, she said in her memoir that 'Haworth and John between them made a biographer of me.' As a biographer, her drive and focus continued unabated after her return to London. As far as her emotional life was concerned, there were compensations in the return to West Cromwell Road; she and Nell had always been very close and during the Haworth years she had felt pulled in two directions whenever Nell needed her. From now on the bond between them became even stronger. There were other compensations, too, for the lost raptures on the Haworth moors, in the shape of new literary pleasures and friendships. Haworth was in some ways a paradise lost, like the one she had known with Eugène; but possibly, once the initial pain started to wear off, she came to feel that Haworth and John had given her what they had to give her, and the time had come to return to London and Nell. However, one can only guess at Winifred's innermost feelings as she brought her furniture and piano and Eugène's cello back to London and took up her life again where she had left off. Given her extreme reticence on the subject of her separation from John, she is unlikely to have voiced these feelings even to close friends.

Once again, as after Eugène's death twenty years earlier, her sister had offered her a home; now as then, it was the obvious solution, the best one for both of them. Nell provided the stability of home affection that Winifred needed to work, but this time round Nell was in even more need of support. Gilbert's death left a huge gap and the coming years would increasingly be dominated by the problem of a house that was becoming too big and the difficulty of finding assistance to run it.

As the short-lived home helps came and went, two presences that provided continuity in the household were the cats who were members of it at the time. A return to the companionship of pets was certainly one of the compensations of Cromwell Road, and Betsy and Madame Nhü at once started to make appearances in letters to Belgium, sending 'fraternal greetings' to Péquet, the Gérin's own cat.

Re-installed in her first-floor apartment while Nell painted above, Winifred was even busier than she had been in her former London life. She was turning over ideas for new biographies, on one at least of which she had already started. Her first task, though, was to see *Charlotte Brontë* through publication. Her correspondence with Oxford University Press has been preserved, and bears testimony to some initial bumps in her relationship with her new publisher. Until the two parties got used to each other's ways, all was not as smooth sailing as it had been in the more relaxed dealings with Nelson's and Leslie Murby.

At 'the Press', decisions were made by more formal and rigorous committee procedures. Winifred's book had to run the gauntlet of OUP's editors and academic readers. Her letter of submission was written in her usual enthusiastic style, citing among her main credentials the familiarity with both Haworth and Brussels that had allowed her to do detailed research and brought Charlotte's world 'vividly alive' for her. Her confidence in her own work was borne out at least in part by the favourable reaction of one of OUP's readers, the Oxford academic Kathleen Tillotson, who thought Winifred's biography the most authoritative, balanced and perceptive to date. She had reservations, though, about the style, finding it vigorous and vivid but 'too highly-coloured for some tastes'.[142]

Other readers and editors agreed about the style, finding it too emotional in tone for what one defined as the 'somewhat dry Clarendon Press manner' ('there is some un-C.P.-like feminine gush') and objecting to certain 'purple passages'. Quiller-Couch, Winifred's English literature tutor at Cambridge, would doubtless have concurred. OUP objected, too, to instances of diffuseness and repetition and the over-use of italics for emphasis. Dan Davin, the most formidable of the senior editors,[143] was almost as damning in a preliminary report on Winifred's manuscript as her Newnham tutor Miss

---

[142] The citations relating to Winifred's dealings with Oxford University Press are taken from unpublished correspondence and memos in OUP's archives [hereafter OUP archives], in this case in the *Charlotte Brontë* file. Consulted and quoted by kind permission of the archivist.

[143] 'No editorial pencil moved so swiftly or with such surgical precision'. Simon Eliot, *History of Oxford University Press* (Oxford: OUP, 2013), Vol. III, p. 577.

Firth had been about her first history essay. 'Author has a very shaky hold on sentence construction, punctuation, and English generally', was Davin's verdict. Evidently such opinions, recorded in internal reports, were toned down in communications with the author, but their gist was conveyed.

Peter Sutcliffe, Winifred's editor at OUP, agreed with some of the criticisms but admired her narrative gifts and told colleagues hopefully, 'I think she would probably agree to follow our house rules for sedateness of manner'.

Forty years earlier, after her bruising encounter with Miss Firth, Winifred had opted to sever the connection and go elsewhere. In this new encounter with academic minds, there was no question of going into a huff or withdrawing; she was too conscious of the desirability of securing OUP as a publisher for that. She defended herself, however, politely but forcefully, protesting against the imposition of a uniform 'house style' on all authors. In response to the criticism that her writing was over-emotional and subjective, she stressed the importance she placed on 'warmth'. Sutcliffe wanted to tone down certain passages expressing feeling, including some in which events were described from Charlotte's point of view rather than objectively. In her defence of this rather novelistic practice Winifred was moved to define what motivated her to write biography: 'There is more to be said than the basic fact; and it is that "more" that made the writing of the book, in my eyes at least, worthwhile.'[144]

Another criticism made was that there was at times an overload of unimportant detail, and here her argument was that from fan mail and meetings with Brontë fans during her time in Haworth, she knew that her readers relished such apparently trivial facts.

More serious than any of these were accusations of inaccuracies, for example in transcribing manuscripts, and of discarding evidence that did not support her own view. The latter criticism reminds one of her father's hint, after her disenchantment with history as taught at Newnham, that her strong likes and dislikes and lack of impartiality made her unsuited to being a historian.

Luckily for Winifred's relations with OUP, Peter Sutcliffe steered her tactfully through the difficult first months of her initiation with 'the Press'. Compromises were reached, but Winifred's work undoubtedly benefited from more stringent editing. Blemishes in her style such as the Gallicisms which pepper her letters as well as her books (one example being the use of Gallic inversions such as 'Notable it is that

---

[144] Letter to Peter Sutcliffe dated 26 March 1965. *Charlotte Brontë* file (OUP archives).

. . . ') could have been weeded out at an earlier stage by a vigilant editor. Sutcliffe recognised her strengths as well as tackling her weaknesses, understanding the importance of intuition, empathy and the sense of place in her biographical approach. He was later to write of her, comparing her approach with that of the academic authors whose 'painstakingly scholarly work' on the Brontës began to proliferate from this period, 'Winifred Gérin regarded the labours of the scholars respectfully, and with some wonder, but that was not her way. She herself became passionately fond of her subjects, and cherished them as friends or daughters. Warmth, compassion, and enthusiasm characterize her work.'[145]

In the years that followed, Peter Sutcliffe became a firm friend as well as her editorial 'father-confessor', as Dan Davin put it. A man of learning and wit, Sutcliffe was a sympathetic editor and genial friend. As an editor his wide knowledge made him invaluable; when travel became difficult for her in her final years he even did research for her on occasion, taking the opportunity on a trip to Edinburgh to look up letters in the John Murray archives for her final biography, on Anne Thackeray Ritchie. As a friend, he was appreciative of Winifred's personal qualities. In his obituary of her in *The Times*, he compared her with Anne Ritchie, writing that both women were 'brimming over with impulsive kindness and a spontaneous readiness to make the best of the world':

> Winifred Gérin, who had found much grief in her life, knew how to transcend it. Anne Ritchie referred to two kinds of people: 'Those who *make* life' and the many who 'unmake it'. Winifred Gérin made life, and there could be no finer tribute to a biographer: but she also made it in the non-literary sense, by the unsparing generosity and warmth of her nature.[146]

He would take her out to lunch when he was in London, or lunch with her and Nell at West Cromwell Road and, later, in the cottage she bought in Oxfordshire; he sometimes accompanied her to literary functions when she was in need of an escort.

Charlotte Brontë: The Evolution of Genius, the first fruit of their collaboration, came out in 1967. This longest and most acclaimed of Winifred's Brontë biographies was successful in showing the evolu-

---

[145] Peter Sutcliffe's entry for Winifred in *Dictionary of National Biography 1981–1985* (Oxford: Oxford University Press, 1990).
Entry in *Oxford Dictionary of National Biography* for 1981–5, OUP.
[146] *The Times*, 1 July 1981.

tion, if not of Charlotte Brontë's genius (can 'genius', an innate ability, really be said to 'evolve'?), of her literary imagination and her character. Winifred explores well the development of Charlotte's imagination, starting with the emotionally over-heated atmosphere of Angria in her youth. The Brontë siblings' total immersion in these imaginary worlds was a recipe for disaster once they had to make their way in the real world. Winifred examines the 'novelettes of passion' written when Charlotte was in her twenties, whose heroines are as infatuated with the brooding Zamorna, a precursor of Rochester, as Charlotte was later to become with Heger. Real-life experience failed to provide anything that lived up to Charlotte's ideal of passionate love, and she herself was well aware of the danger of her addiction to the 'infernal world'. Her adult writing, while continuing to draw on the vivid imaginative visions of her youth, records her painful attempt to come to terms with her actual circumstances. Winifred shows Charlotte ultimately reconciling the warring elements within herself and achieving wholeness and acceptance of her lot.[147]

One of the biography's main contributions to research was generally agreed to be the light shed on Charlotte's time at the Pensionnat and her relations with the Hegers. Apart from the detail of the Brussels background, Winifred was praised for her analysis of the complexities of these relations and for giving the Hegers' viewpoint as well as Charlotte's, Mme Heger's included. While not everyone accepted her interpretation – some, for example, suspecting that Charlotte was not as innocent in what she felt for Heger as Winifred claims – Winifred was felt to have presented it persuasively.

For Winifred, *Villette*, born out of the Brussels experience, represented the culmination of Charlotte's literary and personal evolution:

> Never before had her powers of vision and evocation been so . . . royally displayed. The world without, and the world within, were the illimitable stage for the drama's setting, the drama of her own life presented whole at last. The dream of Angria and the reality of Brussels were fused in one grand explosion of passion and pathos, of rebellion and acceptance, of tribulation and ecstasy. What she had been, and what she would never be, were revealed here eloquently for ever . . . [148]

---

[147] This facet is explored in Barbara Mitchell, *The Biographical Process: Writing the Lives of Charlotte Brontë* (PhD thesis, University of Leeds, 1994).
[148] Gérin, *Charlotte Brontë*, Chapter 25.

Winifred saw Charlotte's life as an evolution in terms not just of literary fulfilment but of fulfilment in the sense of 'creation of character'.[149] As she puts it in the Introduction, 'During her short life she suffered exceptional griefs; their mere relation would be intolerable but for the manner in which she bore them – a manner that places them upon the plane of tragedy.' Just as Winifred's personal experience of Brussels and foreign cultures made her eloquent on the Heger episode, so her own experience of bereavement must have fed into the empathy with Charlotte's that led Pamela Hansford Johnson, reviewing the book in the *Sunday Times*, to say, 'She has that feeling for grief and, above all, loneliness, which sheds great illumination upon her subject.'[150] Apart from Charlotte's religious belief and inward reserves of strength, the most effective support she found in a life without Emily, Anne and Branwell was in creative work, an antidote for grief that Winifred herself had of course herself discovered in bereavement.

After a long period of loneliness and desolation a new support appeared in Charlotte's life in the shape of the Rev. Arthur Nicholls, on the face of it an unlikely suitor. Winifred fills us in on his Irish family background, which pleasantly surprised Charlotte on her honeymoon and came as a similar revelation to Winifred when she researched it on a visit to Banagher, the town where Nicholls grew up. Winifred presents him sympathetically and stresses Charlotte's happiness in the marriage. It would have been hard for Winifred to have anything but liking for a man whose love for animals both tame and wild matched her own. Nicholls, a lover of the outdoors, walked the Parsonage dogs in all weathers and refused to lop the trees around his Banagher home because it would disturb the squirrels.[151]

In one way Winifred's task was made easy, since Charlotte tells us so much about herself in her books and letters. On the other hand, her story had been re-told so often that Winifred's main difficulty was how to add anything of value. She did not approach Charlotte from any particular ideological slant, for example the feminist angle that was to become increasingly common in the 1970s with discussion of the 'woman question'. However, the *Times* reviewer, while acknowledging that Winifred adds no really novel theories or revelations to what was already known, considered that 'she tells Charlotte's story more fully than it has ever been told before. And more persuasively'. Familiar though the story was, 'it has never been done quite like this'.[152]

---

[149] *Ibid*, Introduction.
[150] *The Sunday Times*, 2 July 1967.
[151] Gérin, *Charlotte Brontë*, Chapter 27.
[152] *The Times*, 20 July 1967.

Assessing the biography after Winifred's death,[153] the novelist and biographer Elizabeth Jenkins praised the evocative force of the writing in passages such as the description, in the closing pages, of the equinoctial storms that wailed round the Parsonage as Charlotte lay dying in March 1855:

> The March gales had come in, and to those who know the district their gathering force is a phenomenon not to be underrated. Their mounting fury rocks the sky and shudders in the hollows of the hills; every object in their path is swept aside; the waterfalls are tossed into the air, the rocky boulders hurled into the becks, the solitary trees on the bare hillsides are tattered and torn. In the narrow village streets the windows rattle in their frames, the wooden shutters crash, the chimneys roar, and the very key-holes are a vent for eerie cries. To stand between the front and back doors of the old houses in Haworth at such a time is to hear banshee voices shrieking in the gale.[154]

Other readers were uneasy about some aspects of the account of Charlotte's death, in which Winifred allows herself to be somewhat carried away by her own rhetoric. Despite Charlotte's known reluctance to be torn from the side of the husband she had come to love, with approaching death her 'adventurous spirit' is imagined by Winifred as 'leaping to get away' at the sound of the wind's summons, seeking liberation and a reunion with the dead siblings who have gone before.

However, despite some such reservations, and although some academic reviewers, as always, declined to join in the chorus of approval (Barbara Hardy, for example, deplored the biography's lack of critical insights into the novels and scant reference to literary critics[155]), *Charlotte Brontë* provides a comprehensive account of Charlotte's development and represents the peak of Winifred's achievement as a biographer. Recognition was not slow in coming. In December 1967 Robert Blake, in the *Sunday Times*, chose it as his book of the year, declaring it to be 'one of the great biographies of recent times'[156] (footnote opposite). (Ten years later Richard Holmes, in a review of Robert Gittings's *The Nature of Biography* (1978),

---

[153] Elizabeth Jenkins, 'Winifred Gérin: The Brontë Biographies', *Newnham College Roll Letter* (1983), pp. 34–6.
[154] Gérin, *Charlotte Brontë*, Chapter 27.
[155] Barbara Hardy, review in *Nineteenth Century Fiction*, Vol. 23, No. 2, pp. 240–3.

named *Charlotte Brontë* as one of the outstanding biographies in the fifty years since the publication of Strachey's *Elizabeth and Essex* in 1928, a period Gittings calls a 'golden age of biography'.)[157] Winifred's was regarded as the definitive biography of Charlotte for a considerable time despite the publication of major new studies in the succeeding decades: Margot Peters's in 1975, Rebecca Fraser's in 1988 and Lyndall Gordon's in 1994. It won three awards: the University of Edinburgh's James Tait Black Memorial Prize for biography, the Rose Mary Crawshay Prize for works by female scholars and the Royal Society of Literature's Heinemann award. As the awards stacked up, OUP could feel satisfied with their decision to take on this sometimes unruly new author.

Winifred was already immersed in work for her next project. She had, in fact, two new ones in the pipeline. One of these was, inevitably, a biography of Emily, the remaining member of the quartet. Emily was Winifred's personal favourite and her plan, projected in the happy years of her association with Leslie Murby, had always been to write lives of all four siblings. But not for nothing had she put Emily off until last. She was by far the most difficult of the four to tackle, since there was so little on which to base a biography. The ever-communicative Charlotte left letters enough to fill three volumes in addition to her highly self-revelatory fiction; the ever-reticent Emily, who had no confidants outside the family, left just three letters, her prose juvenilia did not survive and all we have to go on for clues to her inner life are her poems and one inscrutable novel.

Between 1965 and 1968 this last Brontë book was put aside while Winifred worked on something completely different. This was a life of Horatia Nelson, Lord Nelson's illegitimate daughter.

Nelson was a hero of the young Brontës, and had been a hero of the patriotic young Bournes in the Norwood days. His daughter Horatia grew up in the Georgian and Regency period so dear to Winifred's heart. Previously, a veil had been drawn over Horatia's life because of her illegitimacy, and Winifred had long wanted to know more about her.

This new biography was of course a complete departure from her Brontë studies. Curiously, there was an incidental link between the Brontë and Nelson families, namely the Sicilian estate of Bronte and the title 'Duke of Bronte' conferred on Nelson by the King of Sicily in 1799, after which he was wont to sign dispatches 'Nelson and Bronte'; this is believed to have given Patrick Brunty, from Drumballyroney in

[156] *The Sunday Times*, 3 December 1967.
[157] *The Times*, 16 November 1978.

County Down, the idea of changing the spelling of his name when he went up to Cambridge in 1802.

Following the success of *Charlotte Brontë*, Winifred's work schedule became ever busier. Her services were increasingly requested as an editor of Brontë writings (though not by OUP – to her disappointment they did not choose her to edit *Villette* and *The Professor*, as she had hoped, for their planned new edition of the novels). The Folio Society commissioned her to edit Gaskell's *Life* and five of Charlotte's juvenile novelettes; the British Council requested a volume on the Brontës for its 'Writers and their Work' series, and Penguin asked for an introduction for the Penguin English Library edition of *The Tenant of Wildfell Hall*.[158] Her biographical research was often interrupted by such assignments. They could be profitable, and with the start of the inflationary 1970s the money was doubtless a welcome contribution to the cost of maintaining the Kensington house. Approaching old age did not slow her down. If anything, she was driving herself harder than ever.

She found time, though, for family and friends. Her return to London made it easier to see the growing Gérin family, and in the summer of 1967 she paid another visit to Liège. Marthe was now nearly eight, Hubert five. On her previous visit Marthe had been a toddler, Hubert a baby a few months old. They were now people with clearly-defined interests and personalities; she could enter into their concerns and hope to transmit her passions to them as she had to Paul. There was another reason why a visit to Liège was important to her at that time. There had been a third addition to the family, a boy born in October of the previous year. He had been christened Eugène after his great-uncle and Winifred had been asked to be godmother.

Her role in Paul's family was, of course, that of grandmother to all the children rather than just godmother to little Eugène. In photos taken with Eugène in her arms, Winny looks, radiantly, every inch a grandmother. After receiving the news of this pregnancy she had taken time off from her literary labours to do some knitting for the new baby. Around this time, Marthe began to write Winifred and Nell letters in English and Winifred wondered hopefully whether their Belgian great-niece would one day be a writer. When Hubert, whose passions were drawing and the Middle Ages, started to send pictures of knights in

---

[158] See Bibliography for details.

armour, Nell was equally hopeful that he was destined to become an artist.

The following summer, 1968, Winifred invited Paul to leave the two eldest children at West Cromwell Road for a fortnight's stay. There was a new reason why he and Anne-Marie were glad to be relieved of some of their parental duties: in February that year there had been a further addition to the family in the shape of twin boys, Vincent and Emmanuel (had they been girls, Paul and Anne-Marie had planned to christen them Winifred and Hélène).

It was Marthe's and Hubert's turn to experience life in Marraine Winny's 'Mary Poppins' house, which had made such an impact on the young Paul on his first visit to London, and to enjoy the wonders of the black-painted, red-carpeted staircase and high-ceilinged rooms. The cultural and educational experience provided for the two children was as intensive as their father's had been. Marthe and Hubert were shepherded by both great-aunts around the sights. They were taken on the Thames, to Kew, to Windsor. They were encouraged, or instructed, to keep a diary and write accounts of their excursions. Hubert preferred to record his own impressions in drawings, and Winny was reminded of how obsessively she and her three siblings had drawn and coloured in the Norwood days. She began a collection of books that was to grow with each visit of her Belgian great-niece and nephews, starting with the Ladybird series on famous people from history – William the Conqueror, Florence Nightingale, Napoleon. She took the children to see Wellington's tomb in St Paul's. Hubert, who at one stage in his childhood, like the Brontë children, had a collection of toy soldiers with which to re-enact the Battle of Waterloo, was a devotee of Wellington, but on a later occasion young Eugène declared a preference for Napoleon. Winifred proved more open-minded than Charlotte Brontë, who managed to turn an essay on Napoleon set for her by Heger into a eulogy of her hero Wellington, for as a Christmas present she gave Eugène a splendid book on Napoleon.

She was more indulgent with Paul's children than she had been with Paul himself as a boy, although her occasional severity with him had been for what she saw as his own good. She entered into their enthusiasms. Hubert's interest in the Middle Ages recalled Roger's boyhood devotion to things medieval and old heroic legends, and Hubert became her *preux Chevalier*, her valiant knight. She and the children saw the newly-released film *Camelot* and she taught them its songs. She told Hubert about King Arthur and on one of the children's visits dubbed him a Knight of the Round Table in a solemn ceremony.

In the Gérin children Marraine Winny inspired a degree of awe. Like their father before them at their age, they sensed they had to be on their best behaviour with her. They perceived her as a *grande dame*, someone from the upper classes, but with kindness and consideration for the *petit peuple*, as they termed it (people from a humbler background) as well as for children.

On return to London after escorting the children back to Ostend, Winifred wrote to Paul and Anne-Marie, 'The house seems very empty to us after the departure of our dear little guests. The silence would soon have weighed on us painfully had I not, while tidying up, found a splendid drawing of a knight in armour, which consoled me a little for the departure of the Chevalier and his sister.'

Visits to Aunts Winny and Nell in the summer holidays now became a fixture in the children's calendar, as did the marvellous Christmas presents that arrived from London, accompanied by anxious and detailed explanations from Winifred for Anne-Marie about each individual gift.

'You occupy a large corner of my heart, from which nothing can ever remove you,' she told the Gérins in a letter of 1969. Mina Breed, after seeing Winifred with the children, said in her annual Christmas letter to Paul – Mina, who had few relatives of her own, was treated by Winny and Nell as one of the family and had befriended Paul in his youth – 'What a pity she never had children of her own. She would have been such a good mother. I have been surprised to see her with your children and to see how well she seems to understand little ones and get on with them.'

These years saw two new departures that further enriched Winifred's life. The first of them was that in 1968, on the strength of the success of *Charlotte Brontë*, she was invited to become a Fellow of the Royal Society of Literature. Winifred was immensely flattered. She was also surprised. Despite her recent awards and not inconsiderable self-belief and forcefulness, one can at times discern in her a certain diffidence about her academic credentials.

She enrolled as a Fellow on 25 April and afterwards related in a note to Dan Davin of OUP the excitement of signing the RSL roll book with Byron's pen. 'This was a giddy moment I can assure you, but happily the pen seems to write of itself – something of Byron's magic guiding it, no doubt.' This gave the ever-sarcastic Davin, no fan of Winifred's style, an opportunity to annotate her letter privately with the comment that she was not the first to observe that her pen sometimes seemed to write of its own volition![159] (footnote opposite).

From then on, some of Winifred's happiest hours were spent at No

1 Hyde Park Gardens, the gracious building then housing the RSL, with its pleasant garden and view looking south over the Park. She attended the monthly lectures and in January 1969 gave a talk herself on *The Effect of Environment on the Brontë Writings*. Her slight anxiety about her worthiness to join the august company of RSL Fellows is revealed by a postscript to Molly Patterson, the Society's Secretary, in a letter about arrangements for the lecture: 'I have a Cambridge M.A. if you wish to add an air of respectability to the lecture invitation cards.' A reminder to add the 'M.A.' was sent just before the cards were printed, as 'it sometimes inspires more confidence in an audience!'[160]

The addition of 'F.R.S.L.' to the 'M.A.' after her name must have been a great confidence-booster. But with or without such aids, Winifred seems to have been a good speaker. 'You created magic, with your gentle delivery, your passionate sincerity and penetration,' wrote the elderly poet and novelist Richard Church, who chaired her talk. 'I watched the audience: not a cough, not one glance of indifference. You had it in the palm of your hand. And your chairman was in the palm of the other.'[161]

The following year she lectured on *Byron's Influence on the Brontës*. This talk was chaired by Joanna Richardson, one of the new friends Winifred made through the RSL. A generation younger than Winifred, Joanna was a prolific translator and literary biographer, chiefly of French writers, and also wrote about various English poets including Keats. Like Winifred, she was sometimes criticised for weighing down her books with detail and telling readers more about her subjects than they wanted to know; she once claimed that 'you ought to know what sort of marmalade the subject eats for breakfast'.[162] As a person, she could be prickly and outspoken and had a tendency to fall out with friends and colleagues, including those on the RSL Council. To judge from the warmth with which she spoke of Winifred, however, their friendship did not flounder.

Another new friend Winifred probably met at the RSL was Elizabeth Jenkins, who was around her own age. The two admired each other's work and had much in common. Elizabeth had read English and History at Newnham a few years after Winifred, when Pernel Strachey was the Principal, and through Pernel had met Edith

---

[159] *Horatia Nelson* file (OUP archives).

[160] Gérin file, RSL Members Files held by Cambridge University Library [hereafter RSL files].

[161] Letter dated 2 March 1969 (Greenwood papers).

[162] Quoted in Joanna Richardson's obituary in *The Telegraph*, 12 March 2008.

Sitwell and Virginia and Leonard Woolf. In her youth she not only lived in Bloomsbury but was for a brief period on visiting terms with Bloomsbury, or at any rate with the Woolfs, but when Winifred met her she had been living for decades in a Regency house close to Keats's house in Hampstead. Exquisitely furnished, it was an apt setting for a writer of wit and elegance who had written lives of Jane Austen and Lady Caroline Lamb.

Both writers spoke warmly about Winifred after her death. In a note to her obituary in *The Times* Joanna Richardson recalled how Winifred's life of Charlotte Brontë kept her enthralled into the small hours when she read it as a member of the Heinemann award committee. Unlike some of Winifred's academic critics, Joanna felt that Winifred's work achieved just the right balance of sense and sensibility.[163] Elizabeth Jenkins described Winifred's personality in similar terms, as romantic but at the same time sensible.[164] The friendship and esteem of such fellow writers was a huge source of gratification to Winifred as she entered her final decade.

The year 1969 saw the second new development that brought her much happiness. Since leaving Haworth she had found life back in London increasingly stressful. Despite the pleasures of London friendships both old and new, her workload was formidable, domestic problems loomed large and she missed the country walks and contact with nature she had known in Haworth. Gimmerton was sold in 1968, and Winifred's thoughts turned to the possibility of using the money from the sale to buy a weekend retreat not too far from London.

Agatha Pearce, her cousin Cuthbert's widow, had a country house in Goosey, a sleepy hamlet just outside the pretty village of Stanford in the Vale in what is now Oxfordshire, in the heart of the Vale of the White Horse. Agatha, Cuthbert's second wife, fun-loving in her younger days, was relaxing and sympathetic company (she was also invaluable to Winifred as a driver on research trips). Winifred made occasional visits to Greystones, the lovely square stone house Cuthbert had bought in Goosey, with its high gateposts and moated garden, next to a tiny church; in summer there were gatherings in the garden with Cuthbert's daughter by his first wife, Joan Stenhouse, and her family.

---

[163] In a note to Winifred's obituary in *The Times*, 4 July 1981.
[164] In correspondence with Robin Greenwood.

When Agatha reported that a thatched cottage at No. 3 Church Green had come up for sale, Winifred went to look at it, was smitten and took the plunge. From then on her 'Richard III cottage', as she called it, became her refuge whenever she felt the need to flee London, though she was never able to spend as much time there as she would have liked.

Vale Cottage, to give it its real name, thought to date from the sixteenth century, was one of a row of whitewashed cottages on the village green with its venerable lime trees, opposite St Denys Church and an old manor house. Winifred's name for it was a reference to the unsubstantiated local belief that Richard III, then Duke of Gloucester, married Anne Neville in this fifteenth-century church. Some support for this legend is provided by the York and Warwick coats of arms on the south porch, now worn away with age.

Winifred loved her Richard III cottage with its low oak-beamed ceilings. She installed some of the Yorkshire furniture brought from Gimmerton and the mahogany glass-fronted bookcase bought for her and her siblings by their father in the year after Phil's death, when the nursery of their carefree childhood became the 'study'. Emily Brontë's portrait was hung over the brick fireplace. In the ensuing years, the Gérin children came in summer to play on the green in front or the courtyard garden at the back of the house. As she and Nell let out more of the Kensington house, it could no longer accommodate the whole family, and Paul and Anne-Marie would sometimes enjoy a break in the London house while the children spent a few days with Winifred and Nell in Stanford. Friends joined them there; Joanna Richardson later recalled a winter evening by the fireside listening spellbound to Winifred's account of her adventures following the invasion of Belgium.[165]

Although the elation she had felt on the Haworth moors with John was now a thing of the past, in her Oxfordshire village she found a place of respite and serenity in the last phase of her life. In his foreword to her memoir, John, who sometimes visited her there, wrote that in Stanford she had found her 'last spiritual home'.

At the beginning of 1970 Winifred was correcting the last proofs of *Horatia Nelson* as the first ones of *Emily Brontë* arrived. *Horatia* was published that year, *Emily* in 1971.

---

[165] Note to Winifred's obituary in *The Times*, 4 July 1981.

Horatia Nelson was an anomaly among Winifred's subjects, the only one of the women she wrote about who was not herself a writer, although by bringing into the limelight a hitherto shadowy figure she was doing for Horatia what she did for Anne Brontë and, later, Anne Thackeray Ritchie. She thoroughly enjoyed her contacts with Nelson descendants and the research which took her to the Norfolk village churches and rectories where Horatia's clergyman husband had been the incumbent. Nelson relatives and Nelson fans alike were enthusiastic about the project. OUP were much less so and hesitated long before accepting it, unsure that the subject would be of sufficient interest and fearing a flop after the success of *Charlotte Brontë* and before the publication of the book on Emily.

There was less scope in this biography for speculation and interpretation than in the Brontë lives, apart from the question of Horatia's parentage – Nelson's mistress Emma Hamilton never acknowledged that she was Horatia's mother and presented herself in the capacity of her guardian, while Horatia herself never recognised Emma as her mother. Three-quarters of the book deals with Horatia's childhood and adolescence: her happy years, as Nelson's adored daughter, at Merton Place, the house Nelson bought for Emma in Surrey, until his death at Trafalgar; the ensuing years of poverty as Emma sank into debt and alcoholism, dying in destitution in Calais when Horatia was fourteen; Horatia's subsequent welcome into the households of various members of her large family of Nelson relatives. There is charm in the picture given of tranquil family life in the country with these uncles and aunts and cousins, very much in the Jane Austen vein. Horatia lived into old age, but her life after her marriage at the age of 21 to the Rev. Philip Ward, which produced ten children, is condensed into the last quarter of the book.

Much of the interest, in fact, dies with Nelson at Trafalgar a third of the way through, and once Horatia becomes Mrs Ward and the mother of ten children Winifred's task of maintaining our interest in her becomes virtually impossible. Horatia is not quite arresting enough in herself to justify a biography of 160,000 words – the original manuscript ran to 200,000, but OUP insisted on drastic cutting. Despite their reluctance to take the book on, however, when it first came out it surprised them by doing well.

After its publication Winifred continued to enjoy her contacts with Nelson fans and was invited with other writers to a dinner on board *HMS Victory* to celebrate the anniversary of Trafalgar. This would have brought memories of catching the steamer from Portsmouth at the start of childhood holidays on the Isle of Wight, when the sight of the *Victory* was always one of the excitements of the trip.

In October 1971 it was the turn of *Emily Brontë*. If *Horatia* could have done with even more cutting, *Emily* was a slim volume by Winifred's standards. Apart from the obvious reasons for this – the uneventfulness of Emily's short life, the lack of letters or journals – another may have been the wish to avoid undue repetition of what had already been recounted in her previous Brontë books. If this is so, her book on Emily suffered by being the last of the four to be published. With four lives so closely interwoven, it is impossible to narrate any one of them without constant reference to the others. Juliet Barker's *The Brontës*, published over twenty years later, tackled the task by dealing comprehensively with all the members of the family in a single volume – albeit one 1,000 pages long.

Although Winifred always said that Emily was her favourite Brontë, and it was her portrait that hung on the walls of her various houses, this last book of the quartet – on the whole the least subjective and most sober in tone of the four – lacks some of the zest of its predecessors. It would be understandable if Winifred felt some fatigue by the time she came to write it. It was now several years since she had left Haworth. It was a long time since her first rhapsodies on the moors, and her years of research had already been condensed into well over a thousand published pages.

Added to this was the difficulty of illuminating and interpreting Emily's life. As one critic put it, 'In a sense, Emily did nothing and went nowhere'[166] – she did have brief sojourns away from Haworth but spent them longing to be back in the Parsonage. The real interest of her life lies not in its external events but in her writings – her poetry and her one novel – and her inner life.

Emily's poetry is drawn on by Winifred throughout the book as providing a key to her inner life, in particular her visionary qualities. In approaching *Wuthering Heights*, she could perhaps have explored its themes in more depth, but she does examine in detail possible sources for the novel. The biographer of Emily Brontë has to look at the question of how so extraordinary a work could have been produced by a girl of Emily's limited experience. Winifred discusses literary influences on Emily's imagination, and also identifies possible sources of inspiration in the world around her, for example, Branwell's probable influence on the character of Heathcliff as an example of the destructive power of love. She tells us about the Heathcliffian propensities of the builder of Law Hill, the school where Emily taught, who turned on the family that adopted him. Ultimately, of course, whatever the literary and other influences on Emily, there can be no

---

[166] Isabel Quigly, review in *The Tablet*, 13 November 1971.

'explanation' of the imaginative processes that created the strange world of *Wuthering Heights*.

Concerning the question of whether Branwell might have had a hand in writing it, as claimed by his friend William Dearden and many others since, Winifred dismissed the possibility out of hand, as she had already done in her Branwell biography, asserting that no reader of his 'turgid' prose could believe him capable of writing a page of Emily's novel. With regard to another much-debated question, that of whether Emily had begun a second novel before she died, Winifred assumed that this was indeed the case and that the letter found in Emily's desk from her publisher Newby, referring to a second novel, was indeed for Ellis Bell (another possibility is that it was for Acton and referred to Anne's second novel *The Tenant of Wildfell Hall*). Assuming that Emily's second novel existed, Charlotte is often blamed for destroying it, but Winifred thought it more likely Emily destroyed the manuscript herself.

The second major challenge for the biographer is the interpretation of what Emily herself termed 'the world within', as opposed to the one without. Not only does Emily appear to have lived her life on two co-existing planes – the real life going on around her and the world of Gondal – but at moments of heightened being, her Wordsworthian communion with nature seems to have brought her ecstatic experiences many have taken to be spiritual and even mystical. Winifred, at any rate, followed earlier biographers such as May Sinclair in defining the visions referred to in Emily's poems as those of a mystic who experienced moments of oneness with the universe; moment of insight when 'the unseen its truth reveals'. She goes as far as to equate Emily's experiences with those of St Theresa or St John of the Cross, unlike other critics who interpret Emily's poems less literally, in terms of the language commonly used by Romantic poets such as Shelley. A.S. Byatt, reviewing the book for the *Times*, felt that despite Winifred's concern to present Emily as a rounded human being (showing us, for example, the housekeeper baking bread for the family and the financial administrator managing the sisters' railway share investments), she did not escape the tendency to approach Emily the 'mystic of the moors' with 'semi-religious awe'.[167]

Emily's inscrutability makes her a difficult subject at any period of her life, but she becomes particularly enigmatic during the final months of her life when, dying of consumption following Branwell's death, she withdrew into herself, refused to discuss her condition with her family and rejected all offers of medical aid. She had hitherto been

---

[167] *The Times*, 9 December 1971.

strong and healthy. Was her death hastened by non-physical causes? The villagers believed she died of grief for Branwell, due to the popular notion that she was the sister who gave him most support in the harrowing years of his decline. Biographers before Winifred had put forward various theories for Emily's behaviour, Virginia Moore suggesting that she willed her own death,[168] while Muriel Spark saw an element of self-dramatisation in Emily's stoical stance.[169]

Winifred believed that witnessing Branwell's deterioration did affect Emily's life of the imagination and ability to write, but found the main reason for her decline elsewhere. She subscribed to the theory that Emily lost the will to live in her last months, and that this was largely attributable to the invasion of her privacy when Charlotte persuaded her to publish her writings. Winifred suggested that as a result of this violation of the world within by the world without, Emily lost not just the ability to write but the visions that gave her fulfilment, and, like Cathy on her deathbed, wished to 'escape into that glorious world, and to be always there: not seeing it dimly . . . and yearning for it . . . but really with it, and in it'.[170] In certain poems Emily does appear to long for death as the ultimate experience of oneness with nature. In contradiction of this theory of a death wish on Emily's part is Charlotte's description of her sister as being torn reluctantly 'out of a happy life', which Winifred explains away by claiming that Charlotte was in denial about Emily's death wish.

Charlotte, in fact, admitted being as much in the dark as anyone else about what was really going on in Emily's head in her last months, when, fading by the day, she stubbornly denied her family the consolation of sending for a doctor until a few hours before she died. A biographer more interested than Winifred in psychological theories might have explored such hypotheses as the possibility of schizophrenic tendencies in Emily, but Winifred was wary of psychological speculation. The only certainty is that the physical cause of Emily's death was galloping consumption – 'consumption, two months' duration', as recorded by the doctor on her death certificate.

Winifred's final Brontë biography sold well but did not have quite the impact of her life of Charlotte, though C.P. Snow wrote that the 'two together rank as one of the monuments, scholarly, literary, intuitive, of our time'.[171] She was generally felt to have made a good job

---

[168] Virigina Moore, *The Life and Eager Death of Emily Brontë* (London: Rich & Cowan, 1936).

[169] Spark and Stanford, *Emily Brontë: Her Life and Work*.

[170] *Wuthering Heights*, Chapter 15.

[171] Cited in Peter Sutcliffe's entry for Winifred in *Dictionary of National Biography 1981–1985* (OUP).

of an almost impossible task. As she herself says in her preface, 'When every writer who has something to say on the subject has said it, Emily Brontë will still elude us; we can hardly wish it otherwise. It is a part of her fascination to elude definition, like the girl in Branwell's portrait whose eyes are not turned on us, but out of this world.'

In her review, A.S. Byatt referred to this elusiveness and why it exerts such an attraction. 'Biographical studies of the Brontës . . . are almost always tinged with the iconography of the unknown. Like Shakespeare, like Richard III, they come to be repositories for other people's need of intenser, extended experience.'[172] It was this 'need of intenser experience' that had brought Winifred and John together. The publication of this biography of the Brontë who fascinated them the most marked the completion of the project they had planned together so excitedly on the Haworth moors.

OUP threw what Winifred described as a lavish launch party for *Emily* at Ely House, the grand former episcopal palace in Mayfair that housed its London offices. They were so confident of *Emily's* success they had printed 8,500 copies, an ambitious print run for a literary biography. At the age of seventy, Winifred was riding high and her energy seemed unabated. She and her publishers had reason to be pleased with each other, and Peter Sutcliffe was looking forward to her next book. She had been toying with various possible subjects. At one point she was considering Hartley Coleridge, the fragile, diminutive son of the famous poet, with whom Branwell found much in common on a memorable visit to Ambleside in 1840; at another, George Eliot's companion and Charlotte Brontë's critic, G.H. Lewes. The subject she finally chose, however, was not a nineteenth-century literary figure. It came as a complete surprise – or rather shock – to Sutcliffe.

Brimming over with enthusiasm as usual, Winifred informed him, in letters full of excited underlinings – she wrote as emphatically as she spoke – that she was planning to write about Amy Robsart, the ill-fated wife of Elizabeth I's favourite, Robert Dudley, later Earl of Leicester. The newly-crowned Elizabeth was known to be infatuated with Dudley. Required to be in constant attendance on her at court, he barely saw his young wife, who passed her time at various country houses. Since the day in September 1560 when she was found dead, her neck broken, at the bottom of a flight of stairs in Cumnor Place

---

172 *The Times*, 9 December 1971.

near Abingdon, there have been numerous theories as to how she died. The coroner's verdict was 'accidental death', but the rumours said otherwise. Such was the scandal around Amy's sudden demise, in fact, that it made a marriage between Elizabeth and Dudley impossible. Was her death murder, suicide or an accident? If murder, was it arranged by Dudley himself or an accomplice? Sir Walter Scott, who uses the story in *Kenilworth*, has Amy done to death by Dudley's steward, Varney.

This was the murder mystery about which Winifred proposed to write under the title *The Death at Cumnor: An Elizabethan Enigma Re-examined*. Peter Sutcliffe was taken aback at such a complete departure both from her usual historical period and her favoured genre of literary biography, and far from certain that she could pull it off. Dismayed, he did his best to dissuade her from the project, while admitting, 'You are very persuasive, as always.' To himself he probably added that she was being very stubborn, as always. She seemed undaunted by the research involved, cheerfully telling Paul Gérin, 'My new book spans all the Tudor reigns, so I have my work cut out.' Much research would be required, and she would have to head back to Norfolk, Amy's home county, where she had gone to research *Horatia*.

She worked at her usual feverish pace, somehow cramming in much else besides this ambitious project. In 1972 she received a formal invitation from Molly Patterson, the secretary of the RSL, to be a member of its Council. 'Mrs Patterson' had fast become 'my dear Molly'; Winifred was one of many Fellows to whom she became a personal friend, to be invited down to supper after lectures to Molly's flat in the basement at No. 1 Hyde Park Gardens. Molly's dinner parties were renowned both for the good talk and for such gourmet delicacies as the plovers' eggs she supplied on one occasion. 'What wonders you achieve culinary and conversational – to only name a few – and all simultaneously!' wrote L.P. Hartley after one such session. 'It is like magic.'[173]

Winifred accepted the invitation to join the Council with delight. 'My dear Molly, I *can't* be formal with someone I am so fond of as you, though the present occasion probably requires it. I feel the *enormous* compliment paid me by the Council in inviting me to join their number, and can find few words in which to convey these feelings; but I *do* know how to express the sheer pleasure it has given me; so I will rather speak of that. To me, time spent on books and writing is not only the occupation of my life, but its purest pleasure; and I can imagine few proposals more congenial to my tastes than the one the

---

[173] L.P. Hartley file (RSL files).

Council, in its generosity, has made to me. I will concentrate on thinking about the *enjoyment* of those meetings, in the company of people who all mean very much to me, and not on my inadequacies for the post.'[174]

Despite her diffidence about her suitability for the position, Winifred was a success on the Council, getting on well with the other members and exhibiting the balance of sense and sensibility referred to approvingly by Joanna Richardson. At meetings she was wont to express herself with warmth and conviction, but at the same time dispassionately and with wisdom.[175] Lord Birkenhead,[176] a former leading light of the Council whose wife Sheila Berry Smith, the author of books on nineteenth-century literary life, was now a member, considered Winifred to be 'one of the most valuable additions for a long time'.[177]

Meetings were on the first Monday of the month and for Winifred these were very pleasant afternoon hours, spent in the company of writers with congenial literary tastes. Apart from the contentious Joanna Richardson, her fellow council members included the women's activist Baroness Mary Stocks, the historical biographer Vincent Cronin, who had written on the French Revolution, and the publisher John Guest.

These RSL colleagues became friends. Mary Stocks, at whose suggestion Winifred had been invited on to the Council,[178] was an admirer of Elizabeth Gaskell and when Winifred came to write Gaskell's biography it was to Baroness Stocks – like Gaskell 'a Mancunian by adoption and a champion of noble causes'[179] – that she dedicated the book.

Vincent Cronin, son of the novelist A.J. Cronin, was a Francophile like Winifred. Married to a Frenchwoman, he divided his time between his house in Hyde Park Square and the Normandy château of his wife's family. From the latter he sent an affectionate thank-you note for a copy of Winifred's latest book. 'I was clipping a hedge in our dried-up garden, thinking about you, wondering how you were, and promising myself I would write that evening. Then at tea-time I undid a parcel . . . What an excitement – such arrivals in the country are to their London equivalents what a picnic is to an indoor meal.'[180]

---

174 Letter dated 5 May 1972, Gérin file (RSL files).
175 Note by Joanna Richardson to Winifred's obituary in *The Times*, 4 July 1981.
176 Frederick Winston Furneaux Smith, 2nd Earl of Birkenhead.
177 Letter to Winifred from Sheila Birkenhead, 1975 (Greenwood papers).
178 According to a letter from Molly Patterson in Birkenkead file (RSL files).
179 Dedication of *Elizabeth Gaskell*.
180 Letter dated 20 July 1976 (Greenwood papers).

Although a generation younger than her he was a traditionalist after her own heart. An author of lightweight but well-researched historical biographies who specialised in French history, his sympathetic view of Louis XVI and Marie Antoinette accorded with Winifred's own.

The publisher John Guest was a cousin of Elizabeth Jenkins's. He had formerly chaired the Heinemann Award Committee and it was at his recommendation that Winifred was invited onto the committee when Joanna Richardson retired from it in 1973; he believed it should include at least one woman.[181] As an author, he was known for one outstanding book, his sensitive, award-winning wartime memoir *Broken Images*. A homosexual, he had a wide circle of literary friends and a wide repertoire of entertaining literary anecdotes. He later offered Winifred sympathy and support in the difficult last period of her life.

To these fellow council members Winifred sent copies of her books as they came out and received in return elegantly-phrased handwritten notes of appreciation. She and her literary friends formed something of a mutual admiration society; from them she need not fear any bracing criticism of the kind she got from Peter Sutcliffe. For many she rapidly became 'My Dearest Win'. Quite a few were her contemporaries, often in failing health, struggling to get to the meetings at Hyde Park Gardens that were one of the pleasures of their old age. They propped one another up, visiting members who were in hospital and offering support to the bereaved spouse when a council member died.

During Winifred's final years, when she was just managing to hobble to meetings of the Council despite increasing infirmity – 'I hope that I shall not be kicked out of it yet awhile and continue to keep your greatly valued friendship,' she wrote to John Guest two months before her death[182] – it received new blood with the advent of new members from a younger generation of writers such as Melvyn Bragg and Michael Holroyd, with whom she was also soon on friendly terms.

Throughout the decade of the seventies, Winifred's writing and Council work were carried out against a backdrop of growing domestic and family problems. The industrial strikes of the period, too, made life difficult for her and her circle of ageing friends (unlike her old friend Mina Breed, though, who felt the unions had become

---

[181] Letter from Robert Speaight in Speaight file (RSL files).
[182] Letter to John Guest dated 6 April 1981. University of Reading, Special Collections.

too powerful and joined her local Conservative Party, Winifred voted Labour and disliked Margaret Thatcher from the start). There were postal strikes, train strikes, strikes of hospital workers. During the electricity cuts resulting from the miners' strikes she and Nell had to cook on gas stoves; when it was the gas workers' turn to strike they had to prepare meals for their elderly lodger Miss Sorrie, who used gas. In addition, elderly lodgers like Miss Sorrie had to be nursed when ill. The problem of finding domestic help was more intractable than ever. Their Spanish help always seemed to be on holiday or ill just when they most needed her services, and became so 'lazy and insolent' it was a relief when she gave her notice.

Domestic trials were compounded by health problems. Roger developed heart and respiratory troubles and was never really well in his final decade. He had hitherto led a contented life under Holloway's benign regime; now, Winifred said, he had nothing left to live for. She kept up her tiring train journeys to Holloway even though she now often had to nurse Nell, whose health was failing fast. By the mid-seventies heart disorders exacerbated by hyperthyroidism had made her an invalid. She was sometimes seriously ill – Winifred reported sleeping for ten days in an armchair at her sister's bedside after Nell had some kind of heart attack – and failing eyesight robbed her of her main occupation, her painting. As she could no longer manage the stairs up to the second floor, they both moved down a floor and let out more of the house. Winifred would have liked to have a live-in help; she needed someone to stay with Nell when she herself was out doing research. To stand in for the home help during her frequent absences, the second-floor lodger sometimes kept an eye on Nell when Winifred was out, and a student was commissioned to do shopping and other errands.

One of these was to walk Jamie, a newcomer in the household who gave Winifred much joy in her last years. After the death of Betsy left the house without a pet, Winifred could not bear to get another cat to replace her. Instead she acquired a puppy. Like Flossy, Anne Brontë's dog, described in Winifred's biography of Anne as 'one of those spaniels who worm their way immediately into the hearts of their owners',[183] he was a King Charles spaniel, the breed popular with the Merry Monarch, and was 'adorable'. Her King Charles dog and her Richard III cottage did the most to alleviate the strain of those years. Breaks in the country became more and more necessary to her. Apart from anything else, housekeeping in Stanford, where they had some domestic help, was so much easier than at 60 West Cromwell Road.

---

[183] Gérin, *Anne Brontë*, Chapter 15.

The stays in Stanford were all too brief, though. Mina Breed remarked that Winifred put herself under too much pressure of work and 'lived on her nerves'. Although Winifred was always loyal to her friends, she seemed so busy Mina was often loath to phone her and interrupt her work.

Under these circumstances, it was remarkable that Winifred managed to finish the typescript of her Amy Robsart story at all, let alone so soon. She sent it to Peter Sutcliffe, only to be told that he felt it was unpublishable. Whether or not he said 'I told you so', he was naturally both annoyed and sorry that so much energy had been expended on a project that he had foreseen from the start would be unsuited to her. He suggested doing a book on Elizabeth Gaskell instead, as following on naturally from the Brontës. Winifred swallowed her disappointment and accepted the commission, finding Gaskell an attractive subject for many reasons apart from the Brontë link. Not only was she a personality almost impossible to dislike, but Winifred's experience of living in Haworth and her discovery of the character of northerners, rather like that of the heroine of *North and South*, gave Mrs Gaskell's portrayal of the people of the north a personal appeal. She was also attracted by her defence of the poor.

There had been no shortage of studies of Gaskell's work, but there was a lack of comprehensive biographies. Winifred's task was made easier by the publication in 1966 of the entire collection of Mrs Gaskell's surviving letters, on which she was the first biographer to draw.

In January 1975 Winifred, writing to thank the Gérins for their Christmas presents, was able to tell them of a New Year's gift for herself that had come as a surprise. She had been awarded the OBE. In a subsequent letter she described her visit to the Palace in February as rather like being at the court of Elizabeth I. In dwelling on the Beefeaters and the curtseying she was perhaps exaggerating the courtliness of the occasion for the delectation of the Gérins, for her friend the actress Jill Balcon, Cecil Day-Lewis' widow, had warned her that the ceremony was likely to be less solemn than she expected. 'Don't be put off by the string band playing selections from musical comedies interspersed with *Sheep may safely graze*. When my father was knighted the band was playing *Doing what comes naturally*.'[184] Winifred invited her friends to a celebratory party at West Cromwell Road for which she did most of the catering herself. In a thank-you note Jill feared that she must have thoroughly exhausted herself.

---

[184] Letter from Jill Balcon dated 18 January 1975 (Greenwood papers).

With various literary prizes under her belt and 'O.B.E., F.R.S.L' to print on her letter paper, completely eclipsing the once-prized M.A., Winifred's cup of honours was full. But the Gaskell book was written in even more challenging conditions than *Death at Cumnor*. 'My book is progressing, with difficulty but enthusiasm', she told the Gérins. In 1975 Winifred's and Nell's settled Kensington life was shaken to its foundations when they finally and with reluctance took the decision to sell the house they loved, and in which Nell had lived for 30 years. The search began for a buyer and for a suitable ground-floor flat to move to. That summer Marthe, now almost sixteen, came to stay for a month to help out. She did shopping, walked Jamie and stayed with Nell while Winifred went to libraries, or to Oxford to see her publisher. Winifred reported to the Gérins that Marthe had made great progress with her English and read to 'Gui-Gui' in the evenings from the English classics and Agatha Christie. As the eldest of a family of five with four boys to help keep in order, Marthe was capable and responsible beyond her years. She was, in fact, the perfect grand-daughter and the sisters missed her cheerful presence when she returned to Liège. They had hoped to sell the house that autumn; they found their dream flat, but one prospective sale after another fell through and when the year ended they were still in West Cromwell Road.

The first months of 1976 brought several successive blows. Sybil Lock died on 31 December 1975 at the age of 79 and Winifred joined John in Eastbourne in the New Year for the funeral. Then in February she was saddened by the news of the death of her oldest friend, Mina Breed.

It was a friendship that had lasted for sixty years despite the many differences between them. Mina's life, spent in the Beckenham home in which she grew up and was still living when she died, had been outwardly uneventful. Throughout the period of Winifred's romance with Eugène and war adventures, Mina, after a few years working in Geneva, was employed at the Board of Trade and lived quietly with her parents. In the years when Winifred was embarking on her Haworth adventure Mina was nursing her failing parents. She seemed to be contented with her lot and happy for her friend when she found the romantic love Mina had never known and very probably never sought. In quiet, kind letters to friends such as Paul Gérin she reported on the many interests and little incidents of her life: her painting classes, the German lessons undertaken for her job in the Board of Trade's Exports Department, her pleasure in the new pets acquired to keep her company in the house she found big and lonely after her parents' death.

At the end of February, as the house was finally to be sold and just after sending the Gaskell book to OUP, Winifred had a stroke. She had been overworking finalising the manuscript. She was taken to St Stephen's Hospital in Chelsea, from where she scrawled a note to Molly Patterson a few days later thanking her RSL colleagues for the flowers they had sent. A letter to the Gérins to reassure them that she was already making progress was also somewhat untidily scrawled, but her right hand, the writing hand, was in fact unaffected – and so, she was able to report with relief, was her brain; the left arm and leg, however, were impaired, and the untidiness of the handwriting was owing to her inability to hold down the paper with her left hand. She was to be sent home after a month, and gratefully accepted Marthe's offer to come and help out in the Easter holidays, as 'I'm afraid we are in rather a fix.' Over the next few months she made steady progress, but she was left with a limp on the left side.

A letter from Jill Balcon testifies to the courage with which Winifred confronted the challenges of the last phase of her life, and to the affection she inspired in her friends. Since Cecil Day-Lewis's death in 1972 Winifred had been a great support to the younger woman, widowed when she was around the same age as Winifred at the time of Eugène's death. 'You have been such a joy in my life,' Jill wrote, 'I could never do enough for you . . . after all the strains and tragedies you have sustained, you *still* have that deep reservoir of courage and invincible determination to fight through. It's a real example to one who goes under for what would seem to you trivialities. You are so brave and uncomplaining – and you have got the additional worry of Nell . . . but characteristically you shout hurrah for meals on wheels as if they were a gastronomic treat, and you *never moan*.'[185]

In July, by which time Winifred's condition had improved, her life of Elizabeth Gaskell came out – the life of one Brontë biographer by another.

Elizabeth Gaskell, charming, lively, witty, happy and sane, fun to be with as well as a do-gooder, the author of books like *Cranford* written to entertain as well as sombre 'Condition of England' novels, had been good company for Winifred over the difficult past two years. However, coming after the Brontë siblings, Mrs Gaskell seemed to some reviewers tame in comparison and too aimiable to be exciting. For Hilary Spurling, reviewing the book in the *Spectator*, one thing that made Mrs Gaskell less than thrilling as a subject was that whereas Gaskell was driven to write the life of Charlotte Brontë in order to

---

[185] Letter of 1976 (Greenwood papers).

refute accusations of Charlotte's 'coarseness', and Gérin in order to correct some of the romantic myths that had surrounded the Brontës since Gaskell's biography, Gaskell's own life left no wrongs to right.[186]

Unlike Charlotte Brontë, Mrs Gaskell was a woman who seemed to have it all. Charlotte was dissatisfied with her life and had to learn to resolve her inner conflicts. In the life of Elizabeth Gaskell there was no such inner drama to be played out and few such tensions to be resolved, since despite one devastating personal tragedy, the death of her baby son, she appears to have achieved fulfilment as a wife, mother and author, somehow bringing her different selves and activities into harmony with one another.

Praised by many as a delightful study of a delightful woman, Winifred's biography was seen by others as worthy, dutiful, old-fashioned and rather dull, 'like its subject at her most tiresome,' as Hilary Spurling put it. This seems unfair to both Winifred and Gaskell, since Winifred's narrative is an extremely readable one and Mrs Gaskell was, in fact, rarely dull in her books and never in her sparklingly spontaneous letters. A more pertinent criticism was that in contrast to Winifred's Brontë biographies with their dense background detail, at 300 pages her Gaskell book sometimes leaves one wanting to know more about the background to Gaskell's busy, well-peopled life.

Some reviewers, curious to know whether Mrs Gaskell was really as emotionally balanced as she appeared, would also have liked Winifred to delve deeper into Gaskell herself, missing the in-depth psychological investigation common in biographies of the time. Speculation about a subject's subconscious, however – about his or her neuroses, complexes, childhood traumas – had never formed a significant part of Winifred's approach. The biographer Claire Tomalin did not see the need for such delving. Describing the book as a 'humane, gentle and loving biography' she said, not disapprovingly, that Winifred 'takes Mrs Gaskell very much as she would have wished to be taken'.[187] If so, this is the opposite of the psychoanalytical approach aimed at uncovering psychological aspects of which the subject may have been unaware. Elizabeth Gaskell would certainly have welcomed Winifred's reticence; she would have been as averse as Emily Brontë to being the subject of a biography and constantly urged her correspondents to destroy her letters. Winifred's light touch is displayed in her treatment of Gaskell's friendship with Charles Eliot Norton, a charming American 16 years her junior whom she met while

---

[186] *The Spectator*, 24 July 1976.
[187] In Critics' Forum, BBC Radio 3, 10 July 1976.

on holiday in Rome. Then 47, she afterwards described it as the happiest time of her life. Abstaining from any obtrusive analysis of Gaskell's feeling for the younger man, Winifred merely describes it as 'platonic love' and allows the reader to follow the blossoming of the friendship without too much comment from her.

Professor Arthur Pollard, co-editor of Gaskell's letters, approved of Winifred's unobtrusive approach and preferred her 'analysis based on common sense, wide experience, and mature judgement' to psychological analysis that risked being speculative. He welcomed Winifred's common-sense approach, for example, in her chapter on William Gaskell, in which she takes a look at the man Gaskell married and at the marriage itself. In her *Life of Charlotte Brontë* Gaskell deliberately draws a veil over Charlotte's marriage as being a private matter; lifting the veil from Gaskell's own – or indeed assessing any marriage from the outside – is well-nigh impossible. The Gaskells' relationship would seem to have been harmonious but their lives and temperaments diverged widely – William rarely accompanied Elizabeth on her travels and she once told a correspondent that his extreme reserve frustrated her own need to communicate. Winifred recognises the difficulty of gauging happiness and fulfilment in married life with remarks such as 'Time inevitably works changes and emphasises disparities of character, just as first love dispels them, and makes relationships complicated that appeared so simple in the early euphoria of the first exchanges. Both husband and wife were bound to experience this, like the majority of men and women'.[188] Her own experience must have taught her the truth of the observation.

The Gaskell biography, described by *The Economist* as 'as pleasant to read as one of Mrs Gaskell's own novels',[189] was awarded the 1976 Whitbread Literary Award.

The sale of the house, which had been delayed by Winifred's illness, kept her and Nell in London in the summer heat, unable to escape to Stanford, until it finally went through. In October they moved to a ground-floor flat in a mansion block close by, Marlborough Court in Pembroke Road. It had a small garden and a sitting room, dining room, three bedrooms and a study; but it seemed small after the high-ceilinged rooms of West Cromwell Road. Winifred placed Eugène's cello in her bedroom so that it would be the first thing she saw each

---

[188] Quoted by Pollard in *Nineteenth-Century Fiction*, Vol. 32, No. 1, June 1977. The quotation is from Chapter 21 of *Elizabeth Gaskell*.

[189] *The Economist*, 24 July 1976.

day, bringing back the memory of their first morning in Paris. It was a reassuring presence in their new surroundings.

This was the house from which she wrote to the Gérins in the summer of 1977 'Je prépare un nouveau bouquin!'[190] She was reading for this new project in the garden and had bought an electric typewriter, which she found easier for her impaired left hand. Her evenings were dedicated to her sister. Nell could no longer see well enough to read or watch their new colour television, and Winifred read aloud to her every day; this displeased Jamie, who was jealous and did everything he could to divert her attention from her sister.

Visiting the following year, Paul Gérin was sad to find both sisters much aged, but Winifred was working as hard as ever on her new electric typewriter and finding her new subject fully as congenial as the last. For this book she had looked no further than a few streets away in Kensington. She had often passed by a bow-windowed Queen Anne house at No. 16 (formerly 13) Young Street, near the corner of Kensington Gardens. It was the house where Thackeray lived from 1846 to 1853. Here, in 1850, he organised a gathering for one of his greatest fans, the newly-famous Charlotte Brontë, a gathering over which Charlotte's paralysing shyness cast such a blight that Thackeray sneaked out of his own party to take refuge at his club. The event was recorded amusingly by his thirteen-year-old daughter Anne ('Anny'), who inherited her father's liveliness and some of his talent for writing. It was on the life of Anne Thackeray Ritchie that Winifred was now working.

As with Gaskell, Winifred had chosen a tremendously sympathetic personality. A further attraction must have been the many facets of Anny's story that chimed in with Winifred's own. There was the relationship with an adored and adoring father, the love of France (Anny and her sister Minny spent part of their childhood in Paris), the foreign travel with a restless father who was always on the move. There was the taint and tragedy of madness in the family – after the first few years of marriage Anny's mother became insane and spent the rest of her life in care – and Thackeray's fear that her madness might be hereditary (in the event, Minny's daughter had a mental disability). There was the unconventional childhood in which by far the greatest influences were provided by the home environment, while a succession of hopelessly inadequate governesses came and went leaving little trace. Another odd parallel between Anny and Winifred was that they both married much younger men. When Anny married her cousin Richmond Ritchie she was forty to his twenty-three.

---

[190] 'I'm writing a new book.'

The first half of Winifred's book, up to Thackeray's death when Anny and her sister Minny were in their twenties, is as much about Thackeray as his daughter. His genial personality, as towering as his physical stature, fills the stage so endearingly that his sudden death at the age of fifty-one is a loss to the book as well as to his two girls. His own words, quoted from his letters on almost every page, give ample proof that under the cynical, rather snobbish exterior that he often assumed in company and that repelled Charlotte Brontë when she met him, was a heart overflowing with kindness as well as fun. His children's book *The Rose and the Ring*, loved by Winifred as a child when given to her by her favourite governess Miss Hodges, was begun during a holiday in Rome to entertain a friend's sick daughter. In Winifred's portrait of him, Thackeray emerges as a valiant single father doing his best for his girls, his mother and stepfather, needy friends and relatives, while working himself to death in order to leave his daughters financially secure.

Charlotte Brontë, who so revered him as a writer, was unfortunate enough not only to clash with him whenever they met but to dedicate *Jane Eyre* to him before she was aware that, like Rochester, he had a mad wife. The dedication caused embarrassment to both of them, since gossip had it that the book was written by a governess who had been in his employ. In fact Thackeray, though fully as lonely in his predicament and as susceptible to female charms as Charlotte's Rochester, avoided temptation by employing only governesses to whom he felt confident he would not feel attracted!

Anny shared her father's likeable qualities as well as his compulsion to write. Inspired to keep a journal after reading Fanny Burney's, she had Fanny's talent for being around when there were famous people to be met, and for recording these encounters in impressionistic word sketches. An example is her account of being taken as a child to visit Chopin in his Paris apartment and hearing him play. In the course of her long life Anny seems to have known just about everyone in literary London, from Dickens, whose daughters were childhood friends, to Virginia Woolf (before his marriage to Virginia's mother her father, Leslie Stephen, was married to Minny Thackeray, who died in childbirth). Winifred's task was to weave all the threads together into a coherent narrative, which she did with her usual skill.

Meanwhile, in the years she was writing the book the fabric of her own life was threatening to unravel, with the death of another of her oldest and dearest friends (Dorothy Moore, who died in 1977 aged 85), and the health of both siblings a constant preoccupation at a time when she herself was increasingly beset by health complications, including arthritis and heart and circulatory problems. Nell required constant attendance, despite which, and despite her own infirmities, which made travelling difficult, Winifred continued to visit Roger regularly. He died in September 1979, at the age of eighty. Winifred's grief was in some ways reminiscent of Charlotte's at the death of Branwell. It was sorrow at the finality of loss of a brother in many ways already long lost to her but whom she had never ceased to love, and renewed regret at his wasted potential. She remembered him as the companion of her teens and the promising student who was doing well in his studies at the very moment his mind was breaking down. She told the Gérins that she felt desolate but that 'everything is for an ultimate good'. Roger was brought to be cremated at Kensal Green Crematorium. The following year, Holloway Sanatorium was closed. The building stood derelict until the 1990s, when it was restored and became Virginia Park, a gated housing development. Today the grounds in which Roger was a familiar figure for so long are as immaculate as in his day.

Soon after his death, Winifred was cheered by a visit from the three eldest Gérin children. Marthe was now twenty and studying law, Hubert seventeen, Eugène thirteen. 'You can be proud of them,' she wrote afterwards to Paul and Anne-Marie. 'Despite the physical changes in them, they are still essentially the same dear, affectionate, charming children Nell and I have always known. We were greatly impressed by their intellectual and, in the case of the two boys, artistic development. Hubert is already an accomplished artist. His work is exquisite, and if he continues like this I feel sure his work will be recognised. Eugène also has great artistic talent, and our dear Marthe is as she always has been – energetic, generous, lively.' She had often been anxious about Eugène; nervous and insecure in earlier childhood, he had suffered from being the middle child after the arrival of the twins. He was now discovering the way he was to take in life. Hubert did become an artist, as Nell had always predicted, and so did Eugène, whose own bent was for cartoons; Marthe, when she finished her law degree, joined the police force. Their visit to London in 1979 was the last time they would see 'Marraine Winny'.

By 1980 *Anne Thackeray Ritchie* was finished and in the publisher's hands. Well before it came out, Winifred was already at work on a new project. Many years previously Peter Sutcliffe had suggested to her that she should write her autobiography. He was not the only person to have made the suggestion over the years. Like John Lock, like Joanna Richardson and other friends, he had listened enthralled to her accounts of her wartime adventures. Recently, he had reiterated his proposal that she should write down her wartime and other memories and that OUP should publish the memoir. Her title for it was *The Years that Count.*

When Peter had first broached the idea she had been dismissive. She was a biographer, immersed in other people's lives, and her own seemed uninteresting in comparison; it was surely presumptuous to think it worth recording. But in the last few years, particularly since her stroke, her perspective had changed. As a biographer she had always considered her subjects' emotional and intellectual life, the personal qualities that gave their writings the power to move others, more important than the external events that marked their lives. She now came to feel that the emotional development of any human being could be of interest to those who had a similar response to experience, and that her own – though she saw the recording of it as a somewhat self-indulgent exercise – need be no exception.[191]

'You may groan', she wrote to Peter on 21 March 1980, 'to hear that I have finally followed your advice and started writing my "auto-biography" – in *no* sense a complete or conventional autobiography. To be called *The Years that Count*, hence purely selective and relating only to vivid memories. It seems to be going well. It will have *no* foot-notes! quotations! or other contentious matter! and may therefore prove quite unsuitable for OUP – but you gave me the first idea so must be the first to be inflicted by the MS. I talk as if it would ever be finished – which it may well never be, but at least it gives me some creative work, and fills the void left since ATR was finished.'[192]

It was the first year of the rule of Mrs Thatcher, who had become Prime Minister in May 1979. Absorbed in her writing in the new flat that had at first seemed so cramped – she and Nell had by now had grown used to its dimensions – Winifred took less interest than usual in the state of Britain or the world. For months on end, as Nell dozed in the next room, Winifred inhabited, for several hours a day, what L.P. Hartley calls the 'foreign country' of the past. For the first time in her writing career it was her own past she was turning into a 'bouquin'. In those months she lived in turn in Norwood, in Paris, in Aspley Guise. She was in turn being shepherded around the glorious Paris of her adolescence by Cousin Enrico, breathing in the mountain air of Plombières, sitting in the concert hall in Cannes listening to Eugène playing Ravel's *Pavane*. She was with Eugène on the train to

---

[191] Preface to Winifred's memoir.
[192] Ritchie file (OUP archives).

Ostend after the invasion of Brussels, she was on the train to Narbonne in pursuit of him as the Germans advanced on Paris, she was on the plane that took them back to England after the nightmare months in Nice. She was standing once again by his side in the hallway of the house in Virginia Water as he began the sentence that he never finished.

Her narrative of the decades since that day, 16 February 1945, lacked the lustre of the earlier chapters; the Haworth years and the discovery of her literary metier had brought much fulfilment but she did not feel the same impulse to explore them. The 'years that counted' were the years up to 1945.

When not re-living the past at her typewriter, Winifred continued to take an interest in the people she loved in the present. She was feeling her age, but her mind and concern for others were as keen as ever. In the summer of 1980 Paul and Anne-Marie brought the twins for some sight-seeing in London. Winny and Nell were in the cottage; the Gérins stayed in the London flat and spent a day with them in Stanford. Vincent and Emmanuel, now twelve, always remembered playing with Jamie that day on the village green.

In November of that year Winifred was cheered by an invitation to be Vice-President of the RSL. 'I am left speechless by the honour conferred on me,' she wrote in her letter of acceptance to the Council Chairman, C.M. ('Monty') Woodhouse. 'Luckily I do not have to speak, but even to write is difficult to convey my happiness, gratitude and, principally, my sense of *inadequacy* . . . I can truly say that at this end of my life the RSL has brought me, together with my work, the greatest gift of happiness and the possession of some of the best friends I know.'[193]

The start of 1981 found Winifred still working on her memoir. She rarely went out these days except to RSL council meetings and lectures; on 19 March she chaired one on Trollope. She reported in letters that Nell, practically immobile and almost blind, still got some enjoyment out of life. She liked feeding the birds when Winifred wheeled her into the garden, listening to the television and being read aloud to. She still wanted to hear the news of their friends and when Winifred returned from Council meetings Nell always asked for a full report.

Nell died peacefully on 26 March after a brief illness during which she was nursed at home. 'Nell and I were so close, shared so many interests, sentiments, reactions to events, that I feel as if the half of me was gone,' she wrote to John Guest. 'Though our paths – hers towards

---

[193] Letter dated 3 November 1980. Gérin file (RSL files).

Art and mine towards books – diverged, we both had a deep feeling for the *other* art – and she could completely share my taste in reading, and I could share her dedication to Art.'[194] 'Jamie sits by Gui-Gui's armchair and rubs his head against the seat', she told the Gérins. 'He follows me around everywhere, afraid that I will disappear too!'

After Nell's death Winifred somehow drove herself to finish her memoir. By May she was making plans for the Gérins to visit that summer. She urged the whole family to come and stay. She intended to spend the entire summer in Stanford. Marthe, Hubert and Eugène could stay in the London house; there was space in the cottage for their parents and the two youngest children, and the three eldest could come and spend a day in Stanford.

Over the weekend of 20–21 June John paid her a visit. It was just before the publication of *Anne Thackeray Ritchie*, and there had been a launch party at which she had enjoyed meeting her RSL and other friends. She and John talked about her plans for the future. The memoir had been sent to Peter Sutcliffe, who felt, however, that it needed quite a lot more work to make it publishable. She told John, as she had the Gérins, that once the flurry of the publication of the Ritchie book was over her only wish was to go to Stanford and stay there until the end of the summer. Looking further ahead, she said matter-of-factly that she reckoned she had another year of life and work left in her, enough at any rate to get the memoir ready for publication.

Anne Thackeray Ritchie came out on 25 June. *The Times* reviewer noted that although it was the first time Anny had had a full-length biography to herself, no-one familiar with nineteenth-century London could have failed to notice that 'whenever she appears it is the cue for a brightening and lightening of mood as human happiness is seen to be possible.' To read Winifred's book was 'to see all the threads assembled at last into one piece of work, and finally to meet a radiant and talented woman previously glimpsed, as it were, at other people's parties, entirely by herself'.[195]

The sympathy with which Anny and just about everyone in her entourage are presented charmed many readers. Not so Jonathan Raban, who in a Critics' Forum discussion on Radio 3 a couple of weeks later called it a 'whitewash job', complaining that, 'Almost everybody in the book is presented as being frightfully nice, frightfully decent, and frightfully talented . . . in that sort of rather upper-class

---

[194] Letter to John Guest, 6 April 1981. University of Reading, Special Collections.
[195] *The Times*, 25 June 1981.

way in which the readers are treated as servants who aren't allowed to see the dirty secrets behind.'[196] He cited as an example of such a 'dirty secret' Thackeray's treatment of his wife; some biographers had accused him of contributing to her mental breakdown by being an absentee husband, and then finding it convenient to put her away when her mind gave way. Despite having been too quick herself on occasion to apportion blame in some of her past biographies, in her last one Winifred is non-judgemental. She seems to have become similarly non-judgemental in her own life, for example choosing the path of acceptance with regard to the break-up of her marriage. At the time she was writing of Anny Ritchie, who died at the age of eighty-one after a lifetime dispensing the warmth of her personality, Winifred was nearing the same age herself; a mood of mellow benevolence permeates her last book, described by one critic as her 'splendid memorial'.[197] Claire Tomalin, for one, welcomed the kindliness of a biography that was 'a restorative rather than a cutting-down-to-size study; the dead are given their stature, reclaimed warmly for our sympathy and fellow-feeling'.[198] Winifred was happy with the reviews that had appeared so far, and was busy for the couple of days after the book's appearance with press and radio interviews.

Early on Sunday 28 June, Jonathan Hull, the porter at Marlborough Court, called as usual to take Jamie out for his morning walk. When there was no answer to the doorbell he let himself into the flat and found Winifred lying on the bathroom floor. An ambulance was called, but she was pronounced dead on arrival at St Stephen's Hospital. The cause of death was recorded as cardiac thrombosis.

A letter from Winifred to the Gérins dated 26 June arrived several days after the phone call from Agatha telling them of her death. Winifred wrote of her pleasure at the reception of her book, but most of her letter was about the final arrangements for the family's stay in July. The three eldest children were to come on ahead for some sightseeing on their own in London; their parents and the two youngest would spend a night in London before being driven to Stanford by Agatha. She ended with concern about Paul's workload. 'Please don't kill yourself by overworking . . . I want you all here as soon as possible so that you can have a well-deserved rest. I'm waiting for you with open arms. *Je vous attends les bras ouverts. Marraine Winny.*'

---

[196] *Critics' Forum*, BBC Radio 3, 11 July 1981.
[197] Philip Howard, Editor's Choice, *The Times*, 10 July 1981.
[198] *Times Literary Supplement*, 10 July 1981.

Epilogue

Winifred's funeral on 7 July 1981 at Kensal Green crematorium, where Roger and Nell had been cremated before her, was attended by numerous friends and relatives.

She would have been relieved to know that a home was found at once for Jamie with Jonathan Hull, the porter of her apartment building who took him for his daily walks.

A home had already been designated for Eugène's 1810 Cremona cello by Winifred herself in her will. She left it to the Royal College of Music together with a legacy of £5,000 for the foundation of a scholarship to be named the Eugène Gérin scholarship.

Winifred's widower, John Lock, kept the Stanford cottage she had loved and maintained the interior much as it was in her lifetime. In his foreword to her memoir, he wrote that photos not just of her but of Eugène Gérin always hung side by side on its walls. In 2005, after John's death, the cottage was gutted by a devastating fire along with the other houses in the terrace. They have now been restored to their original form.

As related in the Preface, to John Lock's disappointment he was unable to find a publisher for the autobiography Winifred finished just before she died.

Envoi

Cling not to me, Bright Images, for light!
my soul's brief sparkle surely will be doused
in the deep drop t'wards death; but take your flight
unfaded, now, betimes, ere I am housed
helpless in my close grave for evermore.
Fly while yet quick! as in the sunken day
flashing like steely blades, swallows outsoar
the dusk to float upon the lasting ray
of the low-fallen sun. So fly you me
into the quenchless radiance of art
beyond the blight of my mortality
where change and death and sorrow have no part
where only you of all my world shall last
long after I who shaped you shall be past.

The final poem in Winifred Gérin's book of verse
The Invitation to Parnassus (1930)

Bibliography

I. Writings of Winifred Gérin

Poetry

The Invitation to Parnassus and Other Poems, as Bourne, W.E. (London: Erskine Macdonald, 1930).

Selected plays (unpublished)

Juniper Hall (produced by the Under Thirty Theatre Group, Leatherhead, 1952; broadcast for radio by the Canadian Broadcasting Corporation, 1953; broadcast for BBC TV in 1956).
Jane, or Fallacious Inferences (*c.* 1953)
My Dear Master (produced by the Playhouse Theatre, Amersham, and the Leeds Art Theatre, both in 1955).

Biography

Anne Brontë (London: Thomas Nelson & Sons, 1959).
Branwell Brontë (London: Thomas Nelson & Sons, 1961).
The Young Fanny Burney (London: Thomas Nelson & Sons, 1961).
Charlotte Brontë: The Evolution of Genius (London: Oxford University Press, 1967).
Horatia Nelson (Oxford: Oxford University Press, 1970)
Emily Brontë (London: Oxford University Press, 1971).
Elizabeth Gaskell: A Biography (Oxford: Clarendon Press, 1976).
Anne Thackeray Ritchie (Oxford: Oxford University Press, 1981).

Other

Lock, John and Gérin, Winifred, *A Guide to Haworth: The Brontës' Moorland Home* (Haworth: Petty, 1956).
The Brontës, for 'Writers and their Work' series (Harlow: published for the British Council by Longman Group, 1973).

Selected articles

'The effects of environment on the Brontë writings' in *Essays by Divers Hands*, Vol. 36 (London: Oxford University Press, 1970), pp. 67–83.
'Byron's influence on the Brontës' in *Essays by Divers Hands*, Vol. 37 (London: Oxford University Press, 1972), pp. 47–62.

Selected works edited

Charlotte Brontë, *Five Novelettes*, transcribed and edited with an introduction by Gérin (London: Folio Society, 1971).

Elizabeth Gaskell, *The Life of Charlotte Brontë*, edited with an introduction by Gérin (London: Folio Society, 1971).

Anne Brontë, *The Tenant of Wildfell Hall*, introduction by Gérin (Harmondsworth: Penguin, 1979).

II. Main biographical sources used

The Years that Count, 1980–1. Unpublished memoir. In private ownership.

Letters held by Paul Gérin and papers owned by Robin Greenwood (private collection) and by the Brontë Parsonage Museum.

Entry by Peter Sutcliffe in *Dictionary of National Biography 1981–1985* (Oxford: Oxford University Press, 1990).

Entry by Barbara Mitchell in *The Dictionary of Literary Biography*, Volume 155. 'Twentieth-century Literary Biographers' (Detroit: Gale Research, 1995).

Entry by Barbara Mitchell in *Oxford Dictionary of National Biography* (Oxford: Oxford University Press, 2004).

Letters from Winifred Gérin and her sister, Helen Bourne, to G.E. and Dorothy Moore in G.E. Moore papers held by Cambridge University Library.

Gérin files in the archives of Oxford University Press.

Correspondence in the Royal Society of Literature files held by Cambridge University Library.

III. Selected works about the Brontës referred to in this book

Barker, Juliet, *The Brontës* (London: Weidenfeld and Nicolson, 1994).

Benson, E.F., *Charlotte Brontë* (London: Longmans & Co., 1932).

Bentley, Phyllis, *The Brontës* (London: Home & Van Thal Ltd, 1947).

Du Maurier, Daphne, *The Infernal World of Branwell Brontë* (London: Victor Gollancz, 1960).

Fraser, Rebecca, *Charlotte Brontë* (London: Methuen London, 1988).

Gaskell, Elizabeth, *The Life of Charlotte Brontë* (London: Smith, Elder & Co., 1857).

Gordon, Lyndall, Charlotte Brontë: A Passionate Life (London: Chatto & Windus, 1994).

Lane, Margaret, *The Brontë Story: a reconsideration of Mrs Gaskell's Life of Charlotte Brontë* (London: William Heinemann, 1953).

Lock, John and Dixon, W.T., *A Man of Sorrow: the Life, Letters and Times of the Rev. Patrick Brontë 1777–1861* (London: Thomas Nelson & Sons, 1965).

Miller, Lucasta, *The Brontë Myth* (London: Jonathan Cape, 2001).

Peters, Margot, *Unquiet Soul: A Biography of Charlotte Brontë* (London: Hodder and Stoughton, 1975).

Robinson, Mary F., *Emily Brontë* (London: W.H. Allen and Co., 1883).

Sinclair, May, *The Three Brontës* (London: Hutchinson & Co., 1912).

Smith, Margaret, *Letters of Charlotte Brontë*, Vols 1–3 (Oxford: Clarendon Press, 1995–2004).

Spark, Muriel and Stanford, Derek, *Emily Brontë: Her Life and Work* (London: Peter Owen, 1960).

Swinburne, Algernon Charles, *A Note on Charlotte Brontë* (London: Chatto & Windus, 1877).

IV. Selected bibliography

Baumber, Michael, *A History of Haworth* (Lancaster: Carnegie Publishing, 2009).

Bernier, Olivier, *Fireworks at Dusk: Paris in the Thirties* (Boston, Mass., London: Little, Brown & Company, 1993).

Brittain, F., *Arthur Quiller-Couch: A Biographical Study of Q* (Cambridge: University Press, 1948).

Bunker, Stephen, *The Spy Capital of Britain: Bedfordshire's Secret War, 1939–1945* (Bedford: Bedford Chronicles, 2007).

Chisholm, Kate, *Fanny Burney: Her Life* (London: Chatto & Windus, 1998).

Cléry, J.B.C. Hanet, *Journal de ce qui s'est passé de la tour du temple pendant la captivité de Louis XVI, Roi de France* (London, 1798).

Conilleau, Roland, *Plombières-les-Bains: hier et aujourd'hui* (Sarreguemines, France: Pierron, 1986).

Coulter. John, *Norwood in Old Photographs* (Stroud, Gloucestershire: Sutton Publishing, 2002).

Coulter, John, *Norwood Past* (London: Historical Publications, 1996).

De Launay, Jacques and Offergeld, Jacques, *La Vie Quotidienne des Belges sous l'occupation* (Brussels: Paul Legrain, 1982).

Dinsdale, Ann, *At Home with the Brontës: the History of Haworth Parsonage and its Occupants* (Stroud, Gloucestershire: Amberley, 2013).

Findlater, *Lilian Baylis: The Lady of the Old Vic* (London: Allen Lane, 1975).

Forster, Margaret, *Daphne du Maurier* (London: Chatto & Windus, 1993).

Garnett, David, *The Secret History of PWE: The Political Warfare Executive 1939–1945* (London: St Ermin's Press, 2002).

Kanigel, Robert, *High Season in Nice* (USA: Viking, 2002).

Mitchell, Barbara, *The biographical process: Writing the Lives of Charlotte Brontë* (PhD thesis, University of Leeds, 1994).

Partridge, Frances, *Love in Bloomsbury: Memories* (Boston: Little, Brown and Company, 1981).

Phillips, A. (ed.), *A Newnham Anthology* (Cambridge: Cambridge University Press, 1979).

Piggott, J.R., *Palace of the People: The Crystal Palace at Sydenham* (London: Hurst & Co., 2004).

Quigly, Isabel, *The Royal Society of Literature: A Portrait* (London/Cambridge: RSA/Cambridge University Library, 2000).

Ring, Jim. Riviera, *The Rise and Fall of the Côte d'Azur* (London: John Murray, 2004).

Rowse, A.L., *Quiller Couch: A Portrait of 'Q'* (London: Methuen, 1988).

Scott, Pat, Edwards, Alison and Pulfer, Eileen (eds.), *The Perfect Playground: Childhood Memories of the Crystal Palace* (London: The Crystal Palace Foundation, 1990).

Seebohm, C., *The Country House: A Wartime History, 1939–45* (London: Weidenfeld and Nicolson, 1989).

Taylor, John A., *Bletchley Park's Secret Sisters: Psychological Warfare in World War II* (Dunstable: The Book Castle, 2005)

Warwick, Alan R., *The Phoenix Suburb: A South London Social History* (London: The Blue Boar Press, 1973).

Wiser, William, *The Twilight Years: Paris in the 1930s* (New York: Carroll & Graf Publishers, 2000).

Yardley, M.D., *Sydenham High School: Centenary Reminiscences* (privately printed, 1972).

Index